LABOR in the
MODERN SOUTH

Economy and Society in the Modern South

Edited by Philip Scranton and Douglas Flamming

During the past half century, the American South has undergone dramatic economic and social transformations. Gone is the South of cotton fields and cotton mills, of monocrop agriculture and rudimentary industries, of desperate poverty and stultifying racial segregation. Gone is the South that Franklin Roosevelt saw as "the Nation's Number One economic problem." But if that South is gone, how can we explain the rise of the "Sunbelt," and what has economic change meant to southerners—their daily lives, their attitudes, their culture? This series aims to answer these critical questions through a multidisciplinary analysis of the region's economic and social development since World War II. It seeks to present the best new research by historians, economists, sociologists, and geographers—fresh scholarship that investigates unexplored topics and boldly reinterprets familiar trends.

LABOR in the MODERN SOUTH

Edited by Glenn T. Eskew

The University of Georgia Press

Athens and London

In honor of Gary M Fink

© 2001 by the University of Georgia Press
Athens, Georgia 30602
All rights reserved
Designed by Betty Palmer McDaniel
Set in 9.5 on 13 New Baskerville by G&S Typesetters, Inc.
Printed and bound by Maple-Vail
The paper in this book meets the guidelines for
permanence and durability of the Committee on
Production Guidelines for Book Longevity of the
Council on Library Resources.

Printed in the United States of America
05   04   03   02   01   C   5   4   3   2   1

Library of Congress Cataloging-in-Publication Data

Labor in the modern South / edited by Glenn T. Eskew.
        p. cm.
    A collection of 10 papers, 6 of which were presented at a
March 7, 1998, festschrift in honor of Gary M Fink on his
retirement from the Georgia State University Dept. of
History faculty.
    Includes bibliographical references and index.
    ISBN 0-8203-2260-1 (alk. paper)
    1. Labor—Southern States—Congresses.   2. Labor—
Southern States—History—Congresses.   3. Industries—
Southern States—History—Congresses.   4. Southern
States—Economic Conditions—1945- —Congresses.
5. Fink, Gary M.   I. Eskew, Glenn T.   II. Fink, Gary M.

HD8083.S9 L33 2001
331'.0975—dc21   00-050798

British Library Cataloging-in-Publication Data available

Contents

Preface

The essays in this volume reflect current scholarship on labor history in the modern South. Seven of the ten contributions present original primary research, with two historiographical essays and one oral interview completing the collection. Informed by postmodern sensitivities, the authors use the analytical tools of race, class, and gender to bring to the fore the previously overlooked stories of southern, often black and usually female, workers. The focus on the "other" builds on the techniques of social history by adding an appreciation for cultural history. The result is a more nuanced analysis that asks different questions. Rather than debating southern distinctiveness or pondering the absence of unions in the South, the essays challenge the very notion of southern—and American—exceptionalism and consider unionization drives within a layered critique of politics and institutions. In several ways, the contributions to this volume turn basic assumptions upside down. More than simply restoring the voices to southern workers overlooked by previous historians, these essays knock off center the very understanding that gave rise to such scholarship. In place of the old southern labor histories of strikes, unions, and white male workers, these authors posit a new southern labor history that, through its inclusiveness, offers a more complex narrative of work in the modern South.

Six of the authors presented their scholarship at a Festschrift in honor of Professor Gary M Fink, who served twenty-eight years on the faculty of Georgia State University. Held on March 7, 1998, in GSU's Alumni Hall in Atlanta, "Labor in the Twentieth Century South" featured Douglas Flamming, Tera W. Hunter, Bryant Simon, Alex Lichtenstein, Robert H. Zieger, and Judith Stein. The GSU history department, which Fink chaired from 1984 to 1991, the Southern Labor Archives, which he cofounded at GSU with colleague Merl E. Reed, and the Atlanta Seminar on the Comparative History of Labor, Industry, Technology, and Society (SCHLITS), which he helped organize, cosponsored the daylong symposium. The retirements of Reed in 1995 and Fink in 1998 signaled the loss to GSU of two preeminent scholars in labor history. Yet the hiring of Michelle Brattain as Fink's replacement and the scholarship of Clifford Kuhn reflect the department's dedication to the field, as does the faculty's sustained interest in the Southern Labor Archives, SCHLITS, and the Southern Labor Studies Conference. Indeed the widespread university support for the Festschrift and the support for the publication of this volume from Associate Provost Timothy Crimmins, Dean Ahmed Abdelal, and Department Chair Diane Willen signify GSU's continued commitment to southern labor history.

The Department of History at Georgia State University is pleased that this volume of essays will appear in the new series Economy and Society in the Modern South, which is published by the University of Georgia Press. Series editors Philip Scranton and Douglas Flamming provided valuable assistance during the editorial process, as did senior editor Malcolm Call. The editor of this volume appreciates the patience and good humor of the contributors during the lengthy process of revision and publication. Word-processing specialist Elizabeth Adams standardized pagination, and a subvention from Georgia State University covered the cost of manuscript preparation and indexing. Royalties from the sale of the volume will be split between the endowment of the Southern Labor Archives and the Merl Reed Scholarship Fund, which provides stipends to researchers using the collections.

The Pursuits of Post-exceptionalism: Race, Gender, Class, and Politics in the New Southern Labor History

Michelle Brattain

In 1954, Mrs. Dorothy Shiflett, a former textile mill employee in Rome, Georgia, wrote to the National Labor Relations Board (NLRB) to inquire about an unfair labor practice case filed by her union. Shiflett was one of 350 members of the Textile Workers Union of America (TWUA) who claimed to have been illegally blacklisted after a 1948 strike. "Several charges," Shiflett reminded the board, including the union's claim that the strike had been caused, prolonged, and violently aggravated by unfair labor practices, had already been upheld by the board's trial examiner. At the time Shiflett penned her letter, she reckoned the union had current "charges pending before [the] Board which has been there for 1 year." In fact the original case concerning Shiflett and fellow members of Local 787 had been filed nearly five years earlier, in November 1949.[1]

Although she opened with "Honorable Sir," Shiflett's letter did not proceed to plead for the board's sympathy, even though many of the strikers had since fallen on hard times.[2] Her prose crackled with frustration and anger as she then recalled an all-too-familiar story about the long wait for justice from a government agency. Less familiar, perhaps, was Shiflett's rhetorical stance. Shiflett prefaced her complaint with an indirect reminder to NLRB members that she was a voter, a taxpayer, and the wife of a World War II veteran. In fact, she and her husband had voted for Eisenhower because he had promised to speed up "services to the people." In so many words, Shiflett reminded the board that the members of the government and the NLRB worked for her. "Get on the job or get out of Government Service," the letter reproached, "because we are tired of paying a salary to a bunch of dead beats."[3]

Shiflett was a union member, even a *good* union member, who stuck with her TWUA-CIO local and stayed the course for ten months when hundreds of her coworkers crossed the picket line. The wife of a veteran who signed her letter "Mrs. Dorothy Shiflett," she was nevertheless also a worker in her own right. Her letter did not bother with maternal appeals on behalf of her family, and her willingness to call the male members of the NLRB "dead beats" certainly belied popular middle-class stereotypes of 1950s-style femininity.

That Shiflett wrote such a letter is significant. The presence of this kind of letter in the NLRB file—along with many other letters from her coworkers, union representatives, even the congressman from her district—suggests the extent to which Shiflett, an employee in one of the most poorly paid industrial occupations in the nation, may have internalized the liberal, democratic rhetoric of the postwar labor movement. To be sure, that rhetoric often functioned as a hollow diversion to deflect anticommunist criticism, yet once in the hands and hearts of workers like Shiflett, labor movement rhetoric about class and democracy became a potent discourse. It encouraged workers to consider class issues outside the workplace and, more important, to act on them politically.

The problem for historians, of course, is that many people, including Shiflett, wrongly believed this rhetoric could apply to a white working-class democracy. Shiflett ended her letter by comparing the fate of her struggle to the contemporary Civil Rights movement. She concluded with a rebuke to the NLRB and the federal government more generally: "I think if you will check the records of the Supreme Court of the U.S.A.," she challenged, "you will find that it did not take them as long to rule on their Biased School opinion as it is taking you on this case."[4]

So who was Dorothy Shiflett? Was she a feisty "girl striker," an empowered new member of the nascent southern CIO PAC? A "missed opportunity" for conversion at the hands of CIO missionaries of civil rights? A key to the failure of the CIO? A typically southern white worker?

Shiflett certainly fits easily into the conceptual scheme of the new southern labor history. Once depicted as passive fixtures on a static southern scene, twentieth-century southern workers are now more often portrayed as shrewd and capable political actors who defended their rights in active and creative ways, if not always in a manner scholars would prefer. Indeed, many historians have recently suggested that the attitude and experience of southern workers—anti-unionism, racial divisions, and all—may be the norm rather than the exception.[5] Her gumption and her offhand remark about *Brown v. Board of Education* also place her squarely within contemporary debates of the new southern labor history. Recent scholarship has focused particularly on the racial identity of workers, the role of the state, and the significance of political action among other issues. In short, the new southern labor history has effected a minor revolution in the representation of southern workers in just over fifteen years.

Recent debates and conceptual challenges within the field, however, indicate that the revolution is far from over. This essay examines the recent decline of exceptionalism and its analytical successors with particular emphasis on the significance of race, gender, and politics in the new southern labor history. Although recent interest in civil rights, nonunion strategies of resistance, and "whiteness" have probably replaced southern distinctiveness as the field's major preoccupation, it is unclear whether southern labor history has fully incorporated all the potential insights of race and gender studies into its collective tool kit.[6] Of central concern to this essay, and the field, is the well-known debate about labor's "race problem." Examining how race has been addressed—especially by historians of gender and African American labor—this essay suggests new solutions and directions for southern labor history. Only recently have historians begun to move beyond research into *race relations* within unions to examine *race* as a cultural phenomenon affecting all workers. Getting a firmer grip on the analytical tools of race, class, and gender, refusing to deploy them in isolation of one another, and making them do more "work" may expand an understanding of the southern working class and also enhance the significance of such scholarship to southern and American history more generally.

The significance of the new southern labor history's revolution is real, and its impact is starkest in comparison with early-twentieth-century studies of southern workers. Although there were the occasional heroic stories of dramatic protests, much of the older literature, especially contemporary accounts published in the first half of the century, described southern workers in terms of their deviation from the "American" (or northern) standard.[7] Often portrayed as "cheap and contented," in the words of Sinclair Lewis, white employees of the textile mills were depicted as pathologically individualistic and religious, naively trusting the South's ruling class, suspicious of "outsiders," incurably racist, and otherwise under the thumb of the South's mill village paternalists. Depictions of black workers, though less prominent, were similarly unflattering. In the early twentieth century, for example, contemporaries portrayed black workers as lazy, shiftless, immoral, childlike, incapable of skilled labor, and content with their "place" in southern society. Many historians since have similarly interpreted black workers' lack of organized protest as silent quiescence or evidence that black southerners had internalized the American ethic of hard work and individualism.[8] The more extreme versions of the old argument suggested that the South's workers bordered on physical, moral, or mental deformity. Even the Left's somewhat sympathetic and slightly more charitable reading of the southern working class branded the region's workers as having a deficient, if not false, class consciousness.[9]

Although important and well-respected historical accounts of southern labor surfaced prior to the 1980s, the field generally did not bear the marks of the "new labor and social history" that rapidly transformed American labor history in the 1960s and 1970s.[10] As scholars working in the tradition of Herbert Gutman and E. P. Thompson began to uncover a rich tradition of labor republicanism, preindustrial resistance, and other indigenous forms of American labor radicalism among workers in the Northeast and New England, southern labor histories tended to focus on economic factors, individual protests, and the allegedly unique aspects of southern industrialization.[11] For example, pathbreaking books in southern history such as F. Ray Marshall's *Labor in the South* (1967) and George Brown Tindall's *The Emergence of the New South, 1913–1945* (1967) narrated important strikes and union organizing efforts but concentrated more on the economic and institutional histories of labor than the social history of mill workers.[12] Although a group of interested scholars had already coalesced into the Association of Southern Labor Historians in 1965 and begun to lay the documentary foundations for a new scholarship in the Southern Labor Archives established in 1969, southern labor history remained in its formative stages.[13] With important exceptions, the field had yet to create the body of scholarship associated with the new (northern) labor history. As that research uncovered more and more evidence to counter American exceptionalism internationally, southern workers continued to be seen as exceptional within American history.

The nub of the old argument and the self-confirming evidence of southern distinctiveness in the twentieth century is the South's historic lack of unions. Even in the post–World War II period, when the labor movement had reached its peak membership, southerners were underrepresented in labor's ranks. In the early 1950s, when nearly 40 percent of American workers belonged to unions, less than 17 percent of southern workers did.[14] The most popular explanation for southern "anti-unionism" and the backbone of most so-called culturalist arguments was articulated by journalist Wilbur J. Cash in his eloquent and sweeping, if somewhat cranky, *The Mind of the South*, published in 1941. Cash placed the blame for the South's seeming lack of class consciousness on the region's unusual history of agricultural and economic backwardness, the boosterism that informed early industrialization, and especially the multiple failings of workers in the South's largest industry, textiles. Although southern textile millhands had staged one of the largest walkouts in American history in the 1934 General Textile Strike, white workers' failure to create permanent unions, and their apparent complicity in the racist antics of southern political demagogues who maintained the great racial divide in the southern working class, seemingly trapped all workers in a vicious and self-defeating cycle.[15]

Accordingly, textile millhands, New South politics, paternalism, and the 1934 strike became targets for the first rounds of revisionism in the 1980s and early 1990s. Works by David Carlton, I. A. Newby, James Hodges, the collective authors of *Like a Family*, Bryant Simon, Linda Frankel, Douglas Flamming, and others provided compelling counterexamples to the older view of southern textile workers.[16] Although the subject matter varied, the central affinity of these new works was their collective emphasis on workers' *agency*, namely southern workers' ability to shape the course of modernization and change. Where older studies had often posited mill workers as victims of overbearing paternalism and of cultures warped by poverty and racism, the new southern labor history uncovered an authentic, vibrant, familial culture and a native tradition of militancy and collective action in the South.

Like a Family: The Making of a Southern Cotton Mill World, begun by a group of scholars at the University of North Carolina at Chapel Hill in 1982, played a critical role in the new revisionism's success. Perhaps as important as the book's reinterpretation of workers' culture, *Like a Family* placed southern workers within their own historical narrative, spanning generations and encompassing a number of extraordinary economic and social changes spearheaded by mill workers themselves. Saving southern mill workers from the condescension of premodern, timeless inaction or a chronicle of reacting to boll weevils, revivals, and race-baiting, it ultimately gave them the authentic history so often denied by southern exceptionalism. Based on in-

terviews with hundreds of former mill workers, an extensive synthesis of
secondary literature, and a wide variety of archival sources, *Like a Family*
traced the forces that pulled mill workers into "public work," the rise and
fall of the family labor system, the extent to which the workers' own rural,
preindustrial cultures shaped southern mill villages, and the enormous impact of World War I on wages and mobility. In the years after World War I
the flowering of southern popular culture, the rising expectations of a new
generation, and the much contested speedup and stretch-out primed
workers to respond favorably to the New Deal's democratic rhetoric. When
southern mill managements refused to abide by New Deal codes for the
textile industry, southern workers wrote to the Roosevelts and the National
Recovery Administration (NRA), joined the United Textile Workers, and
finally staged the largest walkout in American labor history. The "failure" to
create lasting institutions was no failure at all, the book concluded, for
southern workers applied the lessons of their experiences in the 1934 strike
and decided that the northern-led UTW and the federal government were
unreliable allies anyway.

After *Like a Family*, many of the supporting pillars of southern exceptionalism, such as paternalism, the drag of southern-style religion, the en-
abling New Deal state, and the implacable racism of southern whites, began
to fall.[17] Paternalism was among the first to go. New studies of union activity and paternalism provided evidence that many workers understood "the
price of being dependent on . . . the graces of the mill owner" and the hidden costs of the proverbial Christmas ham. Douglas Flamming argued per-
suasively that paternalism was nothing more than welfare capitalism, a strategy ultimately forced on mill owners by workers' demands and the need to
retain a stable workforce.[18] Other research revealed that southern revival-
ism and the growth of smaller Pentecostal sects "made possible a class-based
religious organization" that informed strikers' perception of class conflict
and sustained union struggles. Such work discounted the fact that southern workers had failed to take advantage of the historic moments that ultimately launched the CIO as conclusive evidence of exceptionalism. Studies of NRA policy indicated that the New Deal had not insulated southern
workers from the economic power of mill owners or protected their nascent unions. Furthermore, the uninspired and easily co-opted leadership
of the UTW had contributed to the failure of southern unions in the wake
of the 1934 strike. Finally, comparative histories of union struggles in the
North and South suggested that for a brief moment in the 1940s the po-

tential for interracial unionism and a labor-based civil rights movement existed in both regions. Labor's "missed opportunity," many argued, was thwarted not primarily by southern racism but by the national politics of anticommunism.[19]

With the proliferation of new studies throughout the 1980s and early 1990s, with a well-established conference devoted to the field, and with several anthologies published and several more in the works, by the beginning of the 1990s southern labor history had "emerged as a cottage industry, at the least, and probably as a major trend," in the frequently quoted words of historian Jacquelyn Hall.[20] Although the revisionism began in textiles, a proliferation of community studies—of tobacco and textile workers in Durham, North Carolina; waterfront workers in New Orleans, Louisiana; longshoremen and tobacco workers in Norfolk, Virginia; steel workers in Birmingham, Alabama; and coal miners in West Virginia, to name just a few—began to re-create the intricate fabric and complex texture of everyday life in many different kinds of southern communities.

However, the field had not entirely escaped either the old southern labor history or the criticisms that had already begun to tarnish the products of the new (northern) labor history. Although the new southern labor history seemed virtually to have banished the old arguments about southern exceptionalism, many monographs and articles still revolved around the same old question of "why no unions."[21] Just as the new (northern) labor historians had often written as though "old" labor historians John R. Commons and Selig Perlman were in the room standing on a ballot box waving the flag of job-consciousness, southern labor historians still focused a large part of their energies on proving that southern workers could be pro-union.[22] The result was many studies of that minority of southern workers who joined unions, but, aside from *Like a Family*, comparatively few studies of the unorganized majority of the South's workers appeared.

In some important respects, the problem of southern exceptionalism seemed to have prematurely pushed the new southern labor history straight from the new working-class history of the 1970s to its successor, the new institutionalism of the 1980s. Historians of northern labor had since begun to reexamine trade unions, shop-floor disputes, and the relationship between unions and structural influences of legislation and the state. But where the "new institutionalism" may have been an important corrective for the tendency toward romanticization in northern labor history, southern labor historians had yet to build a correspondingly large body of scholarship on the southern working class. An institutional, or union-centered, focus may have actually obscured lives of southern workers, most of whom had never joined a union. The implications were particularly acute for the history of women and African American workers of both sexes, who were even less represented in the ranks of organized labor.[23]

Critics of the new southern labor history nevertheless identified a general romanticization of southern workers' lives and labors that encompassed a "race problem" and perhaps a gender problem as well. Criticisms of *Like a Family*, for example, anticipated much of the recent interest in the vexed relationship between history and memory. Given the focus on oral history, community culture, and the positive aspects of the cotton mill village, it was no accident that the authors of *Like a Family* tended to focus attention on the positive aspects of textile workers' lives, rather than the negative aspects, such as poverty, poor health and diet, and racism. Indeed the nature of reminiscences or oral history itself, some critics suggested, may have inevitably cast a rosier and less critical glow on history as recalled by participants.[24] Positive accounts of the mill village probably mixed nostalgia with "authentic," or verifiable, memories. Although *Like a Family* answered the need for long-overdue revision and filled an absolutely essential gap in the history of southern workers, it clearly could not stand alone in representing the history of white textile workers' culture.

Race and racism were primary among those aspects of southern working-class life identified as receiving short shrift in the new southern labor history. Although most labor histories of white workers rested relatively silent on the issue of racism, a wealth of anecdotal evidence suggested that Robert Norrell's 1986 study of Birmingham, Alabama, steelworkers was not an isolated instance of white workers using a CIO union to make economic and workplace gains at black workers' expense. The criticism, however, was not directed exclusively at southern historians. In the late 1980s, a growing circle of critics charged that all of labor history, North and South, "had a race problem." This appraisal was articulated most forcefully by former NAACP labor secretary Herbert Hill in his criticisms of Herbert Gutman's work on the possibilities for interracial unionism in the United Mine Workers. Gutman's article on black UMW leader Richard Davis, Hill charged, was emblematic of the new labor history's tendency to replace history with "myth-making."[25] Although substantial evidence attested to the role that unions had played in maintaining and reinforcing white supremacy in the United States, Hill and other scholars pointed out that the new labor history had often ignored the racism of white workers and labor leaders and marginalized the history of black workers. In David Roediger's apt metaphor, the black worker often entered the American labor history "as an actor in a subplot which can be left on the cutting-room floor."[26] Moreover, in attempting to recapture and celebrate the radical, anticapitalist pasts of American workers, labor historians had inadvertently romanticized those white workers who had contributed to the construction of racial privilege.

At times the new southern labor history also seemed to have a gender problem. Although the South had historically been the site of industries with large numbers of female workers, such as textiles, clothing, tobacco, and food processing, the new scholarship focused disproportionately on male-dominated segments of the labor force and male-dominated trade unions in coal, iron, and steel. From the 1970s to the early 1990s, the introductions to prominent anthologies of southern labor history essays voiced editors' regretful recognition that gender and women workers were underrepresented and expressed their hope that this would change. A critic of the 1991 anthology *Organized Labor in the Twentieth-Century South* observed that the analysis of gender noticeably lagged behind that of race and class.[27] With notable exceptions, such as the work of Jacquelyn Hall, Dolores Janiewski, Mary Frederickson, and Linda Frankel, the revolution in women's labor history seemed to have bypassed southern history.[28] In 1991 Hall remarked that although historians of women had "produced a copious literature on the impact of industrialization, urbanization, consumerism, and commercialized leisure on working class women in the Northeast and Midwest," the counterparts of "charity girls" and "women adrift" seemed to disappear below the Mason-Dixon Line.[29]

Much of the literature in the 1990s has addressed and expanded upon these issues, and perhaps it is a measure of the field's maturity that it, like the "new" social and labor history of the 1970s, has come to seem not so new anymore. Southern labor history has never completely abandoned the methodological and political concerns that informed the original "new" labor history. Southern workers' struggles to organize and win concessions from employers still animate much of the published literature. However, new scholarship on northern and southern workers continues to undermine the notion that southern workers were exceptional. As the full impact of that realization sinks in, southern labor seems to have finally escaped the conceptual trap of "why no unions." In the past ten years, exciting new work in southern labor history has extended the focus to include such nontraditional subjects as labor espionage, migrant workers, convict leasing, and domestic service and has created a scholarship that is not always unified around classic southern themes.

The analytical expansion of the new southern labor history has been especially productive in the fields of race and gender history. New work on labor's "race problem" has moved well beyond the issue of whether or not the American labor movement could, or did, serve black working-class interests and civil rights. Recent scholarship, including published exchanges between prominent labor historians, new empirical work, and periodic assessments of the new literature, has produced a broader discussion on the meaning of biracial unionism, race and mobility within the working class, and the respective records of communists, liberals, and anticommunists.[30]

As Eric Arnesen recently noted, new studies documenting the shape and character of working-class race, racism, and racial subordination were in the works even as Hill and others were assessing labor history's race problem. Where the polemic between Hill and Gutman had been largely ideological, research by scholars such as Joe Trotter and Ronald Lewis added new empirical evidence to the debate about the UMW's record on race. Although the UMW and its white southern members permitted pay differentials and occupational segregation, Lewis argued that in the context of segregation and disfranchisement, the black coal miners nevertheless considered the UMW the most progressive force in their lives. A study of southern West Virginia coalfields likewise revealed that in spite of internal racism, black workers participated in union affairs, held office, and used their position in the UMW to fight prejudice among white workers and discrimination on the job with a variety of creative shop-floor devices.[31]

New work on early-twentieth-century mining, longshoring, building trades, and other industries that had biracial workforces confirmed that Gutman's initial speculations had been overly romantic but also corroborated the existence of at least some of those qualities that initially led historians and contemporaries to be so optimistic about unionism. Black commentary on the labor movement in the early twentieth century suggests that in spite of white workers' failure to treat black workers as equal members, many black workers nevertheless chose to join unions and then use their membership as a position to fight for "equal rights and equal consideration within the labor movement." At a time when segregation severely limited black workers' choices, they chose segregated unionism and the opportunity to fight for their rights over no union at all. Southern labor historians have since produced numerous examples of black and white workers building workable, though imperfect, biracial unions in the early twentieth century.[32]

Histories of southern CIO unions were most prone to what critics described as romanticism. Although the AFL's record of tolerating racism and racial exclusion had long been a commonplace in labor history, the history of the CIO, particularly Left-led unions, had always seemed to hold, in the very least, greater promise. Much of the recent historical scholarship has centered on evaluating how well the southern CIO measured up to the federation's commitment to civil rights and "organizing the unorganized." Robert Korstad and Nelson Lichtenstein's assessment of "opportunities found and lost," in many ways emblematic of the "new" southern labor history, substantiated the early optimism and conventional wisdom on the CIO: The CIO's industrial unionism was a natural partner for civil rights in the 1930s and 1940s, with the potential to transform southern industry and to create a "very different sort of civil rights movement," one that was oriented toward economic issues as well as desegregation. Although the CIO had provided the first effective challenges to white supremacy and white democratic politics, the federation's leadership wavered in the late 1940s and 1950s, as the CIO was gripped by conservatism. When the CIO closed ranks and bunkered down for its postwar organizing campaign, Operation Dixie, the civil rights agenda evaporated.[33]

Other historians identified with this tradition, notably Michael Honey and Michael Goldfield, have placed particular emphasis on the destructive role of internal anticommunism. When the CIO expelled communist unions such as the Food, Tobacco, and Agricultural Workers and eliminated the critical left-wing cadre, which had the greatest commitment to civil rights, the federation "destroyed whatever possibilities existed for racially egalitarian unionism," in Goldfield's words.[34] Finally, Honey argued, when the CIO put racial questions on the back burner, expelled Communists from the Operation Dixie staff, and focused its resources and energies on its area of least strength—white textile workers—"the CIO's period of growth and innovation ended" and so did labor's movement for change in the South.[35]

Subsequent studies, however, severely qualified any assumption about the CIO as having a record, at any point in its history, necessarily more egalitarian than the AFL. Even the success stories of southern workers who did build biracial unions often demonstrated that more than the rhetoric of

CIO or communist leadership was usually required to make white workers see the logic of cross-racial class unity. Where theoretical analyses of how racial division ultimately served the capitalist class fell on deaf ears, the identification of a direct economic mutual self-interest could provide an effective motivation to overcome the culture of segregation. In a study of a United Packinghouse Workers of America (UPWA) local in Fort Worth, Texas, for example, Rick Halpern describes the tenuous relationship between black and white union members in the 1940s as "an accommodation rather than an alliance." As a minority presence in the labor force, pro-union black workers needed at least tacit support from a minimum number of whites. Pro-union white workers, on the other hand, needed black workers' power over a key point in the production process to enforce union demands. White packinghouse workers tolerated black workers' demands for equal treatment, but only when those demands were articulated in "traditional trade-union terms" of seniority and job rights. Although Halpern's case study certainly indicated the possibility of racial egalitarianism in a CIO-style organization, it also indicated the significance of other structural factors in facilitating such cooperation.[36]

Recent work has also confirmed that white workers can use and have used their control over union leadership to sustain white privilege in the shop and the union. Rhetoric and commitment aside, the combination of union democracy and the fragility of southern unions could ultimately make union leadership captive to the views of the rank and file. In a recent article on steelworkers, Bruce Nelson describes a local union leadership trapped between a white majority uncommitted to civil rights and an increasingly impatient group of black workers. In spite of internal pressure from black workers and external pressure from the NAACP, the steelworkers' leaders sought a solution based on what would allow them to remain in sync with the principal white constituency and protect the stability of the union. Although black workers clearly identified their union as an appropriate arena for civil rights, the logistics of interracial unionism forced them to look elsewhere for partners in those struggles. Nelson described a similar dynamic at work in the shipyards of Mobile, Alabama, during World War II. First competition between AFL and CIO unions and then the desire to maintain a fragile accommodation between black and white union members, Nelson argued, forced CIO leaders to be cautious in the pursuit of black workers, to support segregated production facilities, and finally to acquiesce in postwar efforts by whites to limit opportunities for black workers. White union members in Mobile and elsewhere were also implicated in the overwhelming opposition to the wartime Fair Employment Practices Commission that ultimately cut short this unprecedented federal attempt to combat racial discrimination in employment.[37]

Identifying a similar phenomenon of union democracy gone wrong in AFL-CIO political action bodies, Alan Draper suggested that the new southern labor history needed to focus more squarely on the institutional context in which racism operated and the limits it placed on unions. Draper's own research concerned the trials of AFL-CIO state councils during the age of massive resistance, 1955–68, when many southern unions disaffiliated from state bodies or rejected AFL-CIO Committee on Political Education (COPE) policy in retaliation for the national leadership's pro–civil rights positions. In spite of AFL-CIO efforts to fight racism within the labor movement and "do the right thing," Draper argues, the strain between pro–civil rights leaders and pro-segregation members rendered positive AFL-CIO actions largely symbolic. Principled objections to the likes of segregationist George Wallace cost the federation dearly as retaliatory disaffiliations severely undermined the fragile institutional base from which organized labor conducted its political education campaigns. If historians insisted on identifying missed opportunities, he argued, they inadvertently blamed the victim, as union leadership fully understood the power of a labor–civil rights alliance and ultimately paid the price for southern racism.[38]

Much of this recent work has now coalesced into a debate on the relative wisdom of various union strategies of attack on the unorganized South. Korstad and Lichtenstein, Honey, and Goldfield suggest that had different paths been chosen—the communists retained on the CIO staff, left-wing popular front alliances maintained, and black workers targeted for CIO resources and organizing efforts—the CIO might have truly transformed the South. Honey, in fact, frequently describes CIO movements as "choices." For example, he argues that in the postwar period, "the CIO in the South would have to decide whether, and how far, to move forward on the crucial question of race."[39] A radical strategy of confrontation with the larger South's system of disfranchisement, conservatism, and white racial privilege, this counterfactual argument implies, would have succeeded where the conventional CIO failed. Others, such as Draper, Norrell, and Nelson, suggest the many ways that CIO leadership choices were severely constrained by the institution's dependence on the rank and file. Every "choice" was really the product of a complex calculation of costs and benefits. At the local level, this often meant how to confront, avoid, or act on civil rights in a way that maintained both black and white members' loyalty. At a state or national level, this meant how to expand and maintain the southern base as the northern base was eroded by industrial migration. Both sets of authors, those advocating the need for radicalism and those underlining the necessity of realism, show how union leaders usually sought a compromise between principles and pragmatism.

Evaluating the records of biracial unionism, debating the merits of realism, and understanding the constraints on union leaders has added to a new appreciation of race as a complex dynamic dividing potential trade unionists, but the field only recently has begun to address the full implications of labor's "race problem." Historians of the African American working class have provided compelling arguments for thinking about class and racial identity as they existed inside and outside of the workplace in a much more fluid way. Until recently much of the new southern labor history focused on race relations in unions and the workplace. A new institutional history of trade union racial practices and their relationship to other civil rights and political organizations is coming into sharper view, but the new southern labor history has yet to confront fully the non-workplace and extra-union meaning of race. While studies of racial conflict within unions and racial obstacles to unionization are important, more work needs to be done on race as a cultural construction that affects whites as well as blacks. Part of labor's "race problem" is a failure to understand that race is a richer phenomenon that affects whites even when they are not in interracial settings.

Recent work on race and class by David Roediger, Nell Painter, and Alexander Saxton has challenged labor historians to think broadly about how white labor has historically benefited from and maintained the "wages of whiteness" in less tangible ways. In Roediger's view, whiteness, constructed through the process of defining the black "other," was the product of the northern working class's attempt to come to terms with industrial wage work, and thus it was a fundamental aspect of working-class history. Building on the insights of W. E. B. Du Bois, Roediger vividly conveyed the myriad ways that white workers benefited from and contributed to racial privilege in the United States. Although white workers may have objected to wage labor in a manner suggested by the "new" labor history, they did it largely by creating a myth of white labor's supremacy over unfree black labor. This process began long before white workers formed trade unions, and thus its history lay outside as well as inside such working-class institutions. In Roediger's words, "there can be no assumption that the whiteness of the white working class deserves exploration only when we begin to discuss the history of race relations in labor organizations. Rather, race has at all times been a critical factor in the history of U.S. class formation."[40]

The process of reassessing whiteness, and blackness for that matter, seems to call into question, as one southern labor historian so aptly put it, "some of [the new labor history's] most cherished assumptions about class."[41] While the old "new" labor history envisioned class as a cultural phenomenon as well as a matter of relations to the means of production, it nevertheless seemed to assume a predisposition for class consciousness simply to eliminate race consciousness. Working-class activism, it was often presumed, could and would eliminate racial division because racism was an economic problem—the product of economic competition or capital's tool to divide and conquer the working class. Class consciousness would permit workers to "see" and understand the nature of shared oppression. Of course, there is some truth to these claims, but as Roediger and others have argued, such explanations often served to obscure the role that the white working class played in maintaining white racial privilege.

Women's labor history, however, has already provided some instructive clues for how to handle, and where to go with, the rediscovery of whiteness. As women's labor historians have argued for some time, class consciousness does not naturally translate into something broader than white, male, trade union consciousness. As Dolores Janiewski noted in 1985, adding gender and race to Thompson's notion of class consciousness did not produce the making of the southern working class but a "complex six-sided negotiation among unequal partners." In Durham, North Carolina, Janiewski argued, the "raw material" for a mutual class consciousness existed among black and white workers, but it was complicated, and ultimately overcome, since workers' identities were rooted in race and sex, as well as class.[42] Jeanne Boydston's research on northeastern and New England class formation suggested that in the years of the early republic, the wage itself came to be identified as not only white but also *male*. Ruth Milkman's work indicated how cultural and economic factors interacted to define jobs themselves as male or female and to preserve sex discrimination within workplaces and unions.[43] Finally, discrimination against all working women, cultivated first in the household, then the community, and finally in ideology, should warn against continuing to treat inequality as a purely economic constant of job competition. Already southern labor history has provided substantial evidence that consciousness of class seldom occurs in isolation from consciousness of race or gender. Given the ample documentation of the intensely racialized nature of southern society, and the complex interaction of racial and gender ideology that supported it, there are few reasons to think that it could.

In Du Bois's construction, the wages of whiteness have a particular relevance for the history of the South's white working class. The likely source of much of Du Bois's insight is his experience with segregation, which suggests the necessity and profitability of looking more closely at the culture of Jim Crow and how it might have affected workers, workplaces, and workers' institutions in the South. As a Marxist, Du Bois was deeply concerned with class, but as a black resident of Atlanta who witnessed horrific episodes of white vigilantism and intraclass violence firsthand, he developed a shrewd perspective on southern culture. All black residents of the South suffered under segregation, and when someone as erudite and accomplished as Du Bois confronted segregation's demeaning and belittling assaults, it is perhaps not surprising that he developed a canny insight into the ways that the white South reserved particular privileges for whites, even poor whites. At a time when black southerners suffered ritual terrorism, white workers received courtesy and deference.

Southern workers, in particular, had a distinct and palpable experience with the regional culture of race long before they entered a workplace or a union hall. In the context of segregation, Du Bois understood well how "the pleasures of whiteness," in David Roediger's words, provided an extra-wage, psychological compensation for some workers. Although the South's white workers were among the lowest paid in the nation, Du Bois recognized that whiteness bought them city services, better schools, unlimited access to public spaces, the expectation of fair treatment, and the attention of public officials who courted their votes. Race also gave whites a sense of entitlement, which at times proved an important step toward the development of class consciousness. Yet the wages of whiteness prevented the South's white workers from recognizing a common interest with the South's black workers, thus limiting their vision for the possibilities of working-class politics. "There are not today in the world," Du Bois wrote in 1935, "two groups of workers with practically identical interests who hate and fear each other so deeply and persistently and who are kept so far apart that neither sees anything of common interests." Though Du Bois failed to see how the peculiar character of southern industrialization insured that blacks and whites would not in fact have identical interests, his insight into the non-economic impact of segregation on the white worker is a powerful one.[44]

Thus far the new labor history has demonstrated how the labor movement failed to teach white workers a better understanding of race relations, but labor's "race problem" demands that historians consider how workers learned racial etiquette elsewhere. Since race is an artificial and historical construction, scholars must evaluate the role the working class, white and black, played in creating and re-creating race.[45] Du Bois's analysis draws attention to the ways that de jure segregation required the working class to participate in the making of race. For much of the twentieth-century history of the South, race consciousness was not simply foisted upon blacks and whites by a segmented labor market, employers, or the white elite. Even after workers discovered the necessity of interracial organizing to mount a successful campaign against management, unionism in the segregated South often encouraged, and at times obliged, workers to participate in the racism of white society.[46] Segregation laws in many instances required separate meetings of black and white workers. Habitual observations of racial etiquette common in the Jim Crow South often spilled into union culture. White members of Mine Mill in the 1930s cooperated with black members to build an interracial local but reserved some privileges—handshaking and the title "mister"—for whites only.[47] In short, race and racial difference were phenomena that all workers living in the South were forced to experience. Blacks and whites observed and practiced race every day, as segregation compelled whites and blacks to re-create, contest, or affirm the "reality" of race in countless ways. Work, unions, even wages were central to that experience.

If many southern labor historians have yet to act on the recognition of working-class whiteness, historians of black workers in the South, such as Joe Trotter, Earl Lewis, Tera Hunter, and Robin Kelley, have provided strong evidence for the necessity and the enormous potential for thinking about race and class in this way. Whether black workers labored in interracial workplaces or in occupations historically allocated to blacks, their histories suggest that the experience of race and class is interconnected and interspersed across many facets of working-class lives, from household to community to workplace to union hall.[48] Moreover, this research indicates that pre-union conceptions of race inform working-class activism at all levels. Earl Lewis's analysis of the black working-class community in Norfolk suggests that black workers learned about class in part through the experience of race. Experiences in the black community, or "home sphere," shaped early workplace actions, which in turn facilitated a unique historical understanding of class and a "sharp and focused racial critique of the economic system." Class consciousness was so closely connected to race-based experiences, he concluded, that black and white workers seldom saw the commonality of their experience or the logic of joining together as workers. Robin Kelley's schematic for an appreciation of infrapolitics in working-class history similarly delivers a vivid reminder of the private lives of class and race. Without an appreciation for the permeability of boundaries between household and work and public space, Kelley suggests, the hidden transcripts of nontraditional forms of resistance, as well as the more traditional structures of power, remain hidden.[49]

Tera Hunter's recent *To 'Joy My Freedom* provides a vivid example of the complex interplay of race, class, and gender across the boundaries of public and private space. The determination of black working-class women to take back their bodies in Atlanta's dance halls, the "fierce sense of irreverence" characterizing the development of the blues aesthetic, and the intense anxieties black leisure aroused in white employers together suggest the significance of seemingly "private" activities to the public world of work, politics, and class relations. By allowing an escape from the debilitating effects of wage work and permitting an important outlet for self-expression and creation of an alternative ethos, dancing had powerful liberating effects for black women in a society that so often denied them a voice. White employers identified a similar relationship between leisure and work, and, perhaps not surprisingly, their complaints indicated that they realized that leisure did in some sense make domestics "bad workers" from their perspective. Dancing the night away could in fact interfere with wage work, Hunter notes, and in the very least, it was clearly antithetical to the "creation of a chaste, disciplined, submissive, and hard-driving labor force." Hunter also makes it clear that this was not simply a black-white conflict, it was also a site of class conflict. Leisure distinguished class within the black community as well. In a 1905 petition to the Atlanta City Council, the black elite expressed its disapproval of dance halls, informing the council that "the better element [in the black community] does not want them, and the worst element should not be permitted to have them." The energy black workers invested in dancing, dressing up, and their own "work" in the juke joints of Atlanta suggests that leisure was a critical element of black working-class self-identity.[50]

Indeed, a fuller appreciation of the multiple dimensions of race is also necessary to evaluate those rare institutional expressions of interracial solidarity and the counterfactual claims of "opportunities lost."[51] Workplace conflict seldom remained on the shop floor or in the union hall. The bold, radical challenge posed by working-class civil rights activism or interracial unionism was often matched by equally staunch resistance elsewhere. In Memphis the police, the city political machine, and troops of working-class whites lined up against black CIO activists. Understanding other noneconomic and nonworkplace factors, which contributed to the creation of race and racial division, would provide better grounds for gauging how and what forces could have or would have hampered social change had the CIO not compromised radical visions for the South. The larger southern community and white workers in particular were clearly significant variables in the assessment.

Textile workers, central to the original revisionism of the new southern labor history, provide a compelling illustration of how class and class formation contributed to the re-creation of race in the New South. As Du Bois and Cash understood, the New South's largest and whitest workforce came to the mills already shaped by the culture of segregation and race. In the context of segregation and a rigidly segmented labor market, entrance into wage work also powerfully reinforced the experience of whiteness. Indeed textile work and race may be one of the most extreme examples of how whiteness affected southern workers. Recipients of an increasingly respectable wage (by southern standards), inhabitants of all-white mill village communities, beneficiaries of welfare capitalism's token rewards, and voters courted by southern Democrats, textile workers in the first half of the twentieth century historically insisted that they be recognized and treated as *white* workers. While many an organizing campaign failed, numerous workers' strikes and legislative initiatives around the turn of the century attested to how important it was for the South's textile workers—and managers—to maintain whiteness in the mills. In 1896 and 1897, Georgia workers in Rome and Atlanta walked off their jobs when managers placed black labor in "white jobs." South Carolina textile millhands influenced state politics in the early twentieth century and managed the passage of a law banning black workers from machine jobs in the mills.[52]

One should be wary of portraying unreconstructed white textile workers as simply the "anti-heroes of the working class."[53] Even Du Bois and Cash understood that the South's white workers were long-term victims, as well as immediate beneficiaries, of the wages of whiteness. Moreover, as Thomas

Sugrue has argued, employers, rather than workers, had more agency in preserving white ownership of certain jobs. It was surely no accident that textile workers' struggles to exclude black workers achieved more success than their struggles to form industrial unions in the New South. Yet new research on race and class provides powerful evidence that the racial history of southern textile workers is about more than a segmented labor market. The South industrialized in a culture permeated with boosterism pitched as regional self-help in a way that complemented white supremacy. Although the Henry Gradys proclaiming textile mills as the salvation of poor whites surely exaggerated, New South boosters nonetheless explained labor in terms of the culture of race.[54]

The initial ban on black workers also had widespread and important peripheral effects. At the turn of the century, when the passage of Jim Crow laws segregated whites and blacks physically, industrial development separated them economically. In turn, these racialized and gendered social spaces of work and community contributed to workers' self-identity and the way that they were perceived by others. Robin Kelley's examination of black workers' politics shows how the division of labor itself can become racialized, for when dirty, difficult, and dangerous work is defined as "nigger work," it allows the job to be perceived as humiliating and undesirable. It was those black jobs and the exclusion of black machine workers that helped make whiteness meaningful. The mills themselves, which placed whites at machines and blacks in custodial and "outside" jobs, replicated the South's division of labor in a confined social space. As Tera Hunter has observed, the 1897 Atlanta textile strike and the sympathy it elicited "symbolized the powerful forces that diminished economic opportunities for black women and maintained their confinement to domestic work." The South's rigidly segmented labor market limited for black workers the occupational mobility, opportunity, and the chimera of status that it granted to whites. In Du Bois's words, "ambition was not for negroes."[55]

Conditions of labor and employment practices also contributed to material differences in the experience of race. By the 1930s, the segmented labor market produced a growing material disparity in standards of living for blacks and whites, particularly in less urban areas where textile factories provided the main source of wages. Although historians sometimes romanticize the preindustrial freedoms of farms and fresh air, industrial wages in the South dramatically increased the standard of living for the region's whites, most of them former tenant farmers and sharecroppers. A comparison of the standard of living of textile workers versus farmers in one relatively industrial county in northwest Georgia illustrates the point. In 1935 the average textile wage was about forty dollars a month while an average farm family in Floyd County, Georgia, owned total assets worth only thirty-five dollars. In the 1930s, while 90 percent of Floyd County farms did not have telephones, electric lights, or even running water, the county's largest textile mill villages had electricity, indoor plumbing, iceboxes, movie theaters, baseball teams, swimming pools, and laundry services. Textile mill wages enabled many poor whites to employ poorer black domestics, which ultimately contributed in important ways to southern white perceptions of blackness. Moreover, as textile jobs became perceptually linked with the sex of the person who performed the work and as textile mill villages increasingly afforded some workers a modicum of middle-class consumer and domestic comfort, the work undoubtedly contributed to emerging modern notions of family and gender difference within the white working class.[56]

Historians of the South have long been aware that gender shaped the perception of race and informed such extreme practices as lynching and segregation. Outside the workplace, sexualized white-on-black violence maintained hierarchy within the southern working class and, for many whites, mystified the common experiences of black and white working-class southerners.[57] This gendered and sexualized ideology also seeped into employment patterns, contributing in important ways to the shape of the southern workforce. Grievances behind the 1896–97 Rome and Atlanta textile strikes, for example, were articulated in terms of gender as well as race, as white strikers objected to the introduction of black male workers so close to white women workers. For much of the twentieth century the taboo against having black men and white women working together or in relationships of employment authority served as an argument for reserving many shops and even whole industries for white employees only. Southern labor historians have also suggested that such tensions lay behind other kinds of racial conflict at work. Nelson's study of shipyard workers in Alabama during World War II argues that the white assaults on black workers in the 1943 Alabama Dry Dock and Shipbuilding Company riot were motivated in part by anxiety about possible contact between black men and white women. Noting a similar by-product of this dynamic, Daniel Letwin has suggested that in the coalfields, it may have been the absence of white women, and thus the absence of sex-based racial anxieties, that permitted successful interracial organization in the New South.[58]

That the explosive issue of interracial sex should have aggravated on-the-job tensions between black and white workers is perhaps not surprising, but in the past decade, a growing number of historians have attributed an even broader role to gender in the history of southern class formation and early episodes of working-class activism and conflict. Jacquelyn Hall's and Nancy MacLean's work on Atlanta, for example, suggests that unease about the growing population of white female wage workers in the New South lay behind the lynching of Leo Frank as well as middle-class responses to labor activism. Although black women had long comprised a large percentage of the wage labor force, white women began to enter wage work in unprecedented numbers around the turn of the century. Between 1900 and 1920, as thousands of women entered Atlanta's workforce, employment rates for white women rose by 276 percent, and their share of the waged female labor force rose from 28 to 48 percent. The shift upset traditional gender and race prescriptions, as many middle-class whites associated work with black women and thus with stereotypes of black immorality. Given the primacy of concerns about sexuality, vulnerability, and the meaning of female waged work, MacLean argues that white Atlantans fixated on the chastity and alleged rape of "little Mary Phagan" by her supervisor Leo Frank. The "'chivalrous' resolution" in the lynching of Frank, MacLean suggests, not only resolved popular anxiety centered on sex, gender, and work, but ultimately affected the momentum of working-class politics by helping "submerge the radical potential" in the popular mood of class antagonism. Whether that class-based anger could have been expressed in a way that excluded lynching as a resolution to conflict, however, is unclear based on the evidence from other contemporary southern communities.[59] Not long after the lynching, Hall argues, when workers in another Atlanta mill went on strike, many New South observers found it difficult to look beyond sensationalized images of sexual "white slavery" and consider the real implications of the strike with regard to wage slavery. Defamatory attacks on the reputation of female organizer Ola Delight Smith, she suggests, similarly paralleled broader anxieties about the changing role of women in New South Atlanta.[60] Although Hall does not address the simultaneous racial tensions in the mill, her emphasis on workplaces as sexualized spaces adds another dimension to historian Gary Fink's analysis of how and why union organizers made such effective propaganda of the black Fulton Mill workers' role in evicting strikers.[61]

Other historians have linked early-twentieth-century working-class culture and activism to a similar anxiety about the changing definition of masculine independence. The flip side of the situation identified by Hall and MacLean was the impact that changing lines of authority and control had on white southern manhood. The shift from farm to factory, by changing the relationships of dependence and independence within the family, introduced formidable challenges to patriarchal authority within the family and between men in the public world of work and politics. The situation was particularly acute in the mill villages, where managers assumed power once held by fathers over familial dependents. As factory work eroded male autonomy in matters of time and work, it also undermined female dependence by providing young female family members with a wage. Indeed, one historian has suggested that the impact of mill work, coupled with the decline of the South's independent yeomanry, was so devastating that men who did the work took on the stigma of "patriarchal failure." Although it is unclear whether mill workers agreed with Progressive reformers' assessment of mill work as representing male inadequacy, many middle-class observers became briefly obsessed with the specter of "mill daddies" exploiting family members and living off the factory wages of their children in the early twentieth century.[62]

These anxieties about sexuality, masculinity, and Progressive reform's threat to patriarchal authority also found political expression in the white working-class politics of the New South. Although many have interpreted the likes of southern governor Cole Blease as emblematic of a warped and empty working-class politics of racism, Bryant Simon has shown how Bleasism resonated with the concerns, frustrations, and resentments of South Carolina textile mill workers. Although mill workers' support of Blease's antireform platform has been interpreted as either a misguided conservatism or a backward-looking mistrust of state intervention, Simon argues that Blease's program did include measures—such as the protection of suffrage rights, legislation to bar African Americans from the textile factories, and resistance to any state encroachment on parental authority—that addressed what workers considered to be issues of paramount importance. Blease's defense of lynching as the morally sound, manly duty to protect white womanhood likewise spoke to the millhands' gendered understanding of class. The primacy of personal issues of sexuality, autonomy, patriarchy, and parenthood, Simon argues, suggests that "the public and private were never, therefore, as far apart for workers as they have been for historians."[63]

If a consensus is forming over the significance of gendered anxiety as an accompaniment to economic and social change, recent work also attests to the continuing significance of "traditional" women's labor in the development of the New South. Tera Hunter's analysis of the 1881 Atlanta washerwomen's strike, for example, indicates the centrality of black women's labor to the emerging political economy of the New South. Just in time to jeopardize the success of the International Cotton Exposition of 1881, the strike revealed exactly how dependent white Atlanta had become on low-waged black labor and the surprising amount of leverage black washerwomen exercised over their employers. Without the labor of Atlanta's black domestic workers, southern boosters' promises of hospitality, service, docile workers, and white grace to northern investors hung in the balance. The washerwomen's strike built upon existing networks of black activism, complemented black Republican self-activity, and finally threatened "to expose the tyranny in the New South by disrupting this celebration of new-found (North-South) harmony at an early stage of its public relations campaign." As Hunter makes acutely clear throughout the book, the lifestyles of whites depended upon their ability to exploit black labor; but in 1881, as the city anticipated a tenfold increase in city population for the duration of the exposition, there was an unparalleled need for, and dependence on, black women's labor. Although white southern employers had the power to confine black women to the margins of the South's emerging wage labor market, Hunter shows that they could not exercise unilateral power over black women. The washerwomen, shrewdly calculating the stakes of the battle, called the city's bluff when it threatened to impose a heavy licensing fee on washerwomen. The laundresses indicated that they would pay but also made it clear that if they did, they would have no qualms about using their monopoly over licenses to determine how work would be conducted and compensated.[64]

In spite of this growing body of work on gender, there are still nagging gaps in southern working-class women's history. Hunter's work is a notable exception. *To Joy My Freedom* has provided a rich social history that serves both as a counterpart to Kathy Peiss's "charity girls" who "put on style" in the urban North and as a model for "scavenging for clues" and "thinking expansively" about possible historical sources from which to write southern women's labor history. However, the field has not overcome the "regional lacunae" in southern women's history that Hall identified in 1991. There are still a large number of southern working-class women about whom little is known. In some ways this may be a function of the field's institutional and conceptual concerns. With the exception of the tobacco industry, unionized industries that formed biracial unions ordinarily were less likely to be industries that employed large numbers of women. As Hall and Mary Frederickson have pointed out, feminine and racial stereotypes—"Heroines," "Girl Strikers," "promiscuous black women," and "passionless white ladies"—continue to command attention even though an enormous amount of evidence simultaneously suggests the need for a more authentic history of women workers and trade union members.[65]

At times the new southern labor history has been criticized for its romantic preoccupation with the subjects of social history, yet the field has produced a considerable body of literature aimed at reintegrating workers' histories into the political history of the South.[66] Conventional wisdom suggests poor whites and blacks played only a marginal role in the political history of the South since poll taxes and disfranchisement dramatically narrowed the electorate. Organized labor acted on this principle as well; many twentieth-century organization campaigns were motivated at least in part by national labor leaders' desire to create a working-class constituency to counter the electoral power of southern elites and industrialists. Ordinarily, when workers participated in southern politics, their efforts were linked to race-baiting and seemingly antilabor demagogues. Equally well known is the role white working-class southerners played in supporting anti–civil rights legislation in the 1950s.[67]

Yet scholars have shown how at other times in the twentieth century, labor organizations, the Left, and southern workers posed significant, if unsuccessful, challenges to the solid South. Sometimes labor organizations challenged voting restrictions, led registration campaigns, and provided crucial support to the few pro-union southern members of Congress. In the 1930s, Communists and UMW members in Birmingham organized Right to Vote clubs, paid poll taxes, and coordinated the efforts of white union members to aid black members in registering to vote.[68] In the postwar period, the CIO Political Action Committee coordinated grassroots registration and political education campaigns that did at times influence state and national politics. Although organized labor's influence was limited in scope, its ability to mobilize working-class voters under its wing seemed disproportionately large. In 1946 northwest Georgia textile workers provided support critical to the election of Henderson Lanham, the only southern member of the House to vote against the Taft-Hartley Act. In the same southern locale, union organization and PAC actions raised the number of workers in one mill village district who turned out to the polls and cast votes from a mere 19 percent of registered voters in 1942 to well over 70 percent in 1950.[69]

Of course organized labor ultimately lacked the power to make southern workers act on the national leadership's goals of uniting black and white into one big, progressive (nonsouthern) Democratic union movement. But reexaminations of working-class political mores, such as Carlton's and Simon's analyses of Bleasism, suggest that even when workers seemed to choose questionable patrons, they were acting on what they perceived to be their class-based interests. In the postwar era, support of pro-segregation candidates such as George Wallace and Herman Talmadge struck CIO leaders as the worst kind of false consciousness, but both governors championed issues dear to the white working-class voter. In fact Wallace's appeal was specifically pro-union. He defended collective bargaining and other measures favorable to labor as well as worked against right-to-work laws. Talmadge's appeal, though less direct, had clear implications for white working-class voters. To white constituencies, Talmadge's anti–Fair Employment Practices Committee tirades promised to protect jobs; and pro-business boosterism promised better employment opportunities for whites. Recent studies of southern political administrations, such as Patrick Maney's critique of Hale Boggs of Louisiana, suggest that the measured appeal to white workers was no accident. Often southern political leaders, like southern union leaders, conducted their business through a careful balancing act of warring constituencies.[70]

New scholarship also points to the persistent influence of the state and of federal labor policy on the fate of southern workers' organizations. Alan Draper's research on Mine Mill in Birmingham in the 1930s suggests that even when workers overcame the hurdles to interracial unionism, it was actually the National Labor Relations Board (NLRB) that gave them the critical edge in establishing their union local and winning their battle for recognition. Federal policy also had a significant impact on nonunion and nonindustrial workers. As Cindy Hahamovitch's study of migrant farm labor on the Atlantic coast demonstrates, New Deal reform policy created the conditions of stability that allowed migrant farm workers to act collectively, withhold their labor, and force growers to pay a just wage. Ultimately, federal policy undermined this newfound labor control, as a tightening of the labor market during World War II provided impetus for policy adjustments that allowed foreign workers to dilute domestic workers' economic power.[71] The significance of the political shift from New Deal liberalism to postwar conservatism is confirmed in studies of the postwar textile industry. Where federal contracts and the authority of the National War Labor Board (NWLB) had contributed to an unprecedented and rapid growth in textile unionism during World War II, the postwar NLRB—underfunded, understaffed, and increasingly conservative—was incapable of protecting textile workers from the postwar business assault on unions. Marshaling new tools provided by the Taft-Hartley Amendments to the National Labor Relations Act and legal resources provided by a new generation of sophisticated anti-union attorneys, business managed to turn the NLRB into a weapon against organizers and existing unions.[72]

Scholars still appreciate the topics of the "old" southern labor history, such as a consideration of the economic and structural factors that worked against meaningful advances for the South's workers. The old questions that animated the new southern labor history have not been abandoned. Timothy Minchin's *What Do We Need a Union For?* reexamines a classic problem: the failure of the textile workers to extend unionism during the CIO's massive postwar organizing campaign, Operation Dixie. Yet Minchin finds new answers as he explains the failure as a product of rising wages and changing lifestyles of southern workers. Credit, home ownership, and a better standard of living made the price of a strike more risky. Given the peripheral benefits of a union presence elsewhere, southern workers no longer found compelling reasons to take the risk and join. In his second book on the integration of textile jobs, Minchin attributed a similarly powerful role to more explicitly material factors. Even the greater militancy of black workers, who increasingly replaced whites in the late 1960s, did not lead to higher rates of unionization, Minchin argues, because changes in the workforce did not alter "the economic balance of power in the industry."[73]

In a revision of F. Ray Marshall's emphasis on the unique qualities of the South's labor-intensive and highly competitive industries, Bryant Simon also identifies the economics of the textile industry as key but places the emphasis on employers' opposition rather than workers' choices. The answers to "why so few unions in the South," Simon argues, may lie in the region's lack of industries in those capital-intensive sectors of the economy that unionized elsewhere, in the determined anti-union opposition of low-wage employers, and in the failure of southern workers to keep the surplus of white labor in the countryside from crossing their picket lines. Lacking a political base, southern workers had little redress against southern boosters who continued to recruit more of the same kinds of industries and perpetuated a cycle of anti-unionism. Mary Lethert Wingerd's analysis of textile workers in a North Carolina mill town provides a cultural addendum to the classic question based on an adaptation of James Scott's notion of infrapolitics. In Cooleemee, Wingerd agrees, the intensely localized culture permitted management to dominate workers' economic lives, but it also provided workers parochial, but effective and meaningful, ways to express their resistance and assert some control over mill village paternalism.[74]

Other research continues to speak poignantly to the "opportunities lost" in the 1930s and 1940s. Alex Lichtenstein's research on transport workers in Miami shows how post–World War II anticommunism undermined leftist union leadership at a time when leaders were poised to make real progress for black workers.[75] Michael Honey's continuing work on Memphis points to the long-term economic effects of racial discrimination, labor market segmentation, and failure of a labor-based Civil Rights movement in the South. At the height of the Civil Rights movement, the disparities in black and white wealth attested to the extent to which a movement against segregation had left the working class poorly equipped to deal with economic aspects of racial inequality. In the 1960s, 57 percent of the black population lived below the poverty line as compared with 13.8 percent of the white population. Declining economic opportunities and increasing unemployment in the 1950s and 1960s disproportionately burdened black males, who continued to be locked out of employment opportunities in the sectors of the economy that were expanding. Martin Luther King Jr.'s Poor People's Campaign intended to unite progressives around a platform of race and class issues, but his assassination in 1968 ended the impetus behind such a campaign.[76]

Persistent differences in the wealth of black and white southerners, consistently low rates of unionization, and the continuing significance of low-wage jobs in the Sunbelt South renewed interest in southern exceptionalism. "Old" questions still seem relevant. Yet in spite of the virtual explosion of published works in southern labor history in the past ten years and in spite of criticism of romantic tendencies to privilege social history, there remain many workers about whom little is known. New work on previously unexamined sectors of the southern economy—such as factory work in the carpet industry, high-tech employment in the aircraft industry, New

South convict labor, and public sector employments such as teaching, sanitation, and fire fighting—demonstrates just how broad and complex the twentieth-century southern working-class experience has been.[77] Such scholarship will add to the diversity and intellectual rigor of the new southern labor history.

Over three decades ago, when the original "new labor history" first appeared, many practitioners chose to identify themselves as scholars of "working-class history" rather than "labor history." The distinction signified the field's divergence from the narrow institutional histories of labor economics. Abandoning the previous focus on trade union leaders, working-class history examined persistent forms of preindustrial resistance, women's unpaid labor, and precapitalist forms of production and ideology. The conceptual definition dramatically opened up the field, making it accessible and relevant to other practitioners of social, cultural, and intellectual history. That conceptual break also made it possible to apply the labor historians' insights to nontraditional labor topics such as the histories of slavery, the impressment of sailors, and the noneconomic impact of industrial time discipline on the household. In the 1970s, Herbert Gutman found it necessary to preface his book-length critique of Robert Fogel and Stanley Engerman's quantitative analysis of slavery with an explanation of why he, a labor historian, took the time to comment on a book about slavery. Few historians in the post-Gutman generation would hold such a narrow view of labor history as to exclude nonwage work.

A cursory review of the new southern labor history indicates that the field has at times earned a reputation for having just such a narrow view. In 1969 George Rawick warned that historians should not treat the history of the working class as simply the history of formal labor organizations, but scholars often have. Although southern labor historians have now assembled a large body of research, a majority of their research concerns the institutions of industrial or factory labor and trade unions, and thus it continues to represent a fairly narrow slice of the southern working class. Reminding scholars of Rawick's warning, Robin Kelley added his own: if historians overlook noninstitutional forms of individual and collective resistance, they risk losing sight of some of the most frequent and effective forms of working-class protest. This warning has particular relevance for southern labor history, as a large proportion of the region's workers labored in service industries, and the greatest proportion of all southern workers, more than 80 percent in the best of times, never joined unions. As late as 1937,

James Hodges suggests, most of the workers in the South's largest industry had never even seen a union organizer.

The latest work in southern labor history, well represented by the essays in this volume, is just beginning to heed this advice and profit from an expanding range of issues, sources, and methodologies in the field. Although each is clearly informed by analysis of class, the authors are scrupulous in their equal attention to race, gender, politics, culture, and the state. Unions play important roles, but, significantly, they are not the major focus of any of these essays. The South, with all its well-documented peculiarities, provides context but does not serve as the driving concern of these narratives.

Several of the essays, for example, provide new insight into the political and strategic complexities of civil rights policy and politics. Merl Reed and Alex Lichtenstein both examine the myriad obstacles to fair employment during World War II and show how the Fair Employment Practices Commission (FEPC) alone could not overcome discrimination in the workplace. Workplace gains made by African Americans were achieved not by government edict, but by active partnership with various wartime bureaucracies and civil rights organizations, often without the cooperation of organized labor. Judith Stein's essay, although not based on a southern locale, similarly underlines the importance of examining economic and civil rights policy in context and issues a general warning about the folly of judging a policy—either its intent or its effectiveness—at face value. As her analysis of a Richard Nixon–supported affirmative action plan shows, political policies can represent numerous and contradictory levels of motivation. Bob Zieger's essay on CIO PAC and southern regional director Daniel Powell reassesses debate about possibilities for labor-led progressive politics after World War II. Although many historians have blamed the CIO leadership for the failure to create an interracial labor movement or to transform southern politics, Zieger makes a persuasive case that given the CIO's overall marginality, its modest resources, and the increasingly strident nature of political opposition to civil rights, union leaders had little choice but to pursue practical techniques and less provocative agendas. To do otherwise, in Zieger's words, was "to court destruction."

Essays by Tera Hunter, Douglas Flamming, and Bryant Simon provide new insight into the symbolic world occupied by wages, gender, and race in southern culture. Examining black women's protests across the South during World War I and the extremes of white reaction, Hunter also provides an analysis of the underlying dispute about racial roles. She argues that although white political leaders resorted to a rhetoric of "vagrancy" and "patriotism" to justify legal coercion, the true conflict between blacks and whites stemmed from black women's agency and the unusual mobility permitted by a tight market for labor during the war. Douglas Flamming's essay on the wages of "cotton mill daughters" addresses regional divergence but also examines the larger significance of the female wage to southern ideas about gender, class relations, and consumption. Moreover, Flamming suggests how related ideas about gender may have played a broader role in politics and mill policies. Bryant Simon's essay examines the imagined life of black southern domestics and the real fears of southern whites through an analysis of wartime rumors about clandestine "Eleanor Clubs," or unions of domestic workers named for the first lady. Simon argues that the rumors about black domestics organizing unions, advocating political action, and otherwise acting out of place reveal more than just white fears of black maids or unions. The rumors provide insight into white ideas about what blackness and whiteness meant, and into how whites were able to deny their real fears of how the war might upset that racial order.

Together these essays represent a rich scholarship that advances the traditional labor history with a nuanced, multilayered analysis of all the many facets of working-class lives, including the home, fair employment policy, nonunion forms of resistance and activism, and the power of ideas. The result is a more complex understanding of the world of work and the world of the working class in the American South.

Rethinking the advantages of this kind of "working-class" history may be a profitable direction for the new southern labor history. To be sure, scholars will continue to examine when, why, and how unions formed and what role they played in the larger southern political economy. Scholars will continue workplace- and community-centered research on workers. Yet southern labor history has much to gain by enlarging its approach to labor issues. Thinking about class in an expansive way may allow southern historians not only to understand the private and public lives of workers more thoroughly but also to bridge some of the artificial boundaries among other fields and southern and American history.

Returning to Dorothy Shiflett may serve to illustrate the point further. Shiflett worked at a plant that had a functioning union shop for only two years. After the strike, the mill workforce never organized again. As a union member Shiflett was among a minority of the eight hundred workers who manned the Anchor Rome mills, and it is clear that in spite of the short career of Local 787, unionism touched her life in an important way. However, her personal history, as conveyed in her two-page letter to the NLRB, indicates that many events competed with the union in shaping her story. Even when taking into account the overly determined context of the letter and its intended audience, one nevertheless gains insight into other facets of Shiflett's life—her sense of herself and the state, her commitment to the union, her personal grievances, and even her resentments over the *Brown* decision. The direct comparison Shiflett drew between her own case and the school desegregation case suggests that Shiflett forged a significant analytical connection between the state's declining interest in her well-being and its growing attention to civil rights.

When placed in the broader context of her personal experience, Shiflett's letter warns against drawing simplistic conclusions about southern working-class whiteness. When Shiflett's local organized in 1945, the company fought hard and dirty, "playing the race issue to the limit," in the words of one union member. Management circulated photographs of John L. Lewis's white daughter seated next to A. Phillip Randolph and John Davis of the National Negro Congress. Supervisors warned mill workers that "the union would have negroes living side by side with [them] in company owned village houses." Still, such threats did not prevent workers from forming some kind of consciousness of themselves and their collective grievances against mill management. Although many of the white mill-hands who related these stories indicated that they agreed with their managers on the desirability of maintaining segregation of the mill village and their jobs, a majority of workers also dismissed this particular sort of race-baiting in 1945 as a "confusion" tactic. It was probably true that Shiflett's white coworkers realized that the South's segmented labor market insulated them from the pro-integration position of union leaders.

Shiflett's story indicates that race and class did not stand firm in stable relationships. The meaning of whiteness and its influence over workers' behavior clearly responded to changes in context and shifted over time. Isolated historical snapshots of Shiflett in 1945 and 1955 provide contradictory evidence of two well-known types in southern labor history—first, workers as opportunities lost, and then, workers as reactionaries in the making. The two only make sense together when placed in a broader narrative of working-class, political, cultural, and social history.[78]

Shiflett's letter offers tantalizing clues about how she and other southern workers fit in with broader trends in American history. The clear disdain she expressed for the workings of the federal government is evocative of the well-known late-twentieth-century phenomenon of alienation from the state generally and suspicion of federal intervention specifically. The dichotomy that allowed a worker who could see race-baiting for what it was and to nonetheless express vocal opposition to school integration suggests that *Brown* may have been as important a watershed as anticommunism in shutting down possibilities for interracial understanding. She also suggests some possible explanations for the southern, and working-class, shift from support of Democratic to Republican candidates. In isolation, Shiflett's history says little about such trends, but when placed within a broadly conceived working-class history, her story is the first step toward appreciating the role she and other working-class people played in shaping the postwar South.

Southern labor historians do not always make a case for the significance of their research to southern history, but ordinary working-class folk have always been the overwhelming majority of southerners. New studies of labor and politics in the post-disfranchisement, pre–civil rights South increasingly suggest the potential for both labor and political history in extending class, race, and gender analysis to the subject of white Democratic Party politics. Not only does this work enlarge the context for understanding the working class, it also provides new clues toward understanding the paradoxical political stability of the Solid South. Recent studies suggest that white working-class issues, gender anxieties, and social mores played a more critical role in the discourse of southern politics than previously imagined. Indeed, an understanding of how southern Democrats spoke to the concerns of working-class voters while at the same time pursuing inherently conservative social agendas may explain how they managed such diverse constituencies among whites.

Although the logical inconsistencies or false consciousness embodied in southern demagoguery is apparent, southern Democrats proved remarkably flexible. Observers of Cole Blease and Eugene Talmadge often observed that these men represented the interests of business even as they spoke the language of the people. Historians have linked this phenomenon to the rhetoric, style, and language put to work on the stump. Yet such leaders also had a finger on the pulse of southern white working-class emotions, fears, and concerns. Since the Talmadges of the twentieth-century South invested so much energy into courting the votes of poor whites and perfecting a neopopulist appeal to working-class whiteness, workers cannot simply be dismissed as powerless in the southern political sphere. The content of political rhetoric suggests that southern white workers exercised a power over the practice of state and national politics at times disproportionate to the number of votes at their disposal. Even after cataloging the many factors that narrowed the southern electorate, V. O. Key observed, with respect to workers' activity in 1949, that "it is virtually a law of our politics that any considerable minority, if it becomes highly vocal, can command a remarkable deference from political leaders."[79] Southern workers at many times in their history played that role.

American concern over race and over the complex and intertwining connections between race and gender and class suggests that southern labor history is poised to become increasingly central to narratives about the United States. As exceptionalism gives way to a recognition of similarity or convergence over time, southern history seems less regional and more American. The potential for further research in the region is rich. The South provides important resources for case studies of employment and civil rights policy, workplace studies of racially diverse and mixed-sex workforces, as well as material for understanding how public policy succeeds or fails in advancing the rights of workers, women, or people of color. With respect to workers, recent historical studies indicate that the South's working class has been on the losing side of the cutting edge in labor relations, urban poverty, and interclass conflicts. Southern working-class history is now, perhaps more than ever before, American working-class history.

The combined analysis of race and southern working-class politics in particular suggests the significance of southern narratives to American history. Numerous people have observed with regret the southernization of American politics in the late twentieth century. Jesse Helms's "white hand" campaign ads, designed to fan the resentment of the white working class against affirmative action, are a well-known product of the new Republican party.[80] But they would have sat easily within the southern Democratic Party of the 1950s and mingled quite agreeably with Herman Talmadge's pamphlet *You and Segregation*, which included, among other subjects, a tirade against the continuation of the FEPC.[81] Probably many Dorothy Shifletts of the postwar South would feel quite comfortable with the white hand as long as the federal government moved quickly to resolve labor disputes. Given the persistence of indirect racism in America, it could be argued that the South was, unfortunately, many decades ahead of its time in American political and labor history. How the working class functioned in the southern past to create a politics of divisive whiteness may in fact provide insight into the ways that race and economics currently compromise political discourse and critical understandings of racial and class equity. More important, a better conception of southern workers' history clearly has something to contribute to the project of abolishing the discrimination, class inequities, and democratic shortcomings that made the South seem exceptional in the first place.

Notes

Many thanks to Dee Garrison, Robert Zieger, Bryant Simon, Philip Scranton, and the Georgia State graduate students in my 1998 seminar on southern labor history for their helpful comments and suggestions. A special thanks to Andrew Milne, who served as a patient sounding board, read multiple drafts, and made this a much better essay.

1. Dorothy Shiflett to NLRB, Oct. 21, 1954, and Office memo from John C. Getreu, Director Tenth Region, and Lloyd R. Fraker, Chief Law Officer, Tenth Region, to Kenneth McGuiness, Associate General Counsel, Sept. 7, 1956, both in NLRB Case 10-CA-903 (1957), Selected Taft-Hartley Cases 1947–1959, National Archives II, College Park, Maryland. See also Intermediate Report 10-CA-84, Feb. 25, 1949, NLRB Case 10-CA-84 (1951), NLRB Papers. For further information on the strike, see U.S. Congress, Senate Committee on Labor and Public Welfare, *Labor-Management Relations in the Southern Textile Manufacturing Industry: Hearings before the Subcommittee on Labor-Management Relations*, 81st Cong., 2d sess., 1950, and Michelle Brattain, *The Politics of Whiteness* (Princeton, forthcoming), Chap. 5.

2. Apparently a representative from the State Department of Welfare had taken it upon herself to appeal to mill management directly to rehire the strikers because some of them were in "desperate circumstances." See Office Memo, Charles Paschal to John Patton, Apr. 17, 1951. For examples of members of Congress writing on behalf of Anchor Rome strikers, see Representative Henderson Lanham to NLRB, June 16, 1955, and NLRB to Hubert Humphrey, Apr. 30, 1956, both in Case 10-CA-903 (1957).

3. Shiflett to NLRB, Oct. 21, 1954, Case 10-CA-903 (1957).

4. Shiflett was referring of course to the *Brown v. Board of Education* decision. The NLRB ruled in favor of the strikers' cases in November 1954, ordering reinstatement and back pay for dozens of workers, but foot-dragging by company officials forced the board to file petition for enforcement of its order in the Court of Appeals, which was issued in 1956. See *NLRB v. Anchor Rome Mills, Incorporated* (1956). In 1957 Anchor Rome Mills had to pay $1,270 to each of the forty-eight strikers named in the case and offer them their jobs back. In January 1957, eight years after

the strike officially ended in January 1949, the strikers' cases against Anchor Rome mills were finally closed. See "Closing Compliance Report," Jan. 7, 1957, Case 10-CA-903 (1957). On white southern workers, the labor movement, and *Brown* see Numan V. Bartley, *The Rise of Massive Resistance: Race and Politics in the South during the 1950s* (Baton Rouge, 1969), 293, and Alan Draper, *Conflict of Interests: Organized Labor and the Civil Rights Movement in the South, 1954–1968* (Ithaca, 1994), 17–41.

5. For reevaluations of southern exceptionalism, see Robert H. Zieger, "Introduction: Is Southern Labor History Exceptional?," in *Southern Labor in Transition*, ed. Robert H. Zieger (Knoxville, 1997), 1–13, "Textile Workers and Historians," in *Organized Labor in the Twentieth-Century South*, ed. Robert H. Zieger (Knoxville, 1991), 35–59, and Bryant Simon, "Rethinking Why There Are So Few Unions in the South," *Georgia Historical Quarterly* 81 (Summer 1997): 465–84. On the "new southern labor history," see Simon, and for a brief but critical account, see Draper, *Conflict of Interests*, 9–14. Other studies documenting the racial conservatism of northern workers have indirectly contributed to the view of southern workers as "normal" rather than "exceptional." See Kevin Boyle, "There Are No Sorrows That the Union Cannot Heal," *Labor History* 36 (1995); and Thomas J. Sugrue, "Crabgrass-roots Politics: Race, Rights, and Reaction Against Liberalism in the Urban North, 1940–1964," 551–78, Arnold R. Hirsch, "Massive Resistance in the Urban North: Trumbull Park, Chicago, 1953–1966," 552–50, and Gary Gerstle, "Race and the Myth of the Liberal Consensus," 579–80, all in *Journal of American History* 82 (1995).

6. See Bruce Nelson, "Class, Race, and Democracy in the CIO: The 'New' Labor History Meets the 'Wages of Whiteness,'" and comments by Elizabeth Faue, "'Anti-Heroes of the Working Class': A Response to Bruce Nelson"; Thomas J. Sugrue, "Segmented Work, Race-Conscious Workers: Structure, Agency, and Division in the CIO Era," and Nelson's reply, "Working-Class Agency and Racial Inequality," in *International Review of Social History* 41 (1996): 351–420. Eric Arnesen's review of the debate and his important suggestions for more analytical precision are also instructive on the state of the field. See Arnesen, "'Like Banquo's Ghost, It Will Not Down': The Race Question and the American Railroad Brotherhoods, 1880–1920," *American Historical Review* 99 (1984): 1601–33.

7. Bryant Simon remarks that northern labor history "strangely enough . . . never goes by this name, it is simply called labor history." Simon, "Rethinking Why There Are So Few Unions in the South," 471; Zieger, "Textile Workers and Historians," 38.

8. Contemporary views of black southerners as workers were comparatively rare. The index to the classic *Mind of the South*, for example, does not even include non-white workers under the heading of labor or work. On contemporary stereotypical views of black workers, see the description of tobacco workers advanced by a Department of Labor investigator in Tera Hunter's essay in this volume; Arnesen, "'Like Banquo's Ghost, It Will Not Down'"; and Robin D. G. Kelley, "'We Are Not What We Seem': Rethinking Black Working-Class Opposition in the Jim Crow South," *Journal of American History* 80 (June 1993): 75–112.

Robin D. G. Kelley suggests that scholars' identification of such *appearances* among black workers may have had some basis in reality but that the appearances may actually represent a deliberate strategy of deception among workers to hide a less apparent tradition of everyday opposition. See discussion below, and Kelley, "'We Are Not What We Seem,'" 75–112. For historians who interpreted the lack of organized resistance as a kind of quiescence, see, as cited in Kelley, p. 76, n. 4: Lester C. Lamon, *Black Tennesseans, 1990–1930* (Knoxville, 1977); Neil McMillen, *Dark Journey: Black Mississippians in the Age of Jim Crow* (Urbana, 1989); John Dittmer, *Black Georgia in the Progressive Era, 1900–1920* (Urbana, 1977); Jack Temple Kirby, *Darkness at the Dawning: Race and Reform in the Progressive South* (Philadelphia, 1972); Paul D. Casdorph, *Republicans, Negroes, and Progressives in the South, 1912–1916* (Tuscaloosa, 1981); Robert Haws, ed., *The Age of Segregation: Race Relations in the South, 1890–1954* (Jackson, 1978); Margaret Law Callcott, *The Negro in Maryland Politics, 1870–1912* (Baltimore, 1969); I. A. Newby, *Black Carolinians: A History of Blacks in South Carolina from 1895 to 1968* (Columbia, S.C., 1973); George C. Wright, *Life Behind a Veil: Blacks in Louisville, Kentucky, 1865–1930* (Baton Rouge, 1985).

9. Sinclair Lewis, *Cheap and Contented Labor: The Picture of a Southern Mill Town in 1929* (New York, 1929). In his influential *Mind of the South*, W. J. Cash described southern textile workers as men with "chinless faces, microcephalic foreheads, rabbit teeth, goggling dead-fish eyes" and women "characteristically stringy-haired and limp of breast at twenty, and shrunken hags at thirty or forty." W. J. Cash, *The Mind of the South* (1941; rpt., New York: 1969), 120. Similar themes are repeated in Dale Newman, "Work and Community in a Southern Textile Town," *Labor History* 19 (Spring 1978): 204–25.

Many of the classic contemporary accounts of southern industrial workers concern textile millhands. See Marjorie Potwin, *Cotton Mill People of the Piedmont: A Study in Social Change* (New York, 1927); Lois MacDonald, *Southern Mills Hills: A Study of Social and Economic Forces in Certain Textile Mill Villages* (New York, 1928); Harriet Herring, *Welfare Work in Mill Villages: The Story of Extra-Mill Activities in North Carolina* (1929; rpt., Montclair, N.J., 1968); Tom Tippett, *When Southern Labor Stirs* (New York, 1931); Liston Pope, *Millhands and Preachers: A Study of Gastonia* (New Haven, 1942); John Kenneth Morland, *The Millways of Kent* (Chapel Hill, 1958). For a more extensive bibliography, see J. Wayne Flynt and Dorothy S. Flynt, *Southern Poor Whites: A Selected Annotated Bibliography of Published Sources* (New York, 1981). Negative or otherwise exotic stereotypes of southern poor whites were also popularized by contemporary fiction. For a discussion of this literature and its roots, especially on the Left, see Sylvia Jenkins Cook, *From Tobacco Road to Route 66: The Southern Poor White in Fiction* (Chapel Hill, 1976). Robert Zieger reviews the twentieth-century literature on southern textile workers in "From Primordial Folk to Redundant Workers: Southern Textile Workers and Social Observers, 1920–1990," in *Southern Labor in Transition*.

10. Notable exceptions include two anthologies of essays from the Southern Labor History Conference published in the late 1970s, and Melton McLaurin's *Pater-*

nalism and Protest (1971). See, for example, Stephen Brier, "Interracial Organizing in the West Virginia Coal Industry: The Participation of Black Workers in the Knights of Labor and the United Mine Workers, 1880–1894," in *Essays in Southern Labor History: Selected Papers, Southern Labor History Conference, 1976*, ed. Gary M Fink and Merl E. Reed (Westport, Conn., 1977), which was an extension of Herbert Gutman's work, and the essays in Gary M Fink and Merl E. Reed, *Southern Workers and Their Unions, 1880–1975: Selected Papers, The Second Southern Labor History Conference, 1978* (Westport, Conn., 1978). See also Robert H. Zieger, "The Union Comes to Covington: Virginia Paperworkers Organize, 1933–1952," *Proceedings of the American Philosophical Society*, 126 (1982), which extended the new labor history's interest in the New Deal–era and mid-twentieth-century resurgence of unionism to the South.

11. On the new labor history, see David Brody, "The Old Labor History and the New: In Search of an American Working Class," *Labor History* 20 (Winter 1979): 123–26, and Montgomery, "To Study the People: The American Working Class," *Labor History* 21 (Fall 1980): 485–512. Perhaps the best-known example of the "new labor history" is the work of Herbert Gutman, *Work, Culture, and Society in Industrializing America* (New York, 1976). For other early examples of the "new labor history," see also Thomas Dublin, *Women at Work* (New York, 1979); Alan Dawley, *Class and Community: The Industrial Revolution in Lynn* (Cambridge, 1976); Anthony Wallace, *Rockdale: The Growth of an American Village in the Early Industrial Revolution* (New York, 1978); Bruce Laurie, "Nothing on Compulsion: Life Styles of Philadelphia Artisans, 1820–1850," *Labor History* 15 (Summer 1974): 337–66; Daniel Walkowitz, *Worker City, Company Town* (Urbana, 1978); Sidney A. Fine, *Sitdown: The General Motors Strike of 1936–1937* (Ann Arbor, 1969).

12. Robert H. Zieger notes that the sources were also quite different, as Tindall and Marshall did not have access to the same archival sources and were often forced to rely on contemporary accounts of labor struggles. See Zieger, "Textile Workers and Historians," 37; F. Ray Marshall, *Labor in the South* (Cambridge, 1967); George Brown Tindall, *The Emergence of the New South, 1913–1945* (Baton Rouge, 1967).

13. On the history of southern labor history, see Gary Fink's introduction to the *Georgia Historical Quarterly's Special Labor Issue* 81 (Summer 1997): 257–64.

14. For figures on unionization rates and an important recent discussion of southern exceptionalism, see Simon, "Rethinking Why There Are So Few Unions in the South," 465. On southern workers' underrepresentation in unions, see also U.S. Department of Labor, Bureau of Labor Statistics, *Labor in the South*, Bulletin 898 (Washington, D.C., 1947); Charles P. Roland, *The Improbable Era: The South Since World War II* (Lexington, 1976); David R. Goldfield, *Promised Land: The South Since 1945* (Arlington Heights, Ill., 1987); Robert E. Botsch, *We Shall Not Overcome: Populism and Southern Blue-Collar Workers* (Chapel Hill, 1980); Barbara Griffith, *The Crisis of American Labor: Operation Dixie and the Defeat of the CIO* (Philadelphia, 1988); John Shelton Reed, *One South: An Ethnic Approach to Regional Culture* (Baton Rouge, 1982);

Michael Goldfield, "The Failure of Operation Dixie: A Critical Turning Point in American Political Development," in *Race, Class, and Community in Southern Labor History*, ed. Gary M Fink and Merl E. Reed (Tuscaloosa, Ala., 1994); Dale Newman, "Labor Struggles in the American South," *International Labor and Working Class History* 14–15 (Spring 1979): 42–47.

For a review of the literature on black workers' relationship to organized labor, specifically, see Eric Arnesen, "Following the Color Line of Labor: Black Workers and the Labor Movement before 1930," *Radical History Review* 55 (1993): 53–87, and Rick Halpern, "Organized Labor, Black Workers, and the Twentieth Century South: The Emerging Revision," in *Race and Class in the American South Since 1890*, ed. Melvyn Stokes and Rick Halpern (Providence, 1994) 43–76.

15. Cash, *Mind of the South*.

16. David Carlton, *Mill and Town in South Carolina, 1880–1920* (Baton Rouge, 1982); I. A. Newby, *Plain Folk in the New South: Social Change and Cultural Persistence, 1880–1915* (Baton Rouge, 1989); James Hodges, *New Deal Labor Policy and the Southern Cotton Textile Industry, 1933–1941* (Knoxville, 1986); Jacquelyn Dowd Hall et al., *Like a Family: The Making of a Southern Cotton Mill World* (Chapel Hill and London, 1987). See also the essays by Bryant Simon and Linda Frankel in *Hanging by a Thread: Social Change in Southern Textiles*, ed. Jeffrey Leiter, Michael D. Schulman, and Rhonda Zingraff (Ithaca, 1991); Douglas Flamming, *Creating the Modern South: Mill-hands and Managers in Dalton, Georgia, 1884–1984* (Chapel Hill and London, 1992). See also Simon, "Rethinking Why There Are So Few Unions in the South," 469–70; Zieger, "Textile Workers and Historians," especially 37–49.

There are similar counterparts in other southern industries; see below, and Dolores E. Janiewski, *Sisterhood Denied: Race, Gender, and Class in a New South Community* (Philadelphia, 1985); Daniel Rosenberg, *New Orleans Dockworkers: Race, Labor and Unionism, 1892–1923* (Albany, 1988); Robert Korstad and Nelson Lichtenstein, "Opportunities Found and Lost: Labor, Radicals and the Early Civil Rights Movement," *Journal of American History* 75 (Dec. 1988): 786–811.

17. For a point-by-point rebuttal of the culturalist argument, see Simon, "Rethinking Why There Are So Few Unions in the South," 463–79.

18. Quote from Simon, "Choosing Between the Ham and the Union: Paternalism in the Cone Mills of Greensboro, 1925–1930," in *Hanging by a Thread*, ed. Leiter, Schulman, and Zingraff, 98. On paternalism and welfare capitalism, see Flamming, *Creating the Modern South*, 120–45. On paternalism, see also David Carlton, "Paternalism and Southern Textile Labor: A Historiographical Review," in *Race, Class, and Community in Southern Labor History*, ed. Fink and Reed, 17–26.

19. Quote from Linda Frankel, "'Jesus Leads Us, Cooper Needs Us, the Union Feeds Us': The 1958 Harriet-Henderson Textile Strike," in *Hanging by a Thread*, ed. Leiter, Schulman, and Zingraff, 115–16. On religion and southern workers, see also Flamming, *Creating the Modern South*; Bryant Simon, "'I Believed in the Strongest

Kind of Religion': James Evans and Working-Class Protest in the New South," *Labor's Heritage* (Oct. 1992): 60–77; and Pope, *Millhands and Preachers*. On the New Deal and the South, see Hodges, *New Deal Labor Policy*, introduction. On the UTW, see Janet Irons, "Testing the New Deal: The General Textile Strike of 1934" (Ph.D. diss., Duke University, 1988), and Korstad and Lichtenstein, "Opportunities Found and Lost."

20. Hall's comment as quoted in Robert Zieger's introduction to Zieger, *Organized Labor in the Twentieth-Century South*, 3.

21. An important exception to this pattern is Barbara Griffith's 1988 *Crisis of American Labor*, an examination of the failure of the CIO's postwar southern organizing campaign, which argues that the campaign faltered on the fear, apathy, racism, religion, insularity, and general anti-unionism of southern workers. See esp. pp. xiii–xvi, 161.

22. Often credited with the creation of American labor history, John R. Commons and his student Selig Perlman argued in the early twentieth century that American workers were exceptional because they were given the "free gift of the vote" and because they developed a possessive attachment to their jobs or "job consciousness" rather than class consciousness. See John R. Commons, *A History of Labor in the United States*, 4 vols. (New York, 1918–35), and Selig Perlman, *A Theory of the Labour Movement* (New York, 1928). An essential element of many of the new labor historians' works was a rebuttal to Commons and Perlman. The classic rejoinder was Alan Dawley's observation that the ballot box was the coffin of American working-class consciousness. See Dawley, *Class and Community*.

23. On the "new institutionalism" see Philip Scranton, "None Too Porous Boundaries: Labor History and the History of Technology," *Technology and Culture* 29 (Oct. 1988): 722–43; Rogers M. Smith, "Political Jurisprudence, the 'New Institutionalism,' and the Future of Public Law," *American Political Science Review* 82 (1988): 89–108; James G. March and John P. Olsen, "The New Institutionalism: Organizational Factors in Political Life," *American Political Science Review* 78 (1984): 734–49. For oft-cited examples of the new institutionalism, see Christopher Tomlins, *The State and the Unions: Labor Relations, Law and the Organized Labor Movement in America, 1880–1960* (New York, 1985), and David Montgomery, *The Fall of the House of Labor: The Workplace, the State, and American Labor Activism, 1865–1925* (New York, 1987). On the uneven treatment of black workers in American labor history, see David Roediger, "'Labor in White Skin': Race and Working-Class History," in *Reshaping the U.S. Left: Popular Struggles in the 1980s*, ed. Mike Davis and Michael Sprinker (New York, 1998), and Kelley, "'We Are Not What We Seem,'" 89–102.

24. See, for example, Robert Zieger's discussion of *Like a Family* and a similar review by Gavin Wright. Zieger suggests that Hall et al.'s romanticization of mill village life may bear a resemblance to the tendency John Bodnar discovered when interviewing workers at Studebaker. Bodnar found that workers inevitably created "a past" and remembered it in a preconceived and often less critical pattern. Zieger, "Textile Workers and Historians," 43; and John Bodnar, "Power and Memory in Oral

History: Workers and Managers at Studebaker," *Journal of American History* 75 (Spring 1989): 1201–8.

25. Nell Painter, "The New Labor History and the Historical Moment," *International Journal of Politics, Culture and Society* 2 (Spring 1989): 369; Herbert Hill, "Myth-Making as Labor History: Herbert Gutman and the United Mine Workers of America," *International Journal of Politics, Culture and Society* 2 (Winter 1988): 132–33. For a thorough and insightful account of the debate about race among labor historians, see Arnesen, "Following the Color Line of Labor," 53–87.

26. Roediger, "'Labor in White Skin,'" 289.

27. See, for example, Gary Fink and Merl Reed's introduction to *Race, Class, and Community in Southern Labor History*, xv–xvii, and Robert Zieger's introduction to *Organized Labor in the Twentieth-Century South*, 3–12.

28. Early work on southern women workers includes Hall et al., *Like a Family*; Linda Frankel, "Southern Textile Women: Generations of Survival and Struggle," in *My Troubles Are Going to Have Trouble with Me: Everyday Trials and Triumphs of Women Workers*, ed. Karen Brodkin Sacks and Dorothy Remy (New Brunswick, 1984), 39–60; Jacquelyn Hall, "Disorderly Women: Gender and Labor Militancy in the Appalachian South," *Journal of American History* 73 (Sept. 1986): 354–82; Janiewski, *Sisterhood Denied*; Mary E. Frederickson, "Heroines and Girl Strikers: Gender Issues and Organized Labor in the Twentieth-Century American South," in *Organized Labor in the Twentieth-Century South*, ed. Zieger, 84–112. For a review of the literature on women and gender in the textile industry, see Bess Beatty, "Gender Relations in Southern Textiles: A Historiographical Overview," in *Race, Class, and Community in Southern Labor History*, ed. Fink and Reed, 9–16.

29. Jacquelyn Dowd Hall, "Private Eyes, Public Women: Images of Class and Sex in the Urban South, Atlanta, Georgia, 1913–1915," in *Work Engendered: Toward a New History of American Labor*, ed. Ava Baron (Ithaca, 1991), 245.

30. For a thoughtful and thorough review of recent literature on race and the CIO, North and South, see Bruce Nelson, "Class, Race, and Democracy in the CIO," and comments by Elizabeth Faue and Thomas J. Sugrue. See also Michael Goldfield's "Race and the CIO: The Possibilities for Racial Egalitarianism during the 1930s and the 1940s," which provides a thorough summary of the literature to that date and a helpful discussion of criteria to assist in evaluating racial egalitarianism. See also replies by Gary Gerstle, "Working Class Racism: Broaden the Focus," Robert Korstad, "The Possibilities for Racial Egalitarianism: Context Matters," Marshall F. Stevenson, "Beyond Theoretical Models: The Limited Possibilities of Racial Egalitarianism," and Judith Stein, "The Ins and Outs of the CIO," all in *International Labor and Working Class History* 44 (Fall 1993): 1–160.

31. Ronald L. Lewis, *Black Coal Miners in America: Race, Class and Community Conflict, 1780–1980* (Lexington, Ky., 1987); Joe William Trotter Jr., *Coal, Class, and Color: Blacks in Southern West Virginia, 1915–1932* (Urbana, 1990).

32. Eric Arnesen also warns that we should be wary of positing absolute egalitar-

ianism as a yardstick to measure early-twentieth-century labor organizations. Using such an ahistorical measure, he argues, prevents us from seeing how black workers managed to work within such organizations and why they found them preferable to working without unions. See Arnesen, "Following the Color Line of Labor," 53–62, quote from 62. See also Arnesen, *Waterfront Workers of New Orleans: Race, Class, and Politics, 1863–1923* (New York, 1991).

33. Korstad and Lichtenstein, "Opportunities Found and Lost."

34. Quote from Goldfield, "Race and the CIO," 27.

35. Honey, *Southern Labor and Black Civil Rights: Organizing Memphis Workers* (Urbana, 1994); see esp. Chaps. 8 and 9, quote from 273.

36. Halpern, "Interracial Unionism in the Southwest: Fort Worth's Packinghouse Workers, 1937–1954," in *Organized Labor in the Twentieth-Century South*, ed. Zieger, 164–76, quote from 169. In a more recent case study of Louisiana sugar workers and the UPWA, Halpern examined an interracial union that successfully incorporated civil rights measures into the local's program. Although some whites attempted to use anticommunism as a vehicle to weaken the union and its civil rights program, Halpern argued that the local's success in advancing the economic interests of both black and white neutralized opposition and fended off a disaffiliation movement. However, the alliance forged between black and white sugar workers was similarly pragmatic in nature, premised on economic necessity rather than solidarity. See Halpern, "The CIO and the Limits of Labor-based Civil Rights Activism: The Case of Louisiana Sugar Workers, 1947–1966," in *Southern Labor in Transition*, ed. Zieger.

37. Nelson, "'CIO Meant One Thing for the Whites and Another Thing for Us': Steelworkers and Civil Rights, 1936–1974," in *Southern Labor in Transition*, ed. Zieger, 113–45; Nelson, "Organized Labor and the Struggle for Black Equality in Mobile during World War II," *Journal of American History* 88 (Dec. 1993): 952–88; Merl E. Reed, *Seedtime for the Modern Civil Rights Movement: The President's Committee on Fair Employment Practice, 1941–1946* (Baton Rouge, 1991), 190–321.

38. Draper, *Conflict of Interests*, 9–13.

39. Honey, *Southern Labor and Black Civil Rights*, 213.

40. Alexander Saxton, *The Rise and Fall of the White Republic: Class Politics and Mass Culture in Nineteenth-Century America* (New York, 1990); Nell Irvin Painter, "French Theories in American Settings: Some Thoughts on Transferability," *Journal of Women's History* 1 (Spring 1989); W. E. B. Du Bois, *Black Reconstruction in America, 1860–1880*, 3rd ed. (New York, 1992), 700; Roediger, *The Wages of Whiteness: Race and the Making of the Working Class* (New York, 1991), 6–13, quote from 11.

41. Nelson, "Class, Race, and Democracy in the CIO," 351.

42. On gender and how the conceptualization of labor history has often revolved around male models of work and activism, see Alice Kessler-Harris, "Treating the Male as 'Other': Re-defining the Parameters of Labor History," *Labor History* 34

(1993): 190–204, and Ava Baron, "Gender and Labor History: Learning from the Past, Looking to the Future," in *Work Engendered*, 1–46. Faue also notes that historians of women's labor have been questioning such a unitary conception of class for a long time now. In connection with the issue of race in particular, see Faue, "Anti-Heroes of the Working Class," 375–88. Quote from Janiewski, *Sisterhood Denied*, 5.

43. On the history of how the wage became "male," see Jeanne Boydston, *Home and Work: Housework, Wages, and the Ideology of Labor in the Early Republic* (New York, 1990). See also Ruth Milkman, *Gender at Work: The Dynamics of Job Segregation by Sex during World War II* (Urbana, 1987). For a discussion of Milkman's work with regard to new studies of race in particular, see Sugrue, "Segmented Work, Race-Conscious Workers," 398.

44. Du Bois, *Black Reconstruction*, 700–701. For an account of Du Bois's life and particularly his experiences of, and ideas about, race, see David Levering Lewis's magnificent biography of Du Bois, *W. E. B. Du Bois: Biography of a Race* (New York, 1993). For a concise discussion of Du Bois's conception of whiteness, see also Roediger, *Wages of Whiteness*, 11–13.

45. The notion that race is an artificial construction is articulated forcefully by Barbara Fields's "Ideology and Race in American History," in *Region, Race, and Reconstruction*, ed. J. Morgan Kousser and James M. McPherson (New York, 1982), and Fields, "Slavery, Race, and Ideology in the United States of America," *Radical History Review* 181 (May/June 1990): 95–118.

46. For example, although UMW leaders in Alabama occupied an ideological position in between advocacy of either white supremacy or racial equality, they were forced to observe the dictates of segregation in order to deflect criticism of interracial unionism. See Daniel Letwin, *The Challenge of Interracial Unionism: Alabama Coal Miners, 1878–1921* (Chapel Hill, 1998).

47. Draper, "The New Southern Labor History Revisited: The Success of the Mine, Mill, and Smelter Workers Union in Birmingham, 1934–1938," *Journal of Southern History* 62 (Feb. 1996).

48. See, for example, Earl Lewis, *In Their Own Interests: Race, Class, and Power in Twentieth-Century Norfolk, Virginia* (Berkeley, 1991), introduction, 47–58; Robin D. G. Kelley, *Hammer and Hoe: Alabama Communists during the Great Depression* (Chapel Hill, 1990); Janiewski, *Sisterhood Denied*; Trotter, *Coal, Class, and Color*; Tera Hunter, *To 'Joy My Freedom: Southern Black Women's Lives and Labors after the Civil War* (Cambridge, 1997).

49. Kelley, "'We Are Not What We Seem,'" 75–76.

50. Hunter, *To 'Joy My Freedom*, 168–86, quotations from 180 and 173.

51. Lewis, *In Their Own Interests*; Kelley, "'We Are Not What We Seem,'" 75–112.

52. On the Rome, Georgia, strike, and whiteness and textile workers more generally, see Brattain, *Politics of Whiteness*. On the Atlanta strike, see Hunter, *To 'Joy My Freedom*, 114–20. On textile workers in South Carolina, see Carlton, *Mill and Town*,

and Bryant Simon, *A Fabric of Defeat: The Politics of South Carolina Mill Workers in State and Nation, 1910–1948* (Chapel Hill, 1998).

53. This apt phrase was coined by Liz Faue to warn against hasty generalizations about workers' racism as the culprit that did in the American working class. See Faue, "Anti-Heroes of the Working Class," 376–79.

54. Brattain, *Politics of Whiteness*, Chap. 1. On the role that racial ideology plays in southern industrialization, see also Henry M. McKiven Jr., *Iron and Steel: Class, Race, and Community in Birmingham, Alabama, 1875–1920* (Chapel Hill, 1995).

55. On gender, race, and the politics of location, see Kelley, "'We Are Not What We Seem,'" 96–110, quote from 101. On race and the cotton mill campaigns, see Broadus Mitchell, *The Rise of the Cotton Mills in the South* (Baltimore, 1921), 106–35; Hunter, *To 'Joy My Freedom*, 120; Du Bois, *Black Reconstruction*, 701.

56. Numan Bartley, *Creation of Modern Georgia*, 2nd ed. (Athens, Ga., 1990), 169–77. See also Brattain, *Politics of Whiteness*, Chap. 1. The significance of working-class whites' ability to employ black domestic workers is articulated forcefully by Tera Hunter; see *To 'Joy My Freedom*, 108–10, 120. On the tendency of workers and managers to sex-type certain jobs, see Ruth Milkman, *Gender Differences at Work*.

57. One of the most compelling examinations of the whole complex of ideas linking racial violence, gender, and sex is Jacquelyn Hall's, "The Mind That Burns in Each Body," in *Powers of Desire: The Politics of Sexuality*, ed. Ann Snitow, Christine Stansell, and Sharon Thompson (New York, 1983), 328–49.

58. Brattain, *Politics of Whiteness*; Dolores Janiewski, "Southern Honor, Southern Dishonor: Managerial Ideology and the Construction of Gender, Race and Class Relations in the Southern Industry," in *Work Engendered*, ed. Baron; Nelson, "Organized Labor and the Struggle for Black Equality in Mobile during World War II," 980–81; Daniel Letwin, "Interracial Unionism, Gender, and 'Social Equality' in the Alabama Coalfields, 1878–1908," *Journal of Southern History* 61 (Aug. 1995): 519–54. See also Letwin, *Challenge of Interracial Unionism*.

59. See, for example, Bryant Simon's discussion of working-class perceptions of lynching in "The Appeal of Cole Blease of South Carolina: Race, Class, and Sex in the New South," *Journal of Southern History* 62 (Feb. 1996), 57–86, and discussion below.

60. Nancy MacLean, "The Leo Frank Case Reconsidered: Gender and Sexual Politics in the Making of Reactionary Populism," *Journal of American History* 78 (Dec. 1991): 917–48; Hall, "Private Eyes, Public Women," 243–73.

61. Gary M Fink, *The Fulton Bag and Cotton Mills Strike of 1914–1915: Espionage, Labor Conflict, and New South Industrial Relations* (Ithaca, 1993), 67–73.

62. For a discussion of male authority in Old South and New, see Simon, "Appeal of Cole Blease of South Carolina." On gender and the mills, see also Gary Freeze, "Patriarchy Lost: The Preconditions for Paternalism in the Odell Cotton Mills of North Carolina, 1882–1900," in *Race, Class, and Community in Southern Labor History*,

ed. Fink and Reed, 27–40. On images of mill workers and reformers' concerns, see Carlton, *Mill and Town*, and LeeAnn Whites, "The DeGraffenreid Controversy: Class, Race, and Gender in the New South," *Journal of Southern History* 54 (Aug. 1988): 449–78.

63. Simon, "Appeal of Cole Blease of South Carolina," 67–86, quote from 67.

64. Hunter, *To 'Joy My Freedom*, 75–97, quote from 96.

65. For example, just to name a few, we know little about women in female-dominated employment such as the chenille industry, service occupations, the garment industry, agricultural labor, secretarial and public sector work, education, and nursing. Much of the scholarship on women workers has focused on workers who organized or were the subjects of organizing campaigns.

66. Alan Draper, for example, has criticized the new labor history for "describing the South as if the race issue were not paramount" and overlooking the role of the state and economic structures in determining union success. See Draper, "New Southern Labor History Revisited" and *Conflict of Interests*, 9–12.

67. A well-known source of this "conventional wisdom" is W. J. Cash. See *Mind of the South*, 161–81, 250–59, 290–94, 427–29, 432–35. On working-class support of massive resistance, see Bartley, *Rise of Massive Resistance*, 293, and Draper, *Conflict of Interests*, 41–61.

68. Robert J. Norrell, "Labor at the Ballot Box: Alabama Politics from the New Deal to the Dixiecrat Movement," *Journal of Southern History* 57 (May 1991): 201–34; Kelley, *Hammer and Hoe*, 182–84.

69. Michelle Brattain, "Making Friends and Enemies: Textile Workers and Political Action in Postwar Georgia," *Journal of Southern History* 63 (Feb. 1997): 91–138; Flamming, *Creating the Modern South*, 249–62.

70. On Wallace, see Robert Norrell, "Labor Trouble: George Wallace and Union Politics in Alabama," in *Organized Labor in the Twentieth-Century South*, ed. Zieger, 250–72, and Draper, *Conflict of Interests*, 107–22. On Talmadge, see Brattain, "Making Friends and Enemies," 91–138. On the feats of flexibility and balance thrust upon southern political leaders of white and black labor, see Patrick Maney, "Hale Boggs, Organized Labor, and the Politics of Race in South Louisiana," in *Southern Labor in Transition*, ed. Zieger, 230–50.

71. Draper, "New Southern Labor History Revisited"; Cindy Hahamovitch, *The Fruits of Their Labor: Atlantic Coast Farmworkers and the Making of Migrant Poverty, 1870–1945* (Chapel Hill, 1997).

72. Michelle Brattain, "'A town as small as that': Tallapoosa, Georgia, and Operation Dixie," *Georgia Historical Quarterly* 81 (Summer 1997): 395–425; Timothy J. Minchin, *What Do We Need a Union For?: The TWUA in the South, 1945–1955* (Chapel Hill, 1997); Daniel J. Clark, *Like Night and Day: Unionization in a Southern Mill Town* (Chapel Hill, 1997).

73. Minchin, *What Do We Need a Union For?* and *Hiring the Black Worker: The Ra-*

cial Integration of the Southern Textile Industry, 1960–1980 (Chapel Hill, 1999), quote from 255.

74. Mary Lethert Wingerd, "Rethinking Paternalism: Power and Parochialism in a Southern Mill Village," *Journal of American History* 83 (Dec. 1996): 872–902. Simon, "Rethinking Why There Are So Few Unions in the South," 476–84.

75. Alex Lichtenstein, "'Scientific Unionism' and the 'Negro Question': Communists and the Transport Workers Union in Miami, 1944–1949," in *Southern Labor in Transition*, ed. Zieger, 58–85.

76. Michael Honey, "Martin Luther King, Jr., the Crisis of the Black Working Class, and the Memphis Sanitation Strike," in *Southern Labor in Transition*, ed. Zieger, 146–75.

77. On these new fields, see, for example, Randall L. Patton, "'A World of Opportunity . . . Within the Tufting Empire?': Labor Relations in North Georgia's Carpet Industry, 1960–1975," *Georgia Historical Quarterly* 81 (Summer 1997): 426–51; and Jacob Vander Meulen, "Warplanes, Labor, and the International Association of Machinists in Nashville, 1939–1945," 37–57; Mark Wilkens, "Gender, Race, Work Culture, and the Building of the Fire Fighters Union in Tampa, Florida, 1943–1985," 176–204; and James Sullivan, "The Florida Teacher Walkout in the Political Transition of 1968," 205–29, in *Southern Labor in Transition*, ed. Zieger; Alex Lichtenstein, *Twice the Work of Free Labor: The Political Economy of Convict Labor in the New South* (New York, 1996).

78. For accounts of management using rumors about race and integration to dissuade potential union members, see Kenneth Douty to Federal Bureau of Investigation, Sept. 25, 1945, Kenneth Douty correspondence folder, box 2, Northwest Georgia Joint Board Papers, Acc 85-10, Southern Labor Archives, Georgia State University, Atlanta, Georgia; Sworn Affidavits of Ottie Argo, July 1, 1947; Henry Farmer, July 2, 1947; Eugene Ingram, July 2, 1947; James E. Forsyth, July 2, 1947; all in NLRB Case 10-CA-84 (1951), NLRB Papers, RG 25.

79. V. O. Key, *Southern Politics in State and Nation* (New York, 1949), 674.

80. In the campaign ad, a white working-class man tore up a rejection letter, while a voice-over said: "You needed that job, and you were the best qualified. . . . But it had to go to a minority because of a racial quota." On the Helms ad, see Andrew Hacker, *Two Nations: Black and White, Separate, Hostile, Unequal* (New York, 1995).

81. Herman E. Talmadge, *You and Segregation* (Birmingham, 1955).

"Give Her Some out of That": Cotton Mill Girls, Family Wages, and the Question of Female Independence in the New South

Douglas Flamming

In 1917, when Sibyl Queen was ten years old, she quit school to take a job in the Crown Cotton Mill of Dalton, Georgia. She wanted to stay in school, but times were hard. Her father, a millhand at Crown, had become seriously ill. Bedridden, no longer a breadwinner, he became economically dependent on his children. Virtually all cotton mill fathers, not just unemployed ones, were dependent on the labor of their children. Mill work did not pay enough for an adult man to be the sole breadwinner for his family. The poor white families who lived and worked in the mill villages of the New South survived by sending every available worker—young children included—to the mill. Had Sibyl Queen's father remained healthy and fully employed, she still would have left school for the mill in her mid-teens. Daughters like her followed a well-worn path to adulthood: from a sharecropper's farmhouse to a company-owned mill house, from the small wooden mill school to the thundering red-brick mill. Thus, in 1917, ten-year-old Sibyl Queen, tiny and wide-eyed, walked through the mill gate, the same mill gate she would walk through almost every day for the next half century.

At Saturday noon, the end of her first week on the job, Sibyl received her pay envelope and headed home. When interviewed in the 1980s, she clearly recalled the scene: "I got 80 cents a day. Oh, you should have seen me when I drawed my first payday. I come strutting in [the house] like I was a millionaire. Then Daddy said, 'Let's see your paycheck, baby.' He was laying across the bed; he was there [sick] near half the time, and he said, 'That's a big payday for a little girl like you.' So he told my mama, he said, 'Now you give her some out of that.' I had to turn my payday over, to help [the family] make a living. But you know, I was glad to do it. . . . I worked a long, long time that I didn't even open my payday envelope. I just went ahead and handed it over to my mama."[1]

This essay is about the Sibyl Queens of the New South—the daughters of poor white families who spent their childhoods and young adulthoods in Dixie's loud, lint-filled, rapidly growing textile mills. It examines their roles in the family-wage economy and their curious position within the patriarchal family. The South's cotton mill girls were part of a larger world of working-class daughters, North and South, twelve, sixteen, twenty-two years of age, daughters who lived at home but worked in factories, daughters who were at once breadwinners and dependents. In the context of the New South, the phrase "Female Independence," from the subtitle of this essay, sounds like an oxymoron. In early-twentieth-century America, the notion that fathers should be in control of their wives and children was practically universal (at least among fathers), but if American patriarchy had a heartland, it was surely the South. And despite what some have argued, poor-white patriarchy in the New South did not disappear when farm folks moved to the factory. Indeed, in many ways patriarchy seemed strongest in Dixie's cotton mill villages, with patriarchal households ensconced within a paternalistic environment.[2] Still, conditions in mill village households—especially the presence of breadwinning daughters—placed new and unusual pressures on poor-white patriarchy. These pressures gave rise to a new embodiment of southern womanhood—the cotton mill girl. These young women fit no existing stereotype; equal parts traditional and rebellious, they seemed determined to uphold patriarchy even as they sought to subvert it.

A review of the literature on working-class daughters shows that the ordinary working family proved to be a resilient and flexible institution as it encountered the industrial transformations of the late nineteenth and early twentieth centuries. The household was central to the processes of labor migration and workforce participation, and family traditions facilitated the persistence of older cultural norms in the industrial setting.[3] Yet it is difficult to believe that industrialization did not infuse working-class households with new and unsettling tensions, particularly between parents and their wage-earning daughters. As more "working girls" entered America's factories and became essential contributors to the family-wage economy, many working-class households faced the matter of a daughter's wages. Would the daughter get to keep the wages she earned or would she give them to her parents? Who decided? Did a young woman's contribution to the family coffer somehow earn her a greater degree of personal autonomy? If parents were partially dependent on their daughters' wages, could those daughters bargain for greater control over their own affairs?

During the past two decades, scholars from a variety of disciplines— especially labor historians and historians of women—have addressed these issues, which boil down to one central question: Did gainful employment in the industrial labor market emancipate young women from traditional roles, or did it serve to strengthen customary roles within the changing economic system? Most recent works, which deal almost exclusively with the North, say both. Working-class womanhood usually followed a path from a childhood of emergent independence to an adulthood of domestic tradition. Kathy Peiss's study of female working-class leisure in turn-of-the-century New York tells the basic tale. In the dance halls and amusement parks of the teeming city, "young working women had defined a style that in some ways subverted the traditional bases of their dependency—as dutiful daughters in the patriarchal immigrant family and as submissive workers in a capitalist economy." In return for wage work, these working girls won more freedom to act independently in their own free time, and they carried a little of their own money to spend as they pleased. These "cheap amusements" offered working daughters a bit of liberation from family and patriarchy. Yet New York's working girls soon reached the limits of social liberation; their teenage adventures briefly forestalled, but did not alter, the confinements of marriage and motherhood that lay ahead.[4]

Leslie Woodcock Tentler's *Wage-Earning Women* offers an even more pointed argument, namely, that the factory experience exerted a strong conservative pull on young women. Placing female work within the family life cycle, Tentler focuses on the critical period between school and marriage, when working-class daughters invariably worked for wages outside the home. Rather than liberating young women from traditional dependencies and ideas, Tentler argues, factory work reinforced their "domestic destiny," because the "strong and controlling bonds of obligation and loyalty" that held working-class families together "were especially strong for daughters . . . [for whom] wage earning was an essentially domestic obligation." Everything in the system—from patriarchy in the home to low-scale jobs in the factories—encouraged female workers to opt for the relative security and well-being of motherhood. From domestic obligations as a daughter to domestic obligations as a wife: that was the pattern of life for most working-class women.[5]

But what about the South? What about the thousands of Sibyl Queens in the mill villages of the up-country textile towns? In keeping with studies of northern women, one needs to understand what wages did, and did not do, for southern mill women. But first more basic information is needed: one needs to know how much of their wages cotton mill girls got to keep. What was the actual amount? Fortunately, the federal government created the necessary data set back in 1907–8, when agents swarmed through the cotton mills of Dixie and New England. In 1910 the mass of data—undigested but rich—was printed in volume 1 of a massive nineteen-volume report on women and child labor.[6] This information provided a basis for estimating how much each working daughter got to keep.

Most cotton mill girls in the South did not get to experiment with their wages because most did not keep a cent. Sixty percent of them controlled none of their wages. Of those who did retain some of their earnings, most kept about one-third of their wages, on average about eighty-five dollars a year for themselves. When Dixie's cotton mill girls are compared to those in New England, the results are surprising. One might well assume that New Englanders would get to keep more, but southern mill girls were twice as likely to keep some of their wages.[7]

Subconsciously or not, rightly or not, historians usually assume some connection between economic modernization and cultural fluidity. New England mill girls earned more money, had better educations, were more likely to have mothers working for wages outside the home, and were far more likely to have been raised in an urban environment than on a farm. Rapid urban growth, a diverse and burgeoning economy, a heterogeneous population overflowing with recently arrived immigrants, more opportunities for working women, a stronger commitment to education—that was New England. Northern cotton mill girls lived in a region that, by every reasonable index, offered the possibility of greater personal autonomy. Yet in terms of wage keeping, they lagged far behind the cotton mill girls of the South. Interestingly enough, North Carolina's mill girls were the least literate and the most rural of any mill girls in the nation, but they led every other state when it came to keeping some of their wages.[8]

Which young women got to keep something? Was there a pattern, and could it explain the regional divide? The answer has to do with regional economic differences, not regional cultural differences. The South was a low-wage region in a high-wage nation, and southern cotton mill workers earned far less than New England millhands.[9] But there is more to the story. At the time of the federal survey, New Englanders generally viewed textile work as low-status labor. In the fully modernized economy of the Northeast, American-born white men looked down at cotton mill work; it was the dregs, work fit for new immigrants. In the South, cotton mill work was, among white working people, one of the better industrial jobs in the region, an increasingly respectable occupation off-limits to blacks. Most textile workers in New England, though paid more than southern textile workers, were low-wage workers in a high-wage environment. Mill families in Dixie earned relatively steady wages at a time when other southern workers lived constantly on the brink of disaster.

Another piece of the puzzle confirms this view. With the help of regression analysis, it is possible to determine what sort of cotton mill girls got to keep some of their earnings. The determinants of wage keeping were different in New England than in the South. Southern mill daughters who got to keep some wages for themselves usually came from families who were deeply committed to mill work and mill village life. If a mill girl's father and older siblings worked in the cotton mill, she usually kept some wages. In New England, just the opposite was true. Northeastern mill women who kept wages were on the margins of the industry. Their fathers were usually native born and did not work in cotton mills. These girls of Yankee stock actually earned *less* in the mills than their immigrant counterparts, who seldom kept any of their wages. New England wage keepers were not really part of the cotton-mill family economy. Instead, they were working part-time for a little extra money for themselves.[10]

Dixie's millhands were so strapped for money that southern labor historians (this one included) might find it hard to imagine that most New England textile workers—mostly Catholic immigrant workers (French Canadians, Italians, Portuguese)—were in a more precarious economic situation than textile workers in the South. But that is what the evidence suggests. During the early twentieth century, New England textile workers experienced chaotic patterns of unemployment and underemployment. These families could not afford to let their daughters keep any wages. The southern industry, by contrast, had entered a period of increasing production and rising employment. In Dixie, certain cotton mill households—those most deeply ensconced in the mill system—were relatively better off, or perceived that they were. Real wages rose in the textile South while the cost to rent a mill house remained at the same low rate, thus increasing the take-home pay of mill-village households.[11] Parents who were well settled in the mill village, especially those who had several older children working in the mill (and thus greater family income from a steady source), could afford to let their working daughters keep some wages. Southern mill girls earned less than New England mill girls, but, regional peculiarities being what they were, less was more.

Even if southern mill girls were more likely to keep some of their wages because their parents could afford to let them keep some, a puzzle remains. For if their economic outlook seemed relatively stable, southern cotton mill families were quite poor. Parents could have used that cash. Obviously, some parents could afford to let their daughters keep some money, but they did not necessarily have to. So why did they?

The answer is elusive. Maybe the fathers felt guilty that their daughters had to toil in the mill because they—the fathers—could not earn enough to keep the family going. Maybe, that is, the fathers were trying to buy some peace of mind. Maybe the redistribution of wages was a way for mill fathers to reassert their patriarchal control over household resources. Picture, for instance, Sibyl Queen's father, bedridden, economically impotent, telling his wife to let Sibyl keep some of her payday. Or maybe the daughters demanded it—children will do that, in ways subtle and direct—and their parents let them keep some as a means of ensuring family harmony. Or maybe they loved those children. Maybe it broke their hearts to put their children to work like that. Gary Fink's book on the Fulton Bag strike offers touching evidence that parents were deeply concerned about the health and well-being of their mill-working children. But there was not much choice. Being poor in the New South meant doing what you had to do; that was what the family-wage economy was all about. So, maybe, if they could afford it, returning wages was a parent's way of saying "thank you" or "I'm sorry."[12]

Beyond causes, there is the issue of consequences. What did it matter that some mill girls had their own money? The average wage keeper stashed about three dollars in her purse at the end of each two-week pay period.[13] That was not much, but it was certainly more than other poor white girls had to spend. What happened to that money? It went for dresses mostly, and shoes and hats and hairstyles to match. Many also bought new clothes for their kid sisters. Stylish, "modern" dresses set young cotton mill women apart—set them apart quite visibly—from rural women and from an older generation of female millhands. Cotton mill girls loved their mamas, but they sure did not want to dress like them; and, who knows, in a larger sense maybe they did not want to live like them either.[14]

Did such small consumer purchases really matter? In the early-twentieth-century mill village, probably so. When, in all of southern history, had poor white daughters been able to walk into a store, cash in hand, and buy what they wanted? Pretty well never, but that was what this generation of poor white girls was doing. It was their money, and they themselves chose how to spend it—at least those who got to keep something, and southerners led the nation in that category.

Southern labor historians, this one included, have noted the rising consumerism of southern millhands, but they have not really considered the relationship between mill-girl consumerism and mill-family patriarchy. There was so much that simply could not be said between daughters and fathers, between parents and children. Poor-white patriarchy was rooted in the land, in farm-muscle productivity. Could it really survive the mill-village family-wage economy, a system in which fathers had no choice but to say things like "That's a big payday for such a little girl"?

What do we make of the following statement about southern mill girls and family roles that is tucked in the federal government's report of 1910? The *Report* reads: "Nearly always [the child's pay envelope] is turned over to the parent unopened. There is no question as to this—it is taken as a matter of course. It is true, however, that the child at work in the mill has a certain economic independence in the family not accorded to the children not earning wages. . . . The little [mill] girl is not so often asked to 'mind the baby' or to wash the dishes. These duties usually devolve upon the oldest schoolgirl, who, in consequence, develops a strong desire to enter the mill as soon as she can."[15]

The way in which the *Report* blithely associates freedom from household chores with "economic independence" only underscores the conundrum. Whether mill girls kept any wages or not, they seemed to have gained a little bargaining power within the home. Parents cut them some slack, allowed them a little more freedom, and, when possible, returned some of their wages. These were subtle changes, and in many ways they merely reinforced the "domestic destiny" of poor white mill girls. Wage keeping, and bargaining one's way out of household chores, did seem to fire an independent streak in southern mill girls, but because the gap in the patriarchal wall was so narrow, their newfound independence was generally played out well within the traditional confines. But even narrow gaps in the patriarchal wall could have been exciting to those children wanting out. They were also worrisome for the patriarchs who hoped to keep their children in.

Did the mill girls' wages actually affect their outlook or behavior? The more one ponders the actual behavior of female millhands—in Dalton and elsewhere—the more the answer seems to be yes. In her essay titled "Disorderly Women," Jacquelyn Dowd Hall explored the famous textile strike of 1929 in Elizabethton, Tennessee, only she did so with an eye toward gendered behavior and the young women who went on strike. What she found was a group of mill girls who were equal parts respectful and rebellious—young women mostly in the 16–21 age range and usually still living with their parents. When the National Guard arrived to control the strikers, the mill girls alternately flirted with them and cussed them out. A few daring women grabbed rifles away from the Guards and pointed the barrels back at southern manhood. Dressed out flapper-style, they flaunted their sexuality on the picket line but seemingly never had a falling out with their parents. There were a few firebrands, such as a single woman known as Texas Bill, who wore cowboy clothes and was described by one National Guardsman as "the wildest human being I've ever seen." Far more common, however, were the seemingly ordinary working daughters, who, in their own quieter way, were pretty disorderly too. Bessie Edens, for example, lived with her parents and, as a young woman in 1929, imagined a future in which she married and settled down. Later she would do just that, but when interviewed about the strike she recalled how proud she was to have been "a daredevil on the picket line," a woman unafraid of the potential violence, because, after all, she had kept a knife hidden in her undergarments.[16]

These women were disorderly in Elizabethton. They were also, as Hall suggests, disorderly for historians. They did not fit any preconceived models of women's behavior. They were not quite the female union activists observed elsewhere, and they were not quite the cotton mill daughters usually imagined. As Hall writes, the women "were neither traditionalists acting on family values nor market-oriented individualists, neither peculiar mountaineers nor familiar modern women. Their irreverence and inventiveness shatter stereotypes and illuminate the intricacies of working-class women's lives."[17] One can think of Elizabethton's strikers as a bunch of militantly pro-union Appalachian pro-family flappers.

Jacquelyn Hall has a useful term for the process that gave rise to such complicated behavior; she calls it "grounded change." That is a beautiful term to describe the New South, where so much changed so fast, and yet so much that was new seemed rooted in tradition. Of course, all change everywhere is grounded. But in the history of New South working people, the old roots seem especially thick and the new fruit especially peculiar.[18]

Hall's notions of "disorderly women" and "grounded change" are applicable throughout the cotton mill South. An exploration of the history of any mill village from the 1890s through the 1930s reveals disorderly women: sometimes pro-union, other times anti-union; sometimes acting in direct violation of patriarchal norms, other times championing the notion that women should be home managers; sometimes circumspect Protestants, other times blatantly irreverent.

With all this in mind, one should revisit Sibyl Queen in Dalton. Now it is 1934 and the union is in the wind, the General Textile strike is on the horizon. Queen has worked in the mill for seventeen years; she is twenty-seven, unmarried, still lives at home in the mill village; her father has died; her siblings still work in the Crown Mill too. One day, as she walked home from the mill, a local organizer stopped her and asked her to join the union. "You're the one we really want," he said, "[because] if you join we know lots of others will too." On the spot, Queen joined the union. Not long after, she had her brother drive her to her first union meeting. The brother, who refused to join the union, waited outside in the car. Inside, a national representative for the union launched into a get-tough speech. And then he swore. A union representative used curse words—in a mixed audience, men and women—he *cursed*. Sibyl Queen, a devout Christian, could not believe her ears.[19]

When interviewed, she recalled it vividly. "I turned white as a sheet," she said. "I got up right then and walked out. And I never had anything to do with the union again. When I got to the car, my brother said, 'What's wrong, Sibbie, you look like you've seen a ghost.' I didn't say nothing. I just said, 'Drive me home.'" Five years later, in 1939, there was a long and bitter strike at Crown Mill, a strike that pitted pro-union millhands against anti-union millhands. Day after day, Sibyl Queen crossed the picket lines. One young man kept taunting her; each morning as she crossed the lines, he hollered, "Here comes the prettiest little scab in the mill." Management had instructed Queen and the other nonstrikers not to talk back as they crossed the picket line, but the day finally arrived when Queen would take no more lip from this heckler. She yelled back: "I'd rather be a scab than that what's under it!" Later, she would join other anti-union women and men in suing the Crown Mill management for not being tougher on the union.[20]

The significant point in Queen's relationship with the union is that she made the critical decisions herself. She did not ask her mother or brothers what she should do about the union, and it seems unlikely that she would have asked her daddy, had he still been living. Her brother dutifully drove her to the union meeting, but she never felt compelled to explain to him why she walked out. Likewise, despite her concerns about clean speech, when push came to shove at the picket line, she could talk that talk. The New South's female textile workers could be that way. Why? One reason is that they were at once dependent daughters and independent wage earners.

That created tensions for their parents, especially their fathers. Poor-white patriarchy in the New South ran head-on into mill-working daughters. It was a collision that everyone in the mill village felt, but one that few millhands felt comfortable talking about. Mill fathers could be compassionate and self-controlled; in many respects they proved remarkably flexible in their adaptation to industrial life. But there was a darker, more unsettling side—a violent defensiveness. Fathers, brothers, boyfriends—anywhere they looked there was a woman their age or younger earning pretty much what they earned. That was one reason young men were abandoning the mills in droves in the early years of the century. That out-migration of young men from the mills prompted management to improve job opportunities and community activities for adult males.[21]

By the second decade of the twentieth century, in a clear departure from the past, men began to get more cotton mill jobs, better mill jobs, and higher pay than women. Agricultural prices were on an upswing, and since many young men still had an eye for life on the farm, they took their family labor supply away from the mills. To quell out-migration and labor turnover, mill officials improved men's economic possibilities in the mill.[22] That explanation is still accurate, but it may not be enough. There was more than the lure of the land involved; there was also the nagging question of manhood, a question that was packed into every pay envelope that working daughters brought home. When husbands and fathers moved their wives and families from the mill back to the farm, they were making a basic economic decision, to be sure, but one can almost hear these men saying,

"Better to be poor and manly on the farm than poor and sissy in the mill village."

From this perspective, it was no wonder that so many aspects of the new company paternalism—the most popular aspects of it—catered to male culture and bravado. Company-sponsored marching bands were exclusively male. The ferociously competitive cotton-mill baseball leagues allowed men to strut their stuff in public, even if they were dependent on the wages of daughters and sisters in the stands. Welfare capitalism for young women—most notably cooking classes—never caught on; the cotton mill girls would not attend. They got the point. Whereas company cooking classes sought to uplift mill girls who lacked womanly skills, company ballparks offered a stage for young men with exceptional skills.

Finally, the question of manhood had political ramifications as well, as demonstrated by the staunch electoral support that South Carolina's adult male millhands gave to the race-baiting demagogue Cole Blease in the first few decades of the twentieth century. David Carlton demonstrated that mill-working men supported Blease because he promised to protect their families—their patriarchal control of their own families—from the meddling Progressive reformers, whose initiatives often aimed to weaken the parental discretion of poor whites. Going a step further, Bryant Simon shows that those mill-working men hollered long and loud for "Coley" because they sensed that industrial wage work was undermining their manhood. Blease's stump-speech tirades assured them, in no uncertain terms, that they were, indeed, manly white men. He assured them that they could prove the point by murdering black men without fear of punishment. He assured them that he would keep a foot on the Progressives' necks.[23]

But there was another threat to cotton mill manhood—a threat about which Blease and his followers were speechless. They could never rail against mill-working daughters. Yet it was the wages brought home by those daughters, week in and week out, that served as the most persistent and unsettling reminder that poor-white patriarchy was not quite what it used to be. From there, the ironies built one upon another. By fighting the Progressives and asserting their right as white men to run their families as they pleased, mill fathers weakened the fight against child labor, a fight led by the Progressives. By supporting Blease against the Progressives, then, mill-working men helped ensure that their daughters would continue to work in the mill and that those daughters would bring home pay envelopes every other Saturday afternoon, when, once again, the identity of fathers and daughters would be open to question.

Notes

1. Sibyl Queen, interview with author, Dalton, Ga., June 26, 1985 (hereinafter Queen interview).

2. On patriarchy and gender in the southern textile industry, see the works discussed in Bess Beatty, "Gender Relations in Southern Textiles: A Historiographic Overview," in *Race, Class, and Community in Southern Labor History*, ed. Gary M Fink and Merl E. Reed (Tuscaloosa: University of Alabama Press, 1994), 9–16. A helpful review of the scholarship (old and new) on cotton mill paternalism is David L. Carlton, "Paternalism and Southern Textile Labor: A Historiographical Review," in ibid., 17–26.

3. Michael Anderson, *Family Structure in Nineteenth-Century Lancashire* (Cambridge: Cambridge University Press, 1971); John Bodnar, Roger Simon, and Michael P. Weber, *Lives of Their Own: Blacks, Italians, and Poles in Pittsburgh, 1900–1960* (Urbana: University of Illinois Press, 1983); Douglas Flamming, *Creating the Modern South: Millhands and Managers in Dalton, Georgia, 1884–1984* (Chapel Hill: University of North Carolina Press, 1992); Jacquelyn Dowd Hall et al., *Like a Family: The Making of a Southern Cotton Mill World* (Chapel Hill: University of North Carolina Press, 1987); Tamara K. Hareven, *Family Time and Industrial Time: The Relationship between the Family and Work in a New England Community* (New York: Cambridge University Press, 1982); Virginia Yans-McLaughlin, *Family and Community: Italian Immigrants in Buffalo, 1880–1930* (Ithaca, N.Y.: Cornell University Press, 1977).

4. Kathy Peiss, *Cheap Amusements: Working Women and Leisure in Turn-of-the-Century New York* (Philadelphia: Temple University Press, 1986), 187. The broader scholarly debate began with Edward Shorter, "Female Emancipation, Birth Control, and Fertility in European History," *American Historical Review* 78 (June 1973): 605–40, which argued that "industrial growth fragmented the customary 'family economy' by making individual producers of its separate members. And, for the children, at least, independence accompanied wage labor" (615–17). The many studies that followed Shorter's controversial piece usually opposed or modified his view. See, for example, Gary Cross and Peter R. Shergold, "The Family Economy and the Market: Wages and Residence of Pennsylvania Women in the 1890s," *Journal of Family History* 11 (1986): 245–65; Thomas Dublin, *Women at Work: The Transformation of Work and Community in Lowell, Massachusetts, 1826–1860* (New York: Columbia University Press, 1979); Sara Evans, *Born for Liberty: A History of American Women* (New York: Free Press, 1989), 156–62, 182–86; Claudia Goldin, "Family Strategies and the Family Economy in the Late Nineteenth Century: The Role of Secondary Workers," in *Philadelphia: Work, Space, Family, and Group Experience in the Nineteenth Century*, ed.

Theodore Hershberg (Oxford: Oxford University Press, 1981), 227–310; Claudia Goldin and Kenneth Sokoloff, "Women, Children, and Industrialization in the Early Republic: Evidence from the Manufacturing Censuses," *Journal of Economic History* 42 (1982): 741–74; Alice Kessler-Harris, *Out to Work: A History of Wage-Earning Women in the United States* (New York: Oxford University Press, 1982); Louise Lamphere, *From Working Daughters to Working Mothers: Immigrant Women in a New England Industrial Community* (Ithaca, N.Y.: Cornell University Press, 1987); Christine Stansell, *City of Women: Sex and Class in New York, 1789–1869* (New York: Alfred A. Knopf, 1986), 218–21; Louise A. Tilly, "The Family Wage Economy of a French Textile City: Roubaix, 1872–1906," *Journal of Family History* 4 (1979): 381–92; Louise A. Tilly and Joan W. Scott, *Women, Work, and the Family* (New York: Holt, Rinehart, Winston, 1978); Daniel Walkowitz, *Worker, City, Company Town: Iron and Cotton Worker Protests in Troy and Cohoes, New York, 1855–1884* (Urbana: University of Illinois Press, 1978).

5. Leslie Woodcock Tentler, *Wage-Earning Women: Industrial Work and Family Life in the United States, 1900–1930* (New York: Oxford University Press, 1979), 8, 86.

6. U.S. Senate, *Report on Condition of Woman and Child Wage-Earners in the United States*, vol. 1, *Cotton Textile Industry* (Washington, D.C.: GPO, 1910).

7. Among southern mill girls, 38.6 percent kept some of their wages; only 19.8 percent of the New England mill girls kept some of their wages (the chi-square, with 1 d.f., was 81.18, meaning that the results are statistically significant). In North Carolina 45 percent of the mill girls kept some of their wages; in comparison, the figures for other states in the sample were as follows: South Carolina, 39 percent; Georgia, 29 percent; Maine, 25 percent; Rhode Island, 21 percent; Massachusetts, 17 percent. The sample included 1,001 southern female workers and 928 New England female workers, all of whom were under sixteen years of age. *Southern* states here include North Carolina, South Carolina, and Georgia; *New England* states include Massachusetts, New Hampshire, and Vermont. The data was compiled from U.S. Senate, *Report*, 932–1013 (table 30).

8. Average annual earnings for New England mill girls was $324.04, as compared with $240.72 for southern mill girls. Other comparisons between these two groups were as follows: literacy (90.3 percent in New England to 75.8 percent in the South); mothers working for wages (7.5 percent to 5.6 percent); early childhood spent in an urban place (46.7 percent to 4.0 percent); average age (twenty years to nineteen years). Regional definitions and the data source are the same as indicated in the previous note, with one exception: the figures for "early childhood" are calculated from aggregate state figures (not the individual data), which are part of the same *Report*, but which combine data on children under sixteen years of age with data on wage-earning daughters sixteen years and older.

9. Gavin Wright, *Old South, New South: Revolutions in the Southern Economy since the Civil War* (New York: Basic Books, 1986), esp. Chaps. 1, 5.

10. The multiple-regression equations could not be printed here, but the vari-

ables and results can be briefly described. Those wishing to see the full regression results are encouraged to request them from the author. The dependent variable for all of the regressions was a dichotomous (or "dummy") variable indicating whether a mill girl got to keep any of her wages (the variable was equal to 1 if a mill girl kept some of her earnings, and equal to 0 otherwise). The independent variables for both regions were age of the mill girl; the mill girl's individual earnings; work as weaver (1 if working as a weaver, 0 otherwise); family earnings (annual earnings for entire family); younger siblings (number of children in the girl's family under sixteen years of age); older siblings (number of children in family sixteen years or older); single parent (1 if mill girl lived with a single parent; 0 otherwise); mother working for wages (1 for yes, 0 for no); father working in a textile mill (1 for yes, 0 for no).

For southern mill girls, the only two variables that proved statistically significant were "older siblings" (positively related to wage keeping, with a coefficient of .68 and a t-score of 7.26) and "father working in a textile mill" (positively related to wage keeping, with a coefficient of .56 and a t-score of 3.36). For New England mill girls, four variables proved statistically significant: individual earnings (*negatively* related to wage keeping, with a coefficient of −.004 and a t-score of 3.79); family earnings (positively related to wage keeping, with a coefficient of .001 and a t-score of 5.92); younger siblings (*negatively* related to wage keeping, with a coefficient of −.26 and a t-score of 5.03); father working in a textile mill (*negatively* related to wage keeping, with a coefficient of −.64 and a t-score of 2.83). In an expanded regression model for the New England group, mill girls with native-born fathers were more likely to keep wages (coefficient of .57 with a t-score of 2.08) than were mill girls of immigrant fathers. For the data source and regional definitions used in these regressions, see note 7.

11. On mill wages and rents during this period, see Flamming, *Creating the Modern South*, esp. Chap. 5.

12. I offer these "explanations" as suggestive speculations. Perhaps cotton mill parents in New England felt the same way about these emotional and familial dilemmas, but, as argued above, few of them had the financial stability to allow their daughters to keep any wages. Thus, whatever their values about family roles, and whatever their feelings about working daughters, New England cotton mill parents were less likely than southerners to confront actual decisions about their daughters' wages.

13. My calculations from the Senate *Report* data indicate that on average, Dixie's cotton mill girls brought home $9.23 per two-week pay period and that girls who kept some wages usually kept about one-third of what they earned—hence my estimate of $3.00.

14. See Jacquelyn Dowd Hall, "Disorderly Women: Gender and Labor Militancy in the Appalachian South," *Journal of American History* 73 (Sept. 1986): 354–82, esp. 371–80.

15. U.S. Senate, *Report*, 352.

16. Hall, "Disorderly Women," 373, 374–75.

17. Ibid., 357.

18. Ibid., 379.

19. Queen interview.

20. Queen interview; Flamming, *Creating the Modern South*, Chap. 10.

21. On the crisis of poor-white patriarchy and its many ramifications for the southern cotton mill world, see Bryant Simon, *A Fabric of Defeat: The Politics of South Carolina Millhands, 1910–1948* (Chapel Hill: University of North Carolina Press, 1998), which has had a powerful impact on my thinking about southern millhands and which informs much of what I write below.

22. Flamming, *Creating the Modern South*, Chaps. 5–6.

23. David L. Carlton, *Mill and Town in South Carolina, 1880–1920* (Baton Rouge: Louisiana State University Press, 1982); and Simon, *Fabric of Defeat*, Chap. 1.

"The Women Are Asking for BREAD, Why Give Them STONE?": Women, Work, and Protests in Atlanta and Norfolk during World War I

Tera W. Hunter

African American women workers entered the twentieth century confined to the same jobs they had occupied since slavery. The outbreak of World War I offered new prospects, however, marking the first significant change in their opportunities since emancipation. This essay considers the black female workforce in two southern cities, Atlanta, Georgia, and Norfolk, Virginia, during this period. Black women in Norfolk were heavily concentrated in certain industries, most especially in tobacco. Unlike in the rest of the South, they held the majority of manufacturing and mechanical jobs that were open to women. Black women in Atlanta were a minority among industrial workers, but their numbers began to increase in scattered positions throughout the city. In both cases, domestic service continued to dominate their options. However slight their movement may have been into industrial fields, they still encountered much resistance from employers accustomed to controlling their labor. The more things changed, the more they stayed the same, despite African American women's determined efforts to take advantage of their momentary leverage in the labor market. The World War I era offers a window onto this new mobility and the repression it inspired in the South at a time when African Americans would begin to exercise the ultimate protest—packing their bags and leaving.

On the eve of World War I, most African Americans still tilled the soil in the rural South, or cooked, cleaned, washed laundry, and tended to the offspring of white employers in urban areas across the nation. But the war set in motion demonstrable changes in this long-standing pattern. Adult men

marched off or were shipped out to fight for their country, leaving behind
vacated jobs. European immigrants, a mainstay of American industry since
their arrival en masse at the end of the nineteenth century, began returning to fight in their home countries. Meanwhile, as government plants and
private industries struggled to meet the demands of civilians and the military both here and abroad, they were faced with an unprecedented labor
shortage of white men: so they began turning to women and racial minorities to fill in the gaps. These changes stimulated one of the most important
population shifts as well, as African Americans were actively recruited to
leave the South in large numbers and for the first time were able to take advantage of new jobs located in other regions.

Although the war prompted important changes for women's labor force
participation, businessmen and government officials were hesitant to dis-
rupt conventional gender assumptions about work and delayed the official
call for women to enter war-related production until fairly late. Official recognition lagged behind economic pressures of rising prices and diminished
living standards that pushed more women, especially wives, into the labor
market to help their families make ends meet. The most profound change
in women's work was the shift from domestic labor to factory and clerical
work, rather than a tremendous increase in the number of women entering the workforce for the first time. This departure from households to factories and offices was characterized by important racial differences. Black
women, already more than twice as likely to be engaged in waged work than
white women, filled the least-desirable jobs vacated by white women in domestic work in the North and at the bottom of the manufacturing hierarchy everywhere. Less frequently, they replaced the least-attractive jobs vacated by men and boys.[1]

Women of all races were mainly concentrated in industries such as textiles, clothing, foodstuffs, and tobacco products, just as they had been before the war began. Still, they were offered new jobs in munition plants making shells, gas masks, and airplane parts. They could also be seen taking
care of railroad tracks and cars, and working in meatpacking plants, stock-
yards, and metal shops. Black women were the minority within these firms,
as they were in other manufacturing concerns, such as those that made paper boxes, leather goods, hats, furniture, candy, and glass products. Increasing numbers could be found in clerical and sales positions in department stores, mail-order firms, and publishing houses.[2]

There were many local variations on this general theme. Detroit, according to at least one source, provided the best opportunities and the most nonconventional jobs for black women in the nation. They were hired into well-paying jobs in auto plants as machine operators, furnace workers, assemblers, inspectors, and clerical staff.[3] Chicago had the distinction of having one of the largest black populations in the country and also being one of the few cities in which the majority of black women were employed outside of domestic work. Packinghouses were the leading manufacturers that hired them to slaughter hogs, encase beef, trim internal organs, pack fat, and perform other assorted tasks that were all noxious, unhealthy, and dangerous.[4] In Philadelphia, the garment industry employed the largest number of black women in factories, primarily as pressers and trimmers, the least skilled work, though some became machine operators who produced lower-grade clothing such as overalls and house dresses. Blacks in Philadelphia were also occupied in related work in embroidery shops and quilt and cap factories.[5] Pittsburgh, on the other hand, with its concentration of heavy industries like steel and iron, limited occupations for black women— very closely resembling most cities in the South. There, 90 percent of black women were domestic workers in 1910 and as late as 1930—a higher percentage than in Norfolk and Atlanta.[6]

In the South as a whole, changes in black women's jobs outside domestic work developed more slowly.[7] The first hint of measurable change occurred between 1900 and 1910, when the proportion of black women domestics began to decline slightly and the number of seamstresses, dressmakers, tailoresses, and milliners increased.[8] The rising popularity of the fashion industry, mail-order catalogs, and department stores whetted the appetites of middle-class consumers to buy more clothing, which stimulated the demand for seamstresses. Some black women also did piecework at home for some of the thriving clothing manufacturers, though these jobs were mostly reserved for white women and girls. Most black dressmakers became independent artisans or helpers working at home or in shops they owned.[9] They also made small gains in white-collar clerical posts and sales jobs in black-owned insurance and retail shops. A cluster of black women ran businesses alone, with other women, or with spouses, including boardinghouses, lunch rooms, restaurants, groceries, secondhand clothing stores, hairdressing shops, dry goods stores, and ice cream and cold drink parlors. Some peddled their wares on the streets. Though black women were excluded from most factory jobs in the South, except for a few hired as cleaners, between 1900 and 1910 black women entered the commercial laundries more substantially than previously.[10] A nascent underground economy increasingly supplied working-class women with alternative sources of income and employment as gamblers, bootleggers, and prostitutes.[11]

This general pattern for the urban South applied to both Atlanta and Norfolk. By the end of the war in 1920, 82 percent of black women workers were still domestics in Norfolk. Yet black women in this port city held the majority of all manufacturing and mechanical jobs available to women. They were a virtual monopoly in tobacco work. Others were hired as dressmakers in nonfactory settings, though as white women left for better jobs during the war, positions in textile and garment factories, such as Mar-Hof and Chesapeake Knitting Mills, opened up to blacks. At Mar-Hof, the women were primarily responsible for hot and grueling tasks standing over the pressing machines. At Chesapeake Knitting Mills they worked as seamers. Peanut processors and candy manufacturers, like the Bosman and Lohman Company, hired a majority black workforce.[12]

The American Cigar Company was the leading tobacco factory in the city and hired the largest number of black women industrial workers. The company provided typical industrial work for black women not only in Norfolk but across the nation. Tobacco companies employed the second largest number of black women nationwide in industrial work, next to meatpacking plants. The tobacco firms that hired large numbers of black women were located mostly in the South. Black women worked as stemmers in cigar, chewing tobacco, and cigarette firms doing the same kind of work they had done in tobacco factories since the birth of that industry during the antebellum era. At American Cigar, the long-standing division of labor persisted, with black women sorting, picking, stemming, and cleaning tobacco—the dirtiest, least desirable work. Despite gains for black workers during World War I, they were unable to break the color line to gain prized skilled positions as cigar makers anywhere. As one employer explained the rationale, he preferred to hire only "pretty types of rather foreign appearance." Color prejudice and preferences for certain phenotypes were not unique to the tobacco industry, however. In the North, where black women were more likely to make small gains in retail and clerical positions, employers might hire black women with racially ambiguous physical features to work in sight of customers, but those who had "distinctly Negroid" appearances were confined to back rooms.[13]

Conditions in Norfolk tobacco plants were atrocious, as they were in most southern cigar factories. Workers sat for hours on rows of benches without any support for their backs. Makeshift stools or boxes were used as well. Malodorous smells permeated unclean buildings that lacked adequate ventilation, and sunlight was shut out by aprons or burlap bags hung over windows by managers. One report summarized the southern tobacco worker's experience: "It was not uncommon to see workers with handkerchiefs tied over their nostrils to prevent inhaling the stifling, strangling air."[14] Black women were usually separated into the worst sections and floors of the factory, away from white workers. Sanitary facilities for them were inadequate, and provisions for clean drinking water could be reduced to a barrel with a common drinking cup attached by a chain.[15]

Workers put in ten-hour days that could easily stretch into overtime, five and a half days per week, for low wages during a season that typically ran from September through May. In the off-season, tobacco workers had to find other ways of making a living. But even during the season, workers were subject to periods of unemployment, reducing their paltry earnings even further.[16]

The conditions for black women in southern tobacco plants were so abysmal that one investigator for the Department of Labor's Women's Bureau compared them to slavery. "The typical tobacco employer in the Southland thinks of his Negro women workers as his 'property,'" reported Emma Shields.[17] The paternalism of the employer-worker relationship impressed Shields as having inspired mutual "reliance and trust." She perceived a kind of "childlike sense of obedience, loyalty, and allegiance" among workers in relation to the factory management. She understood this as their "fear and suspicion" on the one hand, and "blind submission to authority" on the other, found evidence of resignation and submission in their seemingly pacified countenances as they sang songs and worked.[18] Events in Norfolk during World War I, however, would call these assumptions into question.

Political consciousness and labor unrest became noticeable once war broke out in Europe. When the United States officially entered the war in April 1917, labor shortages became more acute and taxed the capability of businesses to fill vacated and newly created jobs. The federal government sought to neutralize the advantage either to industry or to workers, eliciting a promise from Samuel Gompers, the president of the American Federation of Labor (AFL), to discourage his membership from using the occasion to "change existing standards." But the exceptional strike activity during the war effectively repudiated Gompers's pledge.[19] African American workers were among those who refused to yield to this compromise with the capitalists and the state. As some blacks departed in large numbers to jobs in northern industries to escape Jim Crow, others remained in the South and wielded the new leverage at their disposal to alter the existing standards of racism and poverty.

The first signs that black women in Norfolk were taking advantage of wartime opportunities to organize collectively became apparent by the spring of 1916, when the Working-Women's Union was created by mostly domestic workers. Unfortunately, there is little extant documentation of this organization, beyond what follows. It celebrated its one-year anniversary in May 1917 at the Queens Street Baptist Church and marched in the Labor Day parade of that year as well. Mrs. E. V. Kelly served as president and Mrs. E. L. Cherry as secretary.[20] The national office of the Women's Trade Union League tried to harness this new organizing energy by sending Mildred Rankin, a black organizer, to Norfolk. According to a report she made at the 1919 WTUL convention, there were "a thousand or more" of these women organized in Norfolk and nearby Portsmouth. Rankin was most impressed that the women organized by locale, not trade, though domestic workers appeared to have been dominant. She was also struck by the fraternal structure of their organization, which included sick and death benefits for its membership. "They are exceedingly careful about taking care of the family of a sick member. They will care for her children, clothe and feed them, send them to school or take them into their own homes. They have a hold on each other that is very touching and very remarkable," Rankin reported.[21] These attributes may have surprised Rankin, but they were not exceptional; they were consistent with the structure of many black labor organizations dating back to Reconstruction.[22] Though Rankin was appreciative of the women's initiative and solidarity, she was not able to make progress beyond what the women had already accomplished before her arrival on the scene a year after they were organized.[23] This activity was just one among other attempts to link black workers in Norfolk to regional and national labor organizations.

A similar attempt to draw black women under a national labor umbrella was urged by the *Norfolk Journal and Guide* to stimulate interest in forming a branch of the Women Wage-Earners Association, a Washington, D.C.–based group created by middle-class black women in January 1917. Its roster of officers included leading professionals and social activists such as Mary Church Terrell, former president of the National Association of Colored Women. The group's leadership was self-identified as "public spirited women of the race who have homes of their own and resources independent of service for others for wages." Their main objective was to improve the working and living conditions of all black women workers, to "help those who need help and are unable to help themselves."[24] The group also desired to improve relations between workers and employers; to promote efficient and faithful service; and to provide a home that would serve as a combination of employment agency, residence for unemployed workers, and training school in domestic science. The editors of the black newspaper praised the organization and encouraged women in Norfolk and Virginia to establish local and state branches. No further mention of the Women's Wage-Earners Association was made. Nonetheless, women in Norfolk failed to live up to the image of being "unable to help themselves."[25]

The fall of 1917 brought several strikes by black workers in Norfolk. More than three hundred black women stemmers employed at the American Cigar Company, the largest tobacco factory in the city, led the way by calling a strike in early September. The women demanded higher wages, shorter hours, improved factory conditions, and recognition of their union, the Sisterhood Local No. 1, which was affiliated with the Transport Workers Association (TWA), the city's most effective black union.[26]

The rising cost of living was at the heart of the strike in Norfolk, just as it had prompted protests and food riots throughout the nation, especially among women workers and housewives.[27] The women demanded $1.25 per day, rather than the $.70 they had been receiving. The *Journal* argued in support of their demands, saying, "We do not believe that under present conditions any adult laborer, man or woman, can subsist upon much less than the factory women are making."[28] The *Journal* calculated the cost of house rent, food, fuel, clothing, insurance, church and lodge dues, and other incidentals as necessary expenses that exceeded the wages the stemmers were paid. Large numbers of these women were the primary breadwinners in their families, but even those with husbands and other employed household members were contributing essential resources to their families' survival.

The American Cigar Company rejected the workers' arguments, contending that the demands were unreasonable for unskilled, women workers. Moreover, managers argued, black women at their plant received higher wages than any other workers of their race and sex in the city. Despite their reservations, the managers compromised on wages by offering to raise the average daily pay to $1.00. The wages would be paid on a piece-rate basis, however, determined by the weight of the tobacco after, rather than before, it was stripped. They also agreed to reduce the hours to nine per day. But the company steadfastly refused to recognize the women's union and closed shop despite a monthlong strike.

Indeed, the management blamed the strike on the men in the TWA, apparently in disbelief that the women were capable of organizing protests without outside influence and resentful of the involvement of a well-established union. Their suspicions were not entirely groundless, as the TWA *was* involved in the strike. TWA representatives apparently had submitted the formal demand to the company on behalf of the Sisterhood Local No. 1. But the women as well as the TWA denied that the men had organized the strike. Arkansas Gray, the head of the group, claimed that it was opposed to strikes and only learned about the women's walkout after the fact. On the other hand, the TWA set up a fund that would prove critical to helping sustain the strike for several weeks.[29]

The women initially seemed to agree to the compromise. An announcement of an end to the strike turned out to be premature, however, as the women waited for a sick manager to return to work, then made it clear that they were holding out for union recognition. Meanwhile, other black workers in the city began to follow their lead. Five hundred black men and women at local oyster shucking and packing plants went on strike in early October, forcing several to close down entirely or to shut down those departments that were hurt most severely. The oyster workers, like the tobacco workers, formed an affiliation with the TWA, which was trying to organize black workers in every trade where they had a strong presence. Similarly, the domestic workers and waitresses in the city threatened to go on strike, not coincidentally, for the TWA had been recruiting them. The women wanted $1.00 per day in wages, a five-day work week, and improved working conditions. Neither the oyster shuckers nor the domestic workers appeared to be as effective as the tobacco stemmers, however. Nor were they as strategically positioned as the dock workers in the greater Chesapeake Bay vicinity, who merely threatened to strike for higher wages and won concessions from their employers to avert the walkout. The shuckers and the domestics met more systematic repression.[30]

Local officials called on the force of the federal government to undermine the power of the TWA and its affiliates by investigating the group for violating its original charter as a fraternal order. The local police were authorized to break the strike by arresting oyster shuckers picketing near the ferry landing. Norfolk, the center of the oyster and fish packing industry, was an important food supplier for the war effort. To contain the agitation of the city's white housewives upset over the threat of a domestic workers' strike, police were instructed to arrest "loafing" black women as well. The *Journal* challenged the logic of this repression: "The men and women who are present[ly] asking for a living wage in Norfolk are neither slackers, loafers or law-breakers. They are working people affected by the increase in the cost of living just like thousands of white men who are striking all over the country are affected." As it pointed out, the police did not arrest the three thousand white men on strike at the navy yards. "No government sleuths and legal sharps were sent down to pry into the charter provisions of the unions to which the men belonged." The article concluded with this rhetorical question: "The women are asking for BREAD, why give them STONE?" The domestic workers failed to win their general strike. The oyster shuckers started going back to work within a few days. "The guarded presence of the government agents in the colored section" and the threat of further arrests if agitation continued seem to have effectively deterred both groups.[31]

What do the strikes suggest? African Americans in Norfolk organized some of the most successful protests in the region, largely enabled by the strength of the TWA. Black men in the city dominated dock work and used their leverage in the crucial wartime shipping industry in an essential port city to demand higher wages, union recognition, and other important improvements in their working conditions. The TWA was not satisfied with success in transport industries alone and spearheaded a labor movement to reach out to women and men, skilled and unskilled alike. The cross-fertilization of labor organizing and multiple strikes the TWA helped to inspire provides a window into black workers' consciousness at a pivotal moment. Though overwhelmingly excluded from white unions, black workers used their numerical strength in certain jobs to turn racial exclusivity to their own advantage. They organized a broad-based labor union drive at an unparalleled moment of working-class leverage. It is also evident that their consciousness of the importance of harnessing gender, skill, and racial solidarity extended to support for other black workers outside of their city. The local black newspaper kept its readers abreast of other labor protests in the region, especially news from North Carolina, from which many residents had migrated in recent years. When black women at a Rocky Mount, North Carolina, knitting mill struck in the spring of 1917 and demanded to be treated with respect, blacks in Norfolk cheered them on—deriving inspiration for carrying out similar acts in their hometown.[32]

The black middle class, as far as it can be represented by spokespersons from the *Journal*, supported workers' efforts to organize and fight for their rights during the war. But not even all black workers held identical opinions about how to regard union solidarity. Internal differences based on occupation, age, and family circumstances had undermined the unity of the oyster shuckers during their strike. Both the broad-based working-class solidarity and the support that workers derived from the middle class would diminish in the postwar period. The TWA would be absorbed by the International Longshoremen's Association (ILA), which was much more committed to traditional trade union organizing. While the ILA had the avantage of giving more clout to the Norfolk dockworkers, former TWA members compromised their ability to foster black labor solidarity across skill, occupation, and gender.[33]

The implications of the cigar stemmers' strike must also be understood in the context of the broader industry. Few African Americans belonged to the Cigar Makers International Union because of both discrimination from employers that kept them confined to dirty work and prejudice from fellow white workers. Yet union and nonunion workers alike struck in record numbers during the war. They took advantage of the labor shortage in the industry, as white men deserted the factories in search of better-paying jobs and looked for ways to escape the draft by working in essential war-related production. The Norfolk strike in the fall of 1917 coincided with a wave of cigar workers' walkouts across the nation, not coincidentally, at the beginning of the new season.

In addition, though black women were confined to dirty, dead-end, low-wage labor in the factories, their work involved essential preparation for cigar production. Cleaning and stemming the tobacco was necessary before the actual process of rolling the cigars could begin. Undoubtedly, this boosted their bargaining power and led to some concessions on wages. Their concentration in jobs stigmatized as black women's work in Norfolk, which dated back to the slave industries, would not make it easy to replace them with strikebreakers.[34]

The strikes speak loudest about continued repression and the slow pace of economic justice for African Americans. Despite the escalation of labor organizing in this period, most black workers were unable to make or to sustain relative employment gains. Norfolk had a record migration of blacks into the city in the second decade of the twentieth century, higher than any other southern city. Yet reverse migration of even higher numbers occurred after 1920. As their hopes for improvements were dashed, they continued their journey for better opportunities in the North and Midwest.[35]

The domestic workers' unrest in Norfolk was more representative than the tobacco workers' of the overall thrust of black women's labor protests in southern cities. Furtive labor organizing was afoot in Gainesville, Georgia, and employers took note. "The negro women in their lodges or in some other organization established for that purpose had formed an agreement as to the amount of work, number of hours, and the wage which they would agree upon with the whites," reported one investigator. Black women adopted the motto W.W.T.K. ("White Women to the Kitchen") and instructed their members to abandon service altogether.[36] A secret society may have been responsible for a surreptitious strike among domestics in Rock Hill, South Carolina, in 1919. The workers identified their affiliation in a euphemistic "Fold-the-Arms Club"—a slogan identified with the Industrial Workers of the World. Employers were puzzled by the action and source of discontent. "More difficulty is experienced by Colored labor now than ever before in the history of the city and no one seems to be able to learn just what the trouble is," a reporter explained.[37]

Black women in Houston established the Women's Domestic Union in 1916 and affiliated with the AFL. In New Orleans, Ella Pete organized the Domestic Servants' Union with more than one thousand members and, through negotiations rather than strikes, demanded higher wages and shorter hours. The union faced threats of federal investigations for promoting German propaganda.[38] Other domestics, like the cooks, maids, and nurses in Elizabeth City, North Carolina, took advantage of the labor shortage by demanding higher wages in 1917.[39]

African American household workers in Atlanta likewise used well-worn clandestine union organizing tactics, which became an issue in a political campaign. Joseph M. Brown, son of the Civil War governor Joseph E. Brown, ran for the U.S. Senate against the incumbent, Hoke Smith, in 1914. "There is abundant circumstantial evidence to support the opinion among white people that in these secret societies the negroes discuss and try to regulate the price of cooking, nursing, chopping cotton, cotton picking, etc.," the younger Brown reasoned.[40] Most perturbed by domestic workers who used the "blacklist" through their fraternal orders to censor employers, Brown regarded the threat of uprisings to be the highest insult to white supremacy.

"Every white lady in whose home negro servants are hired then becomes subservient to these negroes," he forewarned.[41] Yet by devoting such energy to assailing household workers and their organizations, Brown inadvertently revealed the power of organized mutuality to challenge unfair labor practices.

To foment the racial fears of the white electorate, Brown raised the specter of interracial labor solidarity between black secret societies and white labor unions. "I have often wondered whether there was any connection between these negro secret societies and the white union leaders of the cities," he speculated.[42] Brown hoped to sully the reputation of his opponent, an ally of the white labor movement, by accusing him of currying favor with blacks. He identified the Georgia Federation of Labor and the Southern Labor Congress as the culprits responsible for organizing black workers to promote social equality—a charge that white labor activists in Atlanta vehemently denied.

The white trade unionists defended themselves against Brown's accusations by reminding the public that "the 'nigger' question is generally the last and most desperate resort of demagogues to win votes." They admitted the importance of black workers organizing in separate unions to prevent undercutting white workers, but they opposed any semblance of racial equality. "'Little Joe' knows that there is not a single white labor unionist in Georgia, or the South, who would stand for that sort of thing," they insisted. Though Joe Brown stirred up trouble by making such an insinuation, he lost the campaign.[43]

The assortment of repressive retaliations against household workers' resistance is itself a measure of black women's effectiveness in foiling the best-laid plans of Jim Crow employers. Employers in Atlanta rallied to forestall the topsy-turvy world Brown had warned against in his Senate campaign. The World War I era evoked memories of the Civil War period, not only in the racist parallels unearthed by the revival of the Ku Klux Klan and the popularity of the pioneering film *The Birth of the Nation*, but also in the resurgence of tactics used by disgruntled employers. The class actions of postwar planters reverberated in the "collectives" urban employers formed to regulate the wages of household workers and stymie competition. White housekeepers in Atlanta formed an organization for "mutual protection against the exactions which come from the inefficient servant."[44] This spirit of collaboration reached Savannah also, as one employer explained: "The women of Georgia have organized in nearly everything under the sun except to help one another in the matter of regulating domestic service." The employers proposed "pledge cards," with connotations of wartime loyalty oaths, to guarantee that the signers would abide by the agreed wages.

One of the most repressive wartime measures levied against black women workers originated as a military promulgation. In May 1918, Enoch Crowder, as the Selective Service director, issued a "work or fight" order to conscript unemployed men into the armed forces. Trade unionists, alarmed by the persecutions that British workers on strike suffered under similar laws, immediately criticized the promulgation. Newton D. Baker, the secretary of war, reassured them of protection, but striking machinists in Bridgeport, Connecticut, were threatened with the order the next year.[45] Southern legislatures and city councils never displayed this Janus face. They deliberately designed their own "work or fight" laws to break the will of black workers, abandoning the original intention of the federal measure, which had been to fill the army with able-bodied *men*, and focusing instead on prosecuting black *women* and forcing them to work in domestic labor, jobs that were unrelated to the business of war.[46]

Conscripting household labor, however, appealed to domestic employers facing their first substantial competition from industries seeking to hire black women. Between 1910 and 1920, the proportion of wage-earning black women in household work dropped from 84 to 75 percent.[47] Occupational choices for black women continued to follow the trend of previous decades, but new options opened as men joined the military and the demand for labor increased. Even before the war broke out, the Atlanta Woolen Mills and other small plants that manufactured women's clothing began hiring black women. The Fulton Bag and Cotton Mill employed 121 black women by early 1914, this time without precipitating a walkout by white workers, as had been the case in the 1890s.[48] Mill managers put black women in segregated groups in the handbag, printing, carding, spinning, and weaving departments. Black women also worked with black men as scrubbers and sweepers in the yards and waste house and performed domestic labor in the cafeteria and nursery. After the war began, cottonseed oil, furniture, lumber, box, pencil, metal, casket, candy, and garment factories hired black women. Only a minority of firms in the city followed suit, however, and the overall numbers in industries remained small.[49] Still, employers of domestic labor resented even mild constraints on their unfettered access to black women's labor.

Patriotism was used to justify the containment of this new mobility. Officials and employers labeled black women who refused to work as domestics as "idlers" even if they were gainfully employed in other fields. A group in nearby Macon, calling itself "friends" of the Negro, sent a warning to black women "slackers" who failed to follow the example of selfless white women who were taking jobs even when they did not need the earnings. All black women, regardless of their economic circumstances or personal preferences, were expected to fulfill their civic duty by engaging in "the labor [for] which they are specially trained and otherwise adapted." Black servants facilitated the entry of white women into war production by releasing them "from the routine of housework in order that they may do the work which negro women cannot do," it was stated. But the Macon group also contended that black women were obligated to serve their country in this way because they owed a special debt to society: the "liberality of the government they are asked to defend has already placed them beyond want." The Macon "friends" concluded their advice with a thinly veiled admonition. "We prefer to appeal to the patriotism and the public duty of those who are idle to accept the employment offered them by their white friends." But if necessary, they vowed to enforce allegiance to "Old Glory" more energetically." [50]

Local "work or fight" laws embodied the "energetic" means to elicit black women's loyalty. They intensified both extralegal violence and legal coercion to force black women into domestic work. A vigilante group in Vicksburg, Mississippi, initiated a crusade to make its community "one hundred per cent American" by ridding the streets of "idle" black workers. The group tarred and feathered Ethel Barrett and Ella Brooks. While the vigilantes escaped punishment, the physically scarred and humiliated victims were forced into court to substantiate their employment as washerwomen. Meanwhile, Barrett's husband fought in France to make the world safe for democracy, although neither he nor his wife was guaranteed the protection of fundamental human rights at home. [51]

Black women were attacked in this patriotic campaign all over the South. Police arrested Maria Parker in Wetumpka, Alabama, because her chosen occupation as a hairdresser was not appropriately servile according to the criteria of the "work or fight" law. The town marshal seized Parker and a washerwoman working on her lot for "vagrancy." This same officer routinely monitored black women's labor output by counting the clothes hanging in their yards and arrested women who fell short of the quotas he established. Just a few miles away, in Montgomery, the police apprehended

Clare Williams and sentenced her to ninety days in the stockade because she worked as a domestic for a black family. It was not enough to work as a servant if one did not labor for whites. Black housewives suffered the worst harassment by this logic.[52]

Atlanta blacks began to organize an assault on "work or fight" persecutions through the NAACP. O. A. Toomer, the secretary of the Atlanta branch, contacted the national office for advice and support. John R. Shillady, the national secretary, responded to Toomer by cautioning him against attacking the laws prematurely. "Many of our northern and eastern cities are passing such laws and they are being sustained by public opinion owing to the war," Shillady wrote. "It may, therefore be dangerous to fight these laws lest the organization be characterized as disloyal in so doing."[53] He urged the Atlanta branch to emphasize curtailing racial discrimination in the application of the laws rather than openly denouncing the measures themselves.

Several months later, however, the national office dispatched Walter F. White to investigate southern conditions, which changed its perspective. "You will remember that when we were discussing the advisability of my making this investigation or study, that there was some doubt in both your mind and in mine as to whether the practice of conscripting Negro labor was extensive as yet," White reported to Shillady. "You will also remember that I said that if the condition was not actual, at present, it was potential and might develop, if not checked at the outset," he continued. "Well, since being here in the South I have learned the condition is not a potential one but rather a full grown development."[54]

Armed with substantial evidence of widespread abuse, the NAACP began an exhaustive campaign to abolish and preempt "work or fight" laws. The exploitation of black women household workers had become a lightning rod for this impetus and catapulted the presence of the NAACP below the Mason-Dixon Line. The material resources and moral support committed to this issue bolstered black resistance and escalated the NAACP's southern membership. Local organizations in the South that were formed expressly to fight wartime repression were inspired to reconstitute as branches of the NAACP.[55]

Buoyed by this esprit de corps, Atlanta blacks protested the inclusion of women in "work or fight" legislation that was pending before the state legislature and Governor Hugh Dorsey. African Americans politely but firmly reminded the governor of the negative ramifications of racist and sexist discrimination on the state's economy in the wake of the dramatic black migration under way. The law passed both houses of the legislature, but the governor vetoed the bill.

When the Atlanta City Council entertained a similar law, the NAACP defeated it as well. Peter James Bryant, a minister and member of the NAACP, summarized the group's strategy: "We went up before His Honor, the Mayor, looked him squarely in the face and told him that the bill meant simply humiliation to black women and that black men had the same respect for their women as white men had for theirs." Bryant and other black men were outraged by the prosecution of gainfully employed women and especially by the harassment of housewives expected to cease taking care of their own husbands, families, and homes in favor of serving whites. They called the law unconstitutional "class legislation" because it was punitive toward mostly working-class women and would not be applied to white women.[56]

African Americans throughout the South attempted to duplicate the Atlanta success but accomplished mixed results. Though trade unions won a victory in New Orleans for black women, those in other cities were not so fortunate. Valdosta and Wrightsville, Georgia; Birmingham and Montgomery, Alabama; and Jackson, Mississippi, passed ordinances specifically mandating black women to carry work verification cards, despite determined resistance.[57] Regardless of whether or not localities mandated the inclusion of women in "work or fight" provisions, women were routinely subjected to harassment. Seventeen-year-old Nellie Atkins and Ruth Warf were arrested in Atlanta for refusing to work as household servants. "You can not make us work," they proclaimed to the police. They proceeded to break windows to vent their anger at the injustice of their arrest, which only fueled the judge to double their sentences to sixty days each in the prison laundry.[58]

The manipulation of household workers during the war revealed another variation on a familiar theme. The South had a long history of disdain for the principles of free labor, especially when the workers were black. White southerners sought recourse in legal and physical coercion to achieve black female subservience because they could not achieve this in any other way during a period of unusual mobility. Beneath the rhetoric of "vagrancy," "idleness," and "patriotism," employers were distressed by black women's relative agency. As women moved into new jobs or migrated north, those who remained in domestic labor and in the South used the threat of leaving to their advantage. Investigations by the NAACP and others confirm that when workers quit or withdrew from the labor market temporarily, demanded higher wages, or expressed discontent in any way, employers summoned "work or fight" laws to retaliate against them.[59] But if "work or fight" laws were designed to contain black mobility and force women to work under oppressive conditions, this strategy backfired. Black women and men were fed up with endless degradation and sought relief by leaving the region en masse.

Black women workers had experienced new opportunities with jobs in industries opening up to them for the first time during World War I. In the case of Norfolk, they strengthened their foothold in the tobacco industry and entered other manufacturing jobs as well. In Atlanta, black women were less concentrated in any one industry and more scattered throughout different factories. However small these gains may have been, they created anxiety for plant managers accustomed to setting the terms of labor without open dissent and for employers of domestic workers acclimated to having a near monopoly on access to black women workers. Black women had organized protests and strikes to combat the unfairness of prevailing standards in traditional occupations and tapped a wealth of support among other women and men across class in their communities, most prominently in local trade unions and branches of national organizations such as the NAACP. In Norfolk, the TWA identified women as vital to its goal of developing a broad-based black labor movement in the city and used its considerable resources to aid their job actions. In Atlanta, the NAACP defined women's issues as community issues, in fighting against repressive "work or fight" laws, although, in doing so, male spokespersons sometimes articulated their prerogatives as men to defend against incursions on access to the labor of their wives. Despite the paternalism implicit in this assumption and the salient image of black women as docile workers, black women workers proved to be quite capable of acting on their own behalf. They were met, however, with a variety of countertactics by equally determined employers eager to maintain their subordination. Many black women left the South during this period because the concessions they gained were not adequate to meet their immediate needs and future ambitions. Once the war was over, whether they had stayed in the South or moved to the North, black women faced more setbacks. As the last hired into wartime jobs, they were the first fired to make room for returning soldiers. A report from the Women's Bureau summed up the situation: the black woman worker during World War I "has been accepted, in the main, as an experiment; her admittance to a given occupation or plant has been conditioned upon no other workers being available, and her continuance hinged upon the same. She was usually given the least desirable jobs."[60] It would take World War II and decades of civil rights protests before black women could safely escape confinement to the worst-paid and least-respected jobs.

Notes

1. U.S. Department of Labor, Women's Bureau, *Negro Women in Industry* (Washington, D.C.: Government Printing Office, 1922), 5–15; Philip S. Foner, *Organized Labor and the Black Worker, 1619–1973* (New York: Praeger, 1974), 120–31; Margaret A. Hobbs, "Workingwomen of America during the War," in *The American Labor Year Book, 1919–1920,* ed. Alexander Trachtenburg (New York: Rand School of Social Science, 1920), 20.

2. U.S. Department of Labor, *Negro Women in Industry,* 2–8, 31–39.

3. Forrester B. Washington, "Reconstruction and the Colored Woman," *Life and Labor,* Jan. 1919, 5–6.

4. Ibid., 3–5; James R. Grossman, *Land of Hope: Chicago, Black Southerners, and the Great Migration* (Chicago: University of Chicago Press, 1989), 184–85, 189–90.

5. Consumers' League of Eastern Pennsylvania, *Colored Women as Industrial Workers in Philadelphia* (n.p., 1919–20), 8–18.

6. Peter Gottlieb, *Making Their Own Way: Southern Blacks' Migration to Pittsburgh, 1916–1930* (Urbana: University of Illinois Press, 1989), 104–11.

7. For more detailed analysis of black women workers in the South, especially Atlanta, see Tera W. Hunter, *To 'Joy My Freedom: Southern Black Women's Lives and Labors after the Civil War* (Cambridge, Mass.: Harvard University Press, 1997).

8. W. E. B. Du Bois, ed., *The Negro Artisan* (Atlanta: Atlanta University, 1902), 90; W. E. B. Du Bois, ed., *The Negro American Artisan* (Atlanta: Atlanta University, 1912), 46; U.S. Department of the Interior, Bureau of the Census, *Report of the Population of the United States at the Eleventh Census: 1890* (Washington, D.C.: Government Printing Office, 1897), pt. 2, pp. 634–35; U.S. Department of Commerce and Labor, Bureau of the Census, *Special Reports: Occupations at the Twelfth Census* (Washington, D.C.: Government Printing Office, 1904), 486–89.

9. On dressmakers see Eileen Boris, "Black Women and Paid Labor in the Home: Industrial Homework in Chicago in the 1920s," in *Homework: Historical and Contemporary Perspectives on Paid Labor at Home,* ed. Eileen Boris and Cynthia R. Daniels (Urbana: University of Illinois Press, 1989), 33–38; Joan Jensen, "Needlework as Art, Craft, and Livelihood before 1900," in *A Needle, a Bobbin, a Strike: Women Needleworkers in America,* ed. Joan M. Jensen and Sue Davidson (Philadelphia: Temple University Press, 1984), 13–16; Ava Baron and Susan E. Kelp, "'If I Didn't Have My Sewing

Machine': Women and Sewing-Machine Technology," in *Needle*, ed. Jensen and Davidson, 47, 50; Gretchen Ehrmann Maclachlan, "Women's Work: Atlanta's Industrialization, 1879–1929" (Ph.D. diss., Emory University, 1992), 33–34, 52.

10. See *Weekly Defiance*, 24 Feb. 1883; *Atlanta Independent*, 26 Mar. 1904, 3 Mar. 1906, 1 Aug. 1906; *Atlanta Constitution*, 5 Aug. 1903, 15 Mar. 1907; Bureau of the Census, *Report of the Population of the United States at the Eleventh Census: 1890*, pt. 2, pp. 634–35; Bureau of the Census, *Special Reports: Occupations at the Twelfth Census*, pp. 486–89; U.S. Department of the Interior, Bureau of the Census, *Thirteenth Census of the United States Taken in the Year 1910*, vol. 4, *Population, Occupational Statistics* (Washington, D.C.: Government Printing Office, 1914), 536–37; Maclachlan, "Women's Work," 19–93.

11. For example, see *Atlanta Constitution*, 17 Sept. 1895, 3 July 1899, 2 Feb. 1909, 8 Feb. 1912.

12. Earl Lewis, *In Their Own Interests: Race, Class, and Power in Twentieth-Century Norfolk, Virginia* (Berkeley: University of California Press, 1991), 36–38, 60–61.

13. U.S. Department of Labor, *Negro Women in Industry*, 37–38; George E. Haynes, *The Negro at Work during World War and Reconstruction: Statistics, Problems, and Policies Relating to the Greater Inclusion of Negro Wage Earners in American Industry and Agriculture* (Washington, D.C.: Government Printing Office, 1921), 27–128.

14. Emma L. Shields, "A Half-Century in the Tobacco Industry," *Southern Workman* 51 (Sept. 1922): 422; Shields, "Negro Women and the Tobacco Industry," *Life and Labor*, May 1921, 144.

15. Haynes, *Negro at Work*, 126–28; Shields, "Half-Century in Tobacco," 422–23; Dolores Janiewski, *Sisterhood Denied: Race, Gender, and Class in a New South Community* (Philadelphia: Temple University Press, 1985), 99–101.

16. Shields, "Half-Century in Tobacco," 422–23; U.S. Department of Labor, Women's Bureau, *Hours and Conditions of Work for Women in Industry in Virginia* (Washington, D.C.: Government Printing Office, 1920), 20–26.

17. Shields, "Half-Century in Tobacco," 420.

18. Ibid.; Lewis, *In Their Own Interests*, 61.

19. David Montgomery, *The Fall of the House of Labor: The Workplace, the State, and American Labor Activism, 1865–1925* (New York: Cambridge University Press, 1987), 370–82.

20. *Norfolk Journal and Guide*, 19 May, 26 May, and 8 Sept. 1917.

21. "Organization Needed in the South," *Life and Labor*, July 1919, 182.

22. See Hunter, *To 'Joy My Freedom*, 70–73, 131–35.

23. Lewis, *In Their Own Interests*, 53; Philip S. Foner, *Women in the American Labor Movement: From World War I to the Present* (New York: Free Press, 1980), vol. 2, p. 65.

24. *Norfolk Journal and Guide*, 3 Mar. 1917.

25. Ibid. See Evelyn Brooks Higginbotham, *Righteous Discontent: The Women's Movement in the Black Baptist Church, 1880–1920* (Cambridge, Mass.: Harvard Uni-

versity Press, 1993), 218–21, 293; Hunter, *To 'Joy My Freedom*, 132, 274; Philip S. Foner and Ronald L. Lewis, *The Black Worker: A Documentary History from Colonial Times to the Present*, vol. 5, *The Black Worker from 1900 to 1919* (Philadelphia: Temple University Press, 1980), 455–56.

26. *Virginia-Pilot and Norfolk Landmark*, 26 Sept. 1917.

27. Foner, *Women in the American Labor Movement*, 494–95; Montgomery, *Fall of the House of Labor*, 370.

28. *Journal and Guide*, 29 Sept. 1917.

29. *Virginia-Pilot*, 25 and 26 Sept. 1917.

30. *Journal and Guide*, 6 and 13 Oct. 1917; *Virginia-Pilot*, 2–6 Oct. 1917.

31. *Journal and Guide*, 6 Oct. 1917.

32. *Journal and Guide*, 3 and 17 Mar. 1917.

33. Lewis, *In Their Own Interests*, 55, 59–61.

34. Patricia A. Cooper, *Once a Cigar Maker: Men, Women, and Work Culture in American Cigar Factories, 1900–1919* (Urbana: University of Illinois Press, 1992), 250, 272–74.

35. Lewis, *In Their Own Interests*, 30.

36. Reed, *Negro Women of Gainesville*, 46.

37. *Savannah Tribune*, 31 May 1919.

38. *New Orleans Louisiana States*, 23 July 1918, in Tuskegee Institute News Clip File (hereinafter cited as TINF).

39. *Journal and Guide*, 25 Sept. 1917.

40. For more details of this and other domestic workers' protests, see Hunter, *To 'Joy My Freedom*; 1914 campaign literature, Joseph M. Brown Papers, Atlanta History Center (hereinafter cited as AHC).

41. Campaign literature, Joseph M. Brown Papers, AHC; Dewey Grantham, *Hoke Smith and the Politics of the New South* (Baton Rouge: Louisiana State University Press, 1958), 270–73.

42. Campaign literature, Joseph M. Brown Papers, AHC. Also see *Atlanta Constitution*, 31 Mar. 1910. The owner of Crawford Coal and Ice Company reported that black men had boycotted his company as a result of their involvement in a secret society. He stated that other firms were facing a similar situation.

43. *Atlanta Journal of Labor*, 24 July 1914. See also *Atlanta Journal of Labor*, 1 May 1914.

44. *Atlanta Constitution*, 8 Oct. 1914.

45. David M. Kennedy, *Over Here: The First World War and American Society* (New York: Oxford University Press, 1980), 269.

46. Walter F. White, "'Work or Fight' in the South," *New Republic*, 1 Mar. 1919, 144–46; Cynthia Neverdon-Morton, *Afro-American Women of the South and the Advancement of the Race, 1895–1925* (Knoxville: University of Tennessee Press, 1989), 73.

47. U.S. Bureau of the Census, *Fourteenth Census of the United States Taken in the Year*

1920, vol. 4, *Population, Occupations* (Washington, D.C.: Government Printing Office, 1923), 1053–56.

48. See Hunter, *To 'Joy My Freedom*, 114–20; Gary M Fink, *The Fulton Bag and Cotton Mills Strike of 1914–1915: Espionage, Labor Conflict, and New South Industrial Relations* (Ithaca: ILR Press, 1993), 40–41.

49. Maclachlan, "Women's Work," 86–87, 90–98; Haynes, *Negro at Work during World War and Reconstruction*, 124–33.

50. *Macon News*, 18 Oct. 1918, in TINF. The federal government also made similar appeals to black women through war propaganda. See for example, the *Portsmouth (Va.) Star*, 21 Oct. 1918, in TINF.

51. Walter F. White, "Report of Conditions Found in Investigation of 'Work or Fight' Laws in Southern States," Group 1, Series C, Administrative Files, National Association for the Advancement of Colored People Papers, Library of Congress (hereinafter cited as NAACP, LC).

52. White, "Report of Conditions Found in Investigation of 'Work or Fight' Laws in Southern States."

53. John R. Shillady to O. A. Toomer, 5 Oct. 1918, Group 1, Series G, Branch Files, NAACP, LC.

54. Walter F. White to Shillady, 26 Oct. 1918, Group 1, Series C, Administrative Files, NAACP, LC.

55. See "Tenth Anniversary Conference of the National Association of Colored People: Reports of Branches," 28 June 1919, Group 1, Series B, Annual Conference Files, NAACP, LC; and A. B. Johnson to James Weldon Johnson, 16 Dec. 1918, Group 1, Series G, Branch Files, NAACP, LC.

56. Rev. P. J. Bryant, Remarks to the 10th Annual Conference of the NAACP, 24 June 1919, Group 1, Series B, Annual Conference Files, NAACP, LC; *Atlanta Constitution*, 9 Nov. 1918. Also see *Atlanta Constitution*, 10 July–25 Aug., 9 Nov. 1918; John Dittmer, *Black Georgia in the Progressive Era, 1900–1920* (Urbana: University of Illinois Press, 1977), 198.

57. White, "'Work or Fight' in the South," 144–46; *Chicago Defender*, 13 July 1918, in TINF; *New York Age*, 19 Oct., 16 Nov. 1918, in TINF.

58. Quoted in *Baltimore Daily Herald*, 10 Sept. 1918, Group 1, Series C, Administrative Files, NAACP, LC.

59. See for example, *New York Age*, 19 and 20 Nov. 1918, in TINF.

60. Haynes, *Negro at Work*, 133.

Fearing Eleanor: Racial Anxieties and Wartime Rumors in the American South, 1940–1945

Bryant Simon

Throughout the early years of World War II, white southerners passed fearsome rumors back and forth about African American uprisings. These stories warned that blacks were on the verge of a bloody rebellion. While perhaps more intense than before, the rumors of the 1940s were certainly not new. Just after the Civil War and then during World War I, whites feverishly talked about race-based social unrest.[1] Obviously, the muffled fears about uprisings corresponded with war and a jump in African American protest, but they also coincided with shifts in labor relations. During the 1940s, the war-induced labor shortage opened new opportunities for African Americans and allowed some to fill jobs previously reserved for whites. With blacks registering economic gains and displaying their newly earned prosperity by wearing fur coats and shiny suits, white southerners warned of revolution.[2] They imagined that African Americans were hoarding ice picks, stockpiling knives, and buying up all the guns at local Sears stores in preparation for Labor Day showdowns.[3]

While the terror that pulsed through southern white communities in the 1940s replayed past fears, there was something different about the World War II–era race rumors.[4] In the same breath that white southerners talked about pitched public battles, they also fretted about private rebellions. African American domestics, more than well-armed men, were the focus of these rumors. The stories predicted that black female household laborers—the same women who cooked white people's food and raised their young children—would rise up against their employers, not on distant streets, but right there in white bedrooms, kitchens, and dining rooms. The threat to white supremacy, therefore, appeared to be immediate and to be happening in the privacy of the home, and there was no escaping the domestic plots.

Some white southerners blamed the apparent domestic turmoil on Hitler, others on the CIO, but most pointed an accusing finger at the Eleanor Clubs: "The Daughters of Eleanor," "The Eleanor Angel Clubs," "The Sisters of Eleanor," or "The Royal House of Eleanor."[5] White southerners were sure that club members admired, or, worse still, worshipped, Eleanor Roosevelt. To many white southerners, even some strong New Deal supporters, Eleanor Roosevelt stood for the most pernicious tenets of liberalism. For starters, she backed labor organizing and spoke out in favor of an expanded welfare state. But what really raised the suspicions of many whites was her public support for civil rights and opposition to white supremacy. White southerners believed that the leaders of the Eleanor Clubs convinced their followers to mimic Eleanor Roosevelt's racial politics. Club members were allegedly under orders to attack long-established relationships between white employers and black employees and eventually to assault the entire Jim Crow order. An angry North Carolina woman fumed in the early 1940s: "All the Negroes are getting so uppity they won't do a thing." "I hear," she added, "the cooks have been organizing Eleanor Clubs, and their motto is 'A white woman in every kitchen by Christmas.'" Everywhere from Louisiana to Virginia whites thought they heard members of these shadowy Eleanor Clubs repeat this very same motto: "A white woman in every kitchen by Christmas."[6]

By Christmas 1942, the stories of Eleanor Clubs and African Americans organizing had become so widespread that alarmed public officials, including the first lady herself, called in the Federal Bureau of Investigation (FBI) to look into the rumors to see if they were true. Worried that the rumors were somehow undermining the war effort, state law officers, journalists, and academics joined in the search for domestic unions and clandestine clubs. All the investigators came to the same conclusion: the Eleanor Clubs did not exist.[7] Despite these widely publicized reports, white southerners in towns and cities, in up-country and low-country farmlands, apparently remained convinced that the Eleanor Clubs had invaded their homes and their neighbors' homes. The actions of African Americans, they told each other, were much too sneaky for a bunch of northern lawmen, uninitiated into the ways of the South, to figure out. "The FBI," wrote a Georgia housewife, "could uncover a Nazi spy more easily than they could these clubs for among themselves negroes are very loyal and so completely secretive as to their inner workings." When a sociology professor told one of her students that the Eleanor Clubs did not exist, the young white southern man, stepping out of place for a moment, cautioned his teacher not to believe everything "she read or heard."[8]

What can be made of these rumors? How should they be "read" as historical sources? Before answering these or any other questions, it is important first to explore the sources themselves. Most stories of the Eleanor Clubs are, not surprisingly, second-, third-, and even fourth-hand reports. Someone heard a rumor from someone else and then relayed it to Eleanor Roosevelt, another political leader, a journalist, a law officer, a government investigator, or an academic. Howard Odum, the respected Chapel Hill sociologist, collected by far the largest number of rumors. Most of the rumors he gathered, and most of the sources used here, came from middle-class white southerners. In the fall of 1942, Odum wrote to friends and associates at universities and colleges around the South asking them to ask their students if they had heard any of the rumors about Labor Day uprisings and Eleanor Clubs he was hearing in North Carolina. Odum's focus on institutions of higher learning obviously skewed his evidence. With few exceptions, only the wealthiest southerners attended college in the 1940s. Because of the nature of these sources, then, the insights one can draw from the rumors of Eleanor Clubs are insights about the thoughts and fears of upper-middle-class white southerners. With this qualification in mind, what, then, can the rumors of Eleanor Clubs reveal about the South during World War II? Why did mostly middle-class, relatively well educated white southerners continue to believe in and spread rumors of Eleanor Clubs even in the face of persuasive evidence that the clubs did not exist? What does this say about who they were and what they cared about?

Answering these questions means taking rumors seriously as historical sources and asking what they are and what they do. More structured than gossip, but less carefully crafted than political rhetoric, rumors are special, and often revealing, forms of speech. Typically rumors are transmitted orally. The rumor teller presents his story as a true story—truer even than the official story—and based on uncommon or secret sources of information.[9] Because they are a kind of unofficial discourse, rarely subjected to rigorous standards of evidence and documentation, rumors can, of course, be misleading and dangerous, blurring the lines between what might be true and what is obviously untrue. Yet for the very same reasons, rumors can also be a more honest and experimental means of "telling" than carefully crafted public pronouncements or political speeches.

Untangling the meaning of rumors first requires placing them in their appropriate context. While rumors can take shape at any time for any reason, they tend to be "most frenzied when the public is expecting a momentous event to occur."[10] In times of economic, political, and social turmoil, people need a way to express their fears and apprehensions.[11] Sometimes they do so through rumors.[12] By repeating rumors, anxious women and men create space to speak about things that they are unsure of, or feel uncomfortable talking about in the open. Yet rumors, like those about the Eleanor Clubs, are more than just puzzling projections of hidden anxieties. Rumors attempt to make arguments and advance theories for why things are the way they are; they make rough sense of the incomprehensible. They offer people explanations for events that frighten them as well as for phenomena that cannot be easily explained. Rumors can also serve important political functions. They can, for instance, discredit the actions of the subjects of the rumors by exaggerating their intentions and the consequences of their actions. Finally, rumors can help to create and reinforce the bonds of community; they point to threats to an established way of life and possible solutions to meet these shadowy challenges.

In the American South, World War II generated the kinds of fierce social and ideological conflicts that typically give rise to rumors. Change tore across the region during the 1940s, attacking along the way deeply entrenched racial and gender systems. Massive federal spending and the huge defense buildup pulled the South out of the depression and transformed it overnight from the nation's number one economic problem into a land of opportunity. As German soldiers marched across western Europe, thousands of new jobs for women and African Americans appeared in the region, especially in the cities. The draft and military service, meanwhile, siphoned off whole battalions of white male workers. The result was an acute labor shortage. As new positions opened up and the federal government bowed to pressure from black activists, setting up the Fair Employment Practices Committee, thousands of African Americans left the farms and low-paying service jobs to enter industries traditionally organized along racial lines. Now, some black men and women were doing white men's jobs. Black agricultural laborers went to work in the shipyards, and black laundresses got positions in automobile plants converted to war production.

And everywhere, Rosie the Riveter traded in her apron for overalls. New opportunities and the labor shortage raised wages across the board, even for those who remained at their old jobs.

As women and African Americans took new jobs, tens of thousands of black men from around the country arrived in the South to drill in the region's many military camps.[13] Some of these black soldiers, especially those from the North, refused to abide by Jim Crow's rigid rules: they sat where they wanted on buses, refused to give way on sidewalks, and went out "stylin" at night. Other African Americans turned the wartime language of patriotic service to their advantage. "Double V" was the call—victory abroad against fascism and victory at home against segregation. Military service and the egalitarian wartime rhetoric, combined with bigger paychecks and increased mobility, translated into a new and more public brand of African American assertiveness.[14] Displaying this newfound independence, southern black women and men flooded into organizations like the National Association for the Advancement of Colored People (NAACP) and the Congress of Industrial Organization (CIO), which were committed to overthrowing white supremacy.[15]

Whites looked on with growing alarm during the early 1940s as African Americans made steady economic, social, and political strides. With each passing day, white fears mounted. Scared and suspicious, some white southerners retreated into a siege mentality. They saw threats to their way of life on every street corner, in every store, and in every kitchen. Integration, the worst fear of many whites, somehow seemed more believable than ever before. And as always in the South, when integration was the topic, talk turned quickly to sex. A brush became a touch, a quick glance a lusty leer. Nervous whites pictured African American men suggestively squeezing white hands when getting change at local stores, whistling at white women, calling them for dates, and sending them chocolates, just like white boys did. As African Americans left their old jobs for higher-paying positions in war-related industries, whites thought they overheard black men say that after the hostilities, "Negroes will marry white girls and run the country."[16]

Some white southerners clearly feared that the war would bring an end to their carefully constructed world of racial privilege and hierarchy. Most whites grew up believing that African Americans were supposed to serve them and make their lives more comfortable.[17] To whites, being white meant having the power and the right to dictate when, where, and for how much black women and men worked. Being black, most whites thought, entailed being dependent on whites and liking this position. African Americans, of course, never accepted these notions about the world. They battled to gain financial independence and autonomy from whites. After Reconstruction they protested most often with their feet, by moving to the "promised lands" of the North and West. During World War II, however, African Americans staged louder, more frequent, more persistent, and more boisterous public protests against white supremacy. Worried that their days of racial domination could be numbered, whites reacted to virtually every black challenge to their authority, both the real and imagined ones. They tried with varying degrees of success to keep African Americans in the grimiest, hardest, lowest-paying jobs. When black women and men displayed their wartime prosperity by putting on the latest fashions, some white southerners attempted to impose rules that would prohibit blacks from trying on shirts, dresses, hats, gloves, and shoes in downtown stores.[18] Across the region, black soldiers who claimed their full rights as American citizens inevitably found themselves face-to-face with angry whites determined to keep them in their "place" with the law if possible and with guns if necessary.[19]

White households were another arena of wartime racial discord. Before the war, more than three-quarters of all African American women who worked outside the home worked in white homes for unbelievably low wages. As the federal government ordered record numbers of tanks, mess kits, and softballs, black southern women left the "service" in droves. Some went to work in defense plants in Atlanta and Norfolk; others escaped to Los Angeles and Detroit. Still others returned to their own homes. Tired of double shift after double shift of paid labor followed by domestic duties, they decided to devote more time to their families now that their husbands or partners earned a living wage. Taking advantage of the acute labor shortage, housekeepers, cooks, washerwomen, and laundresses who stayed on the job demanded higher wages and shorter hours.

Many white southerners had a hard time understanding the growing independence of African American female laborers. Though some acknowledged that the war created new possibilities for these women, many white southerners, it seems, searched for alternative explanations to account for the new assertiveness of household workers. They insisted that these "naturally" loyal and devoted servants quit their jobs or asked for money because of the Eleanor Clubs, not because they did not like the work, the wages, or their bosses. This kind of thinking raises several questions: Why did middle-class southerners rely on rumors of Eleanor Clubs to explain the war-related domestic labor shortage? What "work," to put this question in the idiom of contemporary cultural studies, did the Eleanor Club rumors perform? What did the rumors "do" for, and explain to, white southerners?

Returning to the definition of rumors spelled out earlier in the essay— that is, that rumors are often a projection of fears—clearly in the 1940s, white southerners worried about the future of white supremacy. Yet they refused to see what was going on around them as a homegrown crisis. African Americans, most whites apparently believed or wanted to believe, were happy with the way things were; it was outsiders who got them up in arms. White southerners, concluded a wartime report, "live in constant fear that some outside person or idea will threaten the status quo in respect to race relations." A Birmingham electrical contractor told a federal investigator: "One of my Negro workers asked for a week off while his sister was visiting from Detroit. I'm not going to rehire him because he will be so full of ideas after talking to her."[20] Many identified northern-based unions as yet another invidious agent of change. The Eleanor Clubs, they presumed, were nothing more than unions in disguise. Club members supposedly embraced the foreign ideology of trade unionism, pressing for such "unsouthern" things as wage hikes, cuts in hours, and equal treatment. A Georgia State Womans College sociologist heard from a south Georgia student: "The Negroes have formed unions demanding higher wages and working conditions and it is almost impossible to find any help at all. I don't know about the Eleanor Clubs, but I think they had a hand in trying to organize the Negroes."[21] An Agnes Scott College student's mother told the story of an African American woman who supposedly joined an Eleanor Club and "informed her employer one morning that she had signed up for an 8-hour day with an hour off for lunch. This was a special rule, and members were not allowed to break the rules. If your work is not finished at the end of 8 hours, you just stop work."[22]

If the Eleanor Club rumors spoke to the fears of white southerners, then clearly the pay issue upset them even more than the question of hours. An Alabama office worker complained in the summer of 1942: "Domestic servants are getting organized and you can't do a thing with them. They want more money and less work." Reports claimed that Eleanor Club members demanded nine to twelve dollars per week, or three to four times prevailing prewar rates.[23] At these prices, many white southern women could not afford domestic help, and that could mean that women who rarely cooked or cleaned would find themselves chopping vegetables and scrubbing floors. Expensive domestic labor, furthermore, eroded white women's and men's ideas about "whiteness." Alongside their big houses, shiny new cars, and higher-paying jobs, middle-class whites demonstrated their racial and class position by employing African American labor. If servants and maids charged twelve dollars a week, many whites could not afford to hire "help." Without this domestic labor, whites would be less able to claim the racial and class prerogatives that came along with telling others what to do.

White southerners seem to have pinned just about every domestic disturbance during the war years to the Eleanor Clubs. Even those who could still afford to hire household workers passed on rumors. They complained that Eleanor Club members not only expected higher wages but refused to do anything that fell outside of the scope of their "contracts." The Eleanor Clubs allegedly told washerwomen and laundresses what they should and should not do, which tasks were acceptable and which were not. When employers violated the contract, club members supposedly answered with strikes and sometimes violent acts. According to one story, a wealthy south Georgia planter employed a "Negro cook who lived in a little shack on his farm with her two children." One day his wife directed the woman to do some strenuous washing, and she refused, saying that it was not part of her job. The planter promptly threw the woman and her children out of the shack. A few days later, he claimed he spotted the woman's two boys sneaking around his place. Then, his barn mysteriously caught fire and burned to the ground. Quickly, the local sheriff arrested the older boy and detained the cook, who, according to a white source, "confessed that the whole plot was hatched up in one of the 'Eleanor Clubs,' in Camilla, Georgia, to get revenge on the employer who had wanted her to do some washing that she did not wish to do."[24]

White southerners feared that the Eleanor Clubs, and by implication trade unionism and liberalism, encouraged African Americans to act "uppity" and step out of place. Slippery, unseen leaders allegedly instructed reluctant club members to take bold steps to undermine the Jim Crow order. Southern race relations were constructed around a thick web of rules of etiquette and manners. African Americans were supposed to remove their hats whenever they spoke to a white man; they were told to move off sidewalks when whites passed; they were taught to use only the back door of white homes, never the front; and they were instructed to address whites as Boss, or Mr. or Mrs. In turn, whites learned that they should not use these respectful titles when they addressed African American men and women.[25] The Eleanor Clubs, some whites believed, told servants to call their employers by their first names, not as Mr. or Mrs.[26] Other club leaders were rumored to order members to bathe in their employers' tubs before going home after work.[27] Still other leaders commanded domestics to go right in the front door and sit down and eat with their employers. A Mississippi white woman claimed that one night she arrived home for dinner and found an extra place setting on the table. She asked her housekeeper if the family was expecting company. No, the African American woman brusquely replied, "in the Eleanor Club, we always sit with the people we work for."[28] When a Louisiana housekeeper did not show up for work one morning, her employer drove over to her house and told her to hurry up and get ready. The maid—by then a former maid—pointed to a mirror and roared at the white woman, "You look in that and you'll see your washerwoman. Now get out of here."[29]

In addition to undermining the traditional rules of racial difference and deference, the purported leaders of the Eleanor Clubs also sought to politicize the home. Allegedly these organizations forced their members to make their voices heard in the closely guarded white realm of public power. While conceding that black women were barred from polling stations, club leaders nonetheless told their followers that they could use their labor to hammer home political points. Some clubs, for instance—again allegedly—required members to quit their jobs immediately if their employers said a single harsh word about the first lady or the president.[30]

If black women achieved this kind of independence—if they called their bosses by their first names; if they washed themselves in white people's tubs; if they ate carefully prepared meals at elegant tables; and if they voiced political opinions—then white supremacy could become the relic of a safer and more comfortable past. Whites expressed many of their wartime fears about the future of the Jim Crow order when they repeated the rumors about Eleanor Clubs. Yet it was the imagined setting for the Eleanor Clubs—the household—that gave the rumors their explosiveness and almost palpable sense of danger.

Many white southerners regarded the household as a model for social and racial relationships.[31] Black female labor played a central role in this imagined world. White southerners considered the home filled with African American women cooking, cleaning, and caring for children as both symbol and metaphor for a steady racial order. They saw the ideal home as a place where whites were firmly in control, while African Americans graciously complied with their demands. Whites, furthermore, saw the home as a site of racial peace, a place where smiling and singing black mammies loved white boys and girls and happily took care of them and their parents.[32] Yet these same ideas about racial harmony and the household suggested that if the home was in turmoil, then the larger society was certainly in trouble. When white southerners talked about the Eleanor Clubs, therefore, they fashioned a kind of warning, a sort of awful worst-case scenario, about what would happen if African Americans achieved economic and political independence and unions gained a foothold in white homes and nearby factories.

Whites feared that once black women made decent wages, chaos would reign. African American workers would attack racial hierarchies at home—that is, in white homes—and then quickly do the same in public. African Americans would insist on shopping at the same stores as whites, trying on the same clothes, and going out in public dressed better than white women.[33] Eventually African Americans would turn the entire Jim Crow order upside down. In this new world, whites would be forced to work for blacks. The purported slogan of the Eleanor Clubs—"A white woman in every kitchen by Christmas"—not only suggested that whites would be working in their own kitchens, it also predicted that whites would be working for African Americans. If blacks employed whites, then whiteness would no longer mean anything. This was a nightmare for most whites, and this was what they were talking about when they talked about the Eleanor Clubs.

The idea of African American women organizing unions and acting collectively was not simply mad rantings of paranoid white southerners. At the turn of the century and during World War I, African American women had joined domestic unions and forced their employers to pay them more and define work rules more clearly.[34] Twenty years later, during World War II, African American women again negotiated, sometimes collectively, other times as individuals, for higher wages and shorter hours. Using the labor shortage as leverage, black women made it plain to their bosses that they would quit if their bosses did not give in to their demands. Others probably played tricks on their employers, putting, for instance, an extra plate on the dinner table or running the bathwater just before they went home. Some, it seems, even used the specter of Eleanor Clubs to their own advantage. Well aware of white fears of the clubs, a few domestics apparently whispered just within earshot of their bosses that they or someone else belonged to one of these phantom organizations. Afraid of letting the clubs into their homes, some whites raised the wages and improved the conditions of domestic laborers. Yet no one, not even the most vicious race-mongering politicians, talked about the history of domestic unions when they passed on rumors about Eleanor Clubs. By repeating the Eleanor Club rumor, frightened white southerners created space to speak about something that few were willing to acknowledge openly: the power of African Americans to act in concert with one another and shape white thoughts and actions and even the balance of power in white households.

While rumors can point to hidden fears, they can also suggest theories for why things happen. At the same time, while rumors may help to make sense of the incomprehensible, they can also confine and confuse people, and leave them susceptible to intellectual laziness.[35] This is what happened in the South in the early 1940s. Without much evidence, a number of white southerners apparently came to believe that Eleanor Roosevelt herself was behind the Eleanor Clubs. They insisted that because she supported liberal reforms and tentatively embraced the cause of civil rights, African Americans expected to be treated like whites. Some even fabricated direct connections between Eleanor Roosevelt's actions and the formation of Eleanor Clubs. Whites in Birmingham, Alabama, thought they detected an increase in domestic labor club activity after the first lady visited the city. An Austin, Texas, woman thought that domestics there joined the "Elinor Clubs" after reading one of the first lady's newspaper columns, "preaching race equality."[36]

Why did the rumors focus on Eleanor Roosevelt? Why were the clubs named after her and not another liberal or civil rights supporter? Certainly there were other well-known public figures in the 1940s more liberal than Eleanor Roosevelt and more enthusiastic in their public support for equal rights. Why weren't there rumors of Harold Ickes Clubs or Maury Maverick Clubs?[37]

The answers to these questions certainly have something to do with the heightened tensions of the war years, with Eleanor Roosevelt's relationship to her husband, the president, and with her highly visible role as first lady. Her own politics mattered as well. Beginning in the 1920s, she started to speak out on behalf of the poor and the dispossessed. With the start of World War II, she raised her voice even louder. "No one," Eleanor Roosevelt lamented in 1942, "can honestly claim that . . . the Negroes of this country are free."[38] Discrimination, she insisted, was wrong and so was segregation.

Asked during the war if "negroes should be admitted to the air corps without segregation," Roosevelt answered without hesitating, "Yes!"[39] Pressing to extend democracy, she took cautious aim at the South's Jim Crow order. She supported the NAACP's drive for an antilynching bill and denounced job segregation. "It's not the color of your skin that makes you hirable," she maintained, "you've got to take a person, regardless of his race, creed, or color, when it comes to filling a job."[40]

Predictably, Eleanor Roosevelt's racial politics rattled many white southerners. Some came up with an extraordinary explanation for Roosevelt's racial views. The first lady, these people speculated, must not be entirely white. "I don't mean to be rude," one woman began a letter to Roosevelt, but she wondered, "do you have colored blood in your family as you seem to derive so much pleasure from associating with colored folks?" Roosevelt answered: "I haven't as yet discovered . . . any colored blood, but, of course, if any us go back far enough, I suppose we can find that we all stem from the same beginnings. I have no feeling that the colored race is inferior to the white race."[41] In another context, while denying any knowledge of black ancestry, Eleanor Roosevelt—the second cousin of the president—added that she would not stop her children from marrying a person of color. These pronouncements astounded many white southerners. The war seemed to turn things inside out. Nothing was what it appeared; even Eleanor Roosevelt's apparent whiteness was not reliable. She had to be black, or "colored," as they might say; this was the only explanation that made sense. Only someone black, some were convinced, could or would care about black people and black civil rights, and not cringe at the thought of interracial sex. In the minds of these white southerners, the Eleanor Clubs, therefore, sprang up when black self-interest mixed with white transgression.

Race was not the only fear wrapped in the Eleanor Club rumors. Gender concerns shaped these stories as well. From the time of Marie Antoinette to the days of Hillary Rodham Clinton, commentators have used politically active women as a focus for larger anxieties about the role of women in public life. The wives of state leaders are often portrayed as evil influences or bad mothers who abandon their children and husbands for the thrill of public life.[42] Eleanor's imagined influence over Franklin made her particularly menacing. White southerners seemed to believe that she would use her body—maybe her black body—to enlist the president in her campaign to destroy segregation. Her independence represented yet another danger.

Writing newspaper columns that denounced racial discrimination and speaking out against lynching, Eleanor Roosevelt symbolized an independent woman, that is, a woman like Rosie the Riveter and her coworkers, not entirely controlled by or dependent on a man. Disturbed by what they saw as the first lady's "unwomanly" public persona, many urged her to get back in the home. A Mississippi woman wrote, "I sincerely wish you would give Franklin a break and let him have the spot light." "Why don't you," another woman asked her, "tend to . . . knitting [and] keep Franklin company (as a real good woman should do)." Others instructed her to stop acting like a "female-dictator who would advise her husband." Some thirty years after the war, the reactionary television sitcom character Archie Bunker unintentionally summed up the views of many in the South in the early 1940s. Quarreling with his liberal, feminist adversary Maude, Archie blurted out: "Let me tell you one thing about my president, Richard E. [sic] Nixon: he knows how to keep his wife, Pat, at home. Roosevelt could never do that with Eleanor, she was always on the loose, running around with the coloreds, telling them that they was getting the short end of the stick. She was the one who discovered the coloreds in this country. We never knew they was there."[43]

According to Archie and those who passed along the Eleanor Club rumors, the first lady's public activities encouraged African Americans and women to follow her lead and step out of place. With African Americans and northern women liberating themselves, some white men might have wondered, could white southern women be far behind? Again, what made the Eleanor Club rumors so harrowing was the imagined intimacy between white employers and African American domestic workers, and the sense of personal betrayal that whites felt when their employees quit or questioned their kindness and authority. Clearly politics were not just about public matters—they reverberated throughout the household, the very symbol and metaphor of ordered white racial and gender domination.

While the Eleanor Club rumors warned about threats to white supremacy and patriarchy, they simultaneously tried to bolster these institutions that some perceived as shaky. Seeing this dynamic requires looking at politics from different angles. It requires seeing that some of the hidden and submerged actions of African Americans were political, that they were part of larger struggles over the distribution of public power.[44] When black women and men sat in "white" bus seats, dressed in neat military uniforms, wore fur coats out on Saturday nights, and demanded better pay and working conditions, they sought to control their bodies and alter the boundaries of segregated public space.[45] Whites promptly picked up on this kind of resistance. Some understood that gestures could be, and often were, a form of protest. By responding to these actions, whites recognized public behavior for what it was: an assertion of African American selfhood and autonomy and thus an assault on the Jim Crow order.

Wartime rumors were one way that white southerners dealt with the turmoil of the period. Using rumors rather than formal speech to talk about African American behavior, whites highlighted black protest; but they did so in a way that attempted to subvert and delegitimize the deeper struggles that lay behind these gestures and actions. The stories of Eleanor Clubs called attention to whispered plots, backroom deals, outside influences, and the suspicious actions and heritage of Eleanor Roosevelt. They cited clandestine conversations and secret meetings rather than low wages, long hours, and capricious work rules as the reasons for African American challenges to segregation. The rumors slyly suggested that African Americans had no real grievances—that their protests sprang from the nefarious manipulations of the first lady and a bunch of other outsiders, not from years of exploitation. Blacks, they contended, loved their white bosses and appreciated their place in southern society. According to the rumors, the discontents voiced by the members of the Eleanor Clubs were manufactured by corrupt northerners and agents of Eleanor Roosevelt for their own selfish purposes. In this way, the rumors erased African Americans and their complaints from the story. Ironically, the rumors also erased the agency of whites by asserting that white privilege and abuses had nothing to do with African American protests.

In a rather complicated twist, then, rumors, just by being rumors, generated a sense of exaggeration that turned what was real—that is, African American discontent—into something fantastic. The stories trivialized African American behavior while alerting whites to black anger. Rumors also provided whites with a way to reassure each other that the system of white supremacy was still intact and that they were still in control.

In the end, the Eleanor Club rumors were emblematic of the larger drama of race in America in the 1940s. If, as scholars have pointed out, the war years marked the start of the Civil Rights movement, then they also marked the beginning of what would quickly explode into a full-scale campaign of massive resistance.[46] The stories about the Eleanor Clubs were an opening shot in a vicious and deadly struggle to retain the Jim Crow order.

In an even larger sense, the rumors exposed the absurdity of racism. Story after wild story about Eleanor Clubs and African American domestics showed what strange, evil products sprang from making a hard fact out of the fiction of racial difference. When a society is based on lies, anything is believable.

Notes

1. Arthur I. Waskow, *From Race Riot to Sit-In, 1919 and the 1960s: A Study in the Connections between Conflict and Violence* (Garden City, N.Y.: Doubleday, 1966); Dan T. Carter, "The Anatomy of Fear: The Christmas Day Insurrection Scare of 1865," *Journal of Southern History* 62 (Aug. 1976): 345–64; Stephen Niessenbaum, "An Insurrection That Never Happened: The 'Christmas Riots' of 1865," in *True Stories from the American Past*, vol. 2, ed. William Graebner (New York, 1997), 1–17; and Steven Hahn, "'Extravagant Expectations' of Freedom: Rumor, Political Struggle, and the Christmas Insurrection of 1865 in the American South," *Past and Present* 157 (Nov. 1997): 122–32.

2. A character in Erskine Caldwell's novel, *Trouble in July* (Savannah: Bechive, 1977), 125, hints at white resentment over African American economic success. Any number of lynchings in the South, moreover, took place because of this same resentment. See W. Fitzhugh Brundage, *Lynching in the New South: Georgia and Virginia, 1880–1930* (Urbana: University of Illinois Press, 1993).

3. Sears stores themselves were the subject of rumors as "local storekeepers [fearful of competition] circulated rumors that [the] Sears . . . were blacks and that they sold by mail because 'these fellows could not afford to show their faces as retailers.'" Grace Elizabeth Hale, *Making Whiteness: The Culture of Segregation in the South, 1890–1940* (New York: Pantheon, 1998), 179.

4. The best source on the rumors is Howard Odum, *Race and Rumors of Race: The American South in the 1940s* (1943; rpt., Baltimore: Johns Hopkins University Press, 1997). See also Odum papers at the Southern Historical Collection, University of North Carolina, Chapel Hill, N.C. (hereinafter SHC). For other published accounts see Allida Black, *Casting Her Own Shadow: Eleanor Roosevelt and the Shaping of Postwar Liberalism* (New York, 1996), 87; Doris Kearns Goodwin, *No Ordinary Time: Franklin and Eleanor Roosevelt: The Home Front in World War II* (New York, 1995), 370–71; George B. Tindall, *The Emergence of the New South* (Baton Rouge, 1967), 717; Pete Daniel, *Standing at the Crossroads: Southern Life in the Twentieth Century* (New York, 1986), 141–42; and William Cooper and Thomas Terrill, *The American South: A History* (New York: McGraw, 1996), 669.

5. Odum, *Race and Rumors of Race*, 73, 79.

6. For more on the importance of Christmas in African American culture, see

Nissenbaum, "An Insurrection That Never Happened," esp. 3–9. On the slogan and how ubiquitous it was, see Odum, *Race and Rumors of Race*, 74–77.

7. On police reports about the Eleanor Clubs, see Eleanor Roosevelt's FBI File, published by Scholarly Resources, Roll 1, Enclosure 4. On the state level, South Carolina's wartime governor, Richard M. Jeffries, asked the sheriff in each county of the state to investigate stories about Eleanor Clubs and report back to him. See their reports in the Richard Manning Jeffries Papers, Folder 50–51, South Caroliniana Library, Columbia, South Carolina. See also Eleanor Roosevelt's denial in the *New York Times*, 23 Sept. 1942.

8. Mrs. J. H. Gibbs, Palmetto, Georgia, to Eleanor Roosevelt, 16 Nov. 1942, Eleanor Roosevelt Papers, Box 1642, Franklin D. Roosevelt Library (hereinafter FDRL).

9. Memo, J. W. Martin to Eugene Horowitz, "Definition of Rumor," 2 Sept. 1942, Folder 5, World War II Rumor Project, AFC 1945/001, American Folklife Center, Library of Congress, Washington, D.C.

10. Gordon W. Allport and Leo Postman, *The Psychology of Rumor* (New York, 1947), 33–47.

11. Jean-Noel Kapferer, *Rumors: Uses, Interpretations, and Images* (New Brunswick, N.J.: Transaction Publishers, 1990), 93.

12. Hahn, "'Extravagant Expectations' of Freedom," 122–32. For more on rumors see Luise White, "Between Gluckman and Foucault: Historizing Rumor and Gossip," *Social Dynamics* 20 (Winter 1994): 75–92; Patricia A. Turner, *I Heard It through the Grapevine: Rumor in African American Culture* (Berkeley, 1993); and Arlette Farge and Jacques Revel, *The Vanishing Children of Paris: Rumor and Politics before the French Revolution* (Cambridge, Mass., 1991).

13. Nancy and Dwight MacDonald, "The War's Greatest Scandal: The Story of Jim Crow in Uniform," pamphlet (New York, 1943). See also Harvard Sitkoff, "Racial Militancy and Interracial Violence in the Second World War," *Journal of American History* 58 (Jan. 1971): 661–81; and James Albert Burran, "Racial Violence in the South during World War II" (Ph.D. diss., University of Tennessee, 1977).

14. On the southern home front, particularly labor relations, see Morton Sosna, "More Important than the Civil War: The Impact of World War II on the South," in *Perspectives on the American South: An Annual Review of Society, Politics, and Culture*, vol. 4, ed. James C. Cobb and Charles R. Wilson (New York, 1987), 145–61; Daniel, *Standing at the Crossroads*, 135–49; Tindall, *Emergence of the New South*, 687–731; James C. Cobb, *The Most Southern Place on Earth: The Mississippi Delta and the Roots of Regional Identity* (New York, 1992), 198–202; and the essays in Neil R. McMillen, ed., *Remaking Dixie: The Impact of World War II on the American South* (Jackson, Miss., 1997).

15. On the emergence of the NAACP during the war, see Daniel, *Standing at the Crossroads*, 149; Patricia Sullivan, *Days of Hope: Race and Democracy in the New Deal Era* (Chapel Hill, 1996). On the CIO and race, see Robert Korstad and Nelson Lichtenstein, "Opportunities Found and Lost: Labor, Radicals, and the Early Civil Rights

Movement," *Journal of American History* 75 (Nov. 1988): 786–811. Scholars disagree about the CIO's commitment to "overthrowing white supremacy." (See Merl Reed's essay in this collection.) But few white southerners in the 1940s engaged in these kinds of debates; *they* were convinced that the CIO wanted to bring Jim Crow down.

16. Odum, *Race and Rumors of Race*, 22, 57, 62, 63, 64, 115, 117, 122. More generally see, Thomas Sancton, "Trouble in Dixie: The Returning Tragic Era," *New Republic*, 4 Jan. 1943, 11–14.

17. For insight into white views of black labor, see Melton A. McLaurin, *Separate Pasts: Growing Up White in the Segregated South* (Athens, 1987), 21, 135.

18. On anxieties over dress, see "Grandmom" from Atlanta to Johnston, 17 Dec. 1943, Box 19, General Correspondence, no folder designated, South Carolina Department of Archives and History.

19. Burran, "Racial Violence in the South during World War II"; Bryant Simon, *A Fabric of Defeat: The Politics of South Carolina Millhands, 1910–1948* (Chapel Hill, 1998), 220–30.

20. Cobb, *Most Southern Place*, 203; and Paul Duncan, "Report on Rumors," 8–15 Aug. 1942, Folder 15, World War II Rumor Project, AFC 1945/001, American Folklife Center, Library of Congress, Washington, D.C.

21. Classification, Eleanor Clubs, B. Dekle, Georgia State Womans College (Valdosta), 27 Jan. 1943, Odum Papers, Box 59, Folder—Observation Reports, Black/White Relations, 4/5 (1943), SHC. See also W. W. Brown to Jeffries, 19 Sept. 1942, Jeffries Papers, Folder 50, South Caroliniana Library, Columbia, South Carolina.

22. Classification, Eleanor Clubs, Report from Mamie Sue Parker, Agnes Scott College, 18 Feb. 1943, Odum Papers, Box 59, Folder—Observation Reports, Black/White Relations, 4/5 (1943), SHC.

23. Paul Duncan, "Report on Rumors," 8–15 Aug. 1942, Folder 15, World War II Rumor Project, AFC 1945/001, American Folklife Center, Library of Congress, Washington, D.C. See also J. A. Durrenberger to Odum, n.d., "Race Relations in Valdosta and in South Georgia in General," Odum Papers, Box 59, Folder—Observation Reports, Black/White Relations, 4/5 (1943), SHC.

24. Classification, Story (Eleanor Clubs), Report from Mamie Sue Parker, Agnes Scott College, 16 Feb. 1943, Odum Papers, Box 59, Folder-Observation Reports, Black/White Relations, 4/5 (1943), SHC.

25. On the rules of Jim Crow, see J. William Harris, "Etiquette, Lynching, and Racial Boundaries in Southern History: A Mississippi Example," *American Historical Review* 100 (1995): 387–410.

26. Odum, *Race and Rumors of Race*, 69. Classification, Reported by: Jannie Owen, College: La Grange College, Department: Sociology, 25 Jan. 1943, Folder—Observational Reports on Black/White Relations (1943), 2/5, SHC.

27. Odum, *Race and Rumors of Race*, 69.

28. This rumor is recounted by Goodwin, *No Ordinary Time*, 370–71.

29. Ibid.

30. Odum, *Race and Rumors of Race*, 74. Two stories recounted how Savannah domestics put white women who criticized Eleanor Roosevelt on a supposed blacklist. See Georgia State Womans College (Valdosta), Department: Sociology, 2 Feb. 1943, Folder—Observational Reports on Black/White Relations (1943), 2/5, SHC.

31. See Elizabeth Fox-Genovese, *Within the Plantation Household: Black and White Women of the Old South* (Chapel Hill, 1988), and especially, Stephanie McCurry, *Masters of Small Worlds: Yeoman Households, Gender Relations, and the Political Culture of the Antebellum South Carolina Low Country* (New York, 1995).

32. Hale, *Making Whiteness.*

33. Over and over again, white southerners talked about dress and clothes, especially about African American women insisting on trying on the same dresses as whites. See LSU Department of Sociology, 14 Jan. 1943, Odum Papers, Box 58, New Folder—Blacks and World War II, Articles from LSU Students (1943); and Georgia State Womans College (Valdosta), Department of Sociology, 8 Feb. 1943, New Folder—Observational Reports on Black/White Relations (1943) 1 of 5, SHC.

34. For information on past organizing campaigns, see Tera Hunter, *To 'Joy My Freedom: Southern Black Women's Lives and Labors after the Civil War* (Cambridge, 1998), 74–97.

35. Alex Kotlowitz makes a similar point in a recent article on American race relations. See Kotlowitz, "Colorblind," *New York Times Magazine*, 11 Jan. 1998, 22–23.

36. Mrs. J. H. Gibbs, Palmetto, Ga., to Eleanor Roosevelt, 16 Nov. 1942, Eleanor Roosevelt Papers, Box 1642, FDRL; and Willie K. Jones to Eleanor Roosevelt, 5 Apr. 1944, Box 1684, Eleanor Roosevelt Papers, FDRL.

37. There were some serious limits to Eleanor Roosevelt's liberalism. Asked in 1943 how she would feel if she were a "Negro," the first lady answered, "I should feel deeply resentful." "There are many things in our democracy," she lamented, "which are not as yet democratic." But, Eleanor was quick to add, "if I were either a colored soldier or his sweetheart, I should try to remember how far my race has come in some seventy-five odd years." She also advised caution when it came to social relations. "I have never," she wrote an angry white southerner, "advocated social equality or intermarriage." Eleanor Roosevelt, *If You Ask Me* (New York, 1946), 137–38, and Roosevelt to L. W. Bates, 23 Feb. 1942, Eleanor Roosevelt Papers, FDRL.

38. William T. Youngs, *Eleanor Roosevelt: A Personal and Public Life* (Boston, 1985), 185.

39. *Chicago Defender*, 10 Apr. 1943.

40. *Pittsburgh Courier*, 6 Sept. 1941.

41. Roosevelt, *If You Ask Me*, 68; and Black, *Casting Her Own Shadow*, 87. See a comment on Bertie Mae Loner to Roosevelt, 3 Mar. 1944, Eleanor Roosevelt Papers, Box 2462, FDRL. M. E. Rivers to Russell, 15 June 1942, Box 139, Folder 3, Russell Papers, University of Georgia. Another historian, who is a sixth-generation

North Carolinian, recalled to me that her mother believed that Eleanor Roosevelt was black.

42. For more on the idea of the "bad mother," see Lynn Hunt, *The Family Romance of the French Revolution* (Berkeley, Calif., 1992), 89–123; and Molly Ladd-Taylor and Lauri Umansky, eds., *"Bad" Mothers: The Politics of Blame in Twentieth-Century America* (New York, 1998). On Eleanor Roosevelt, see Audie Calvert to Eleanor Roosevelt, 13 June 1942, Eleanor Roosevelt Papers, and Youngs, *Eleanor Roosevelt*, 198.

43. Videotape, *"All in the Family" Twentieth Anniversary Special* (Columbia/Tristar Studios, Video Release 1999).

44. Robin D. G. Kelley, "'We Are Not What We Seem': Rethinking Black Working-Class Opposition in the Jim Crow South," *Journal of America History* (June 1993): see especially 86, 103–4. See also Fairclough, *Race and Democracy*, 82–83.

45. In another odd twist, white southerners asserted that the tensions on city buses during the war years were caused by "Pushing Clubs." Members of these clubs allegedly pushed people on buses. Again these rumors, like the Eleanor Club rumors, attempted to rob African Americans of their agency. See for examples, Jonathan Daniels to J. Edgar Hoover, 11 Mar. 1944, and Hoover to Daniels, 31 Mar. 1944, FDR Papers, OF4245C, Box 6, File, Office of Product-Management, FDRL.

46. See Sullivan, *Days of Hope*; and John Egerton, *Speak Now against the Day: The Generation before the Civil Rights Movement in the South* (Chapel Hill, 1994).

Bell Aircraft Comes South: The Struggle by Atlanta Blacks for Jobs during World War II

Merl E. Reed

In the summer of 1940, the federal government began dispersing defense contracts around the nation, and the South became a prime beneficiary. As the defense program expanded into a war emergency, old shipyards, idled or closed since the first great war, reopened, and new ones also dotted the Gulf and Atlantic coasts. Army, navy, and marine training camps sprang up. Industries began converting to wartime production, reinvigorating the South's conventional, but still lagging, industrial base. Soon, however, other types of economic activity even more vital to the war effort began to appear. Airplane production became a significant part of the southern economy, a trend that continued in the postwar years. Parts manufacturers and assembly plants in Louisiana, Texas, Oklahoma, Alabama, Tennessee, Maryland, and Georgia soon began turning out aircraft.[1]

Early in 1942, headlines in the *Atlanta Journal* reported that the Bell Aircraft Corporation of Buffalo, the nation's second largest producer of military planes, would operate "one of the most efficient and modernized" plants in nearby Marietta. The news aroused great excitement. President Lawrence D. (Larry) Bell told a crowd of more than a thousand Atlantans and invited dignitaries at a victory dinner that final plans for the facility would be completed by March. The federal government, not the Bell corporation, had chosen the site, and Georgia's U.S. senator Walter George, who introduced President Bell to the gathering, surely had influenced that decision.[2]

The Atlanta area had much to offer. With nearly 480,000 inhabitants in 1940, a diversified industrial base comprising more than nine hundred factories, and far-flung railroad and airline connections, the Gate City had long been recognized as the commercial and banking capital of the Southeast. Now Bell Aircraft's anticipated arrival would constitute an additional, and also unprecedented, economic windfall. The population, 35 percent African American in the city and 29 percent in the metropolitan district, also provided an adequate labor supply. Scheduled to open in the fall, the plant by one report would have a peak employment of forty thousand by the end of 1943. Unmentioned at this time, the facility would assemble what became known as the B-29 bomber.[3]

President Bell expressed enthusiasm about Atlanta's labor resources, but either he had been misinformed about its racial composition or he chose to ignore it. "We are perfectly delighted with the kind of labor you have— 88 or 89 per cent pure Anglo Saxon, all good old American blood. Problems of espionage and sabotage should be at an absolute minimum here." The plant's workforce would be 80 percent semiskilled and unskilled, the executive-level positions to be filled by local people, making it an entirely Atlanta operation. Bell intended to employ women, but only after the male labor supply had been exhausted. He confidently predicted that this new venture "would abolish unemployment of all kinds in this area."[4]

Given Larry Bell's Anglo-Saxon preferences, how this happy outcome could be accomplished in Georgia's mixed-racial and segregated society was unclear. Of the forty-three thousand Atlanta-area job-seekers registered by the United States Employment Service (USES) at that time, over a quarter were African Americans. Officials believed that an intensive registration program would yield four thousand to six thousand more blacks. To John Beecher, a field examiner of the President's Committee on Fair Employment Practice (FEPC), the conclusion was obvious. Atlanta blacks would be excluded in Bell Bomber's plans. The newspaper account "reveals the fact that Mr. Bell reassured the local leaders concerning the company's prospective racial policies," he wrote a superior in Washington. Beecher also noted that Boisfeuillet Jones, a prominent Atlantan who met with company officials, "gathered that they would employ Negroes but only unskilled and in limited numbers."[5]

The Atlanta Urban League (AUL), which had campaigned for black jobs since the darkest days of the depression, also became vitally interested in Bell Aircraft's employment plans, and particularly the opportunities for training. The AUL began sponsoring occupational training courses for African Americans in the early 1930s and tried with some success to find jobs for them in the federal housing projects. When the national defense program began in 1940, AUL leaders took heart, because the Congress prohibited discrimination. Indeed, the AUL's parent organization, the National Urban League, had played a leading role in getting that ban enacted.[6]

Local and state authorities, however, controlled the distribution of federal funds, and the Atlanta public school system gave only a guarded response to AUL inquiries about classes for African Americans. In August, Superintendent Willis A. Sutton wrote of the "great difficulty" in getting started and of "not yet being sure of our ground." But he did expect that the program would apply "to colored as well as white."[7] When that expectation failed to materialize, AUL leaders embarked on a determined but futile campaign for black defense training. As their disappointments mounted, they surely could not have realized that these efforts would provide an important learning experience, one that by February of 1942 would prepare them to take on Bell Aircraft.

Meanwhile, after receiving the August 1940 communication from Superintendent Sutton, AUL leaders watched helplessly as planning for the defense training program got under way primarily for whites. In February 1941, a three-hour meeting with state and local officials produced more frustration. Georgia blacks had access to only 12 defense training courses out of 147 available statewide, AUL executive secretary William Y. Bell explained, and black Atlantans fared even worse. The program would offer them only 4 courses out of 55 in the city and Fulton County, giving instruction in cement finishing, machine crating, scaffold building, and trade cooking, pursuits only indirectly related to defense needs. Meanwhile, white trainees would study airplane and auto mechanics, blueprint reading, radio servicing, electrical and sheet metal work, machine shop tools and die making, and aircraft welding, among others.[8]

State training officials vigorously defended the program with arguments repeated endlessly during the war period. Providing African Americans with skills wasted resources because they could not find employment in Georgia's segregated labor force. When white workers went into defense industries, however, blacks could fill the void in nondefense trades. To prepare black workers for such tasks, state officials proposed adding instruction in greasing and servicing automobiles at Atlanta's segregated Booker T. Washington High School. Negro schools lacked equipment, another reason for denying them defense training. Of course, the claim that skilled blacks could not find work, if not already questionable, soon would be blatantly false. By early 1942, the pages of the black-owned *Atlanta Daily World* continuously carried AUL-sponsored notices of job openings in sheet metal work and machine shop practice, among others, all in war industries outside the South.[9]

Executive Secretary William Bell refused to accept such explanations. Indeed, Bell noted that Commissioner John Studebaker of the United States Office of Education (USOE) had instructed state officials to accept black applicants regardless of immediate employment prospects. "Irrelevant," state officials replied. They advised Bell to see a number of other bureaucrats who allegedly had more power to act. In this encounter, Bell had experienced the classic runaround. On departing, he stated that Georgia, as the custodian of federal funds, had an obligation to eliminate discrimination, especially by withholding funds from uncooperative local school systems.[10]

As the AUL's Bell doggedly continued his campaign, follow-up telephone calls elicited more evasions. The real blame for the training muddle, he was told, lay with Washington officials, who failed to enforce the nondiscrimination clauses. Yet in what appeared to be an unusual flash of candor, the assistant state supervisor of trade and industrial education, J. R. Womack, admitted that the state might have an obligation to keep local school systems from discriminating. But Womack was not going to "stick his neck out," and he advised Bell to follow the same course. Meanwhile, Womack's superior, K. G. Ludtke, tried to discount the type of instruction given to Georgia whites. In a short time it would be obsolete, and blacks should not be concerned about it.[11]

Shortly, even the pseudo defense training available to African Americans came under attack when the Atlanta Federation of Labor put pressure on the federally appointed Local Advisory Committee (LAC) to discontinue courses in carpentry and brick masonry at Washington High. The union representative "undemocratically protested teaching Negroes this trade," the *Atlanta Daily World* reported. At the same time, a third course, greasing automobiles, was "so ridiculous, it's hardly worth discussion," just another example "of how the south deprives its black citizens of opportunity." White youths could sign up for more than fifty courses, "the rankest sort of discrimination."[12]

Executive Secretary William Bell had become equally exasperated. "This leaves one course in greasing and polishing cars which is euphemistically called auto mechanics, and a second course on defense cooking," he wrote an officer of the National Association for the Advancement of Colored People (NAACP). "Local officials say the entire training matter hinges around the lack of equipment," but that was not "strictly true." Washington High had facilities "for more work than [is] now being carried." Meanwhile, in June of 1941, Bell had hopes that the newly created FEPC, with the power to investigate discrimination in the defense training program, would make a difference. Nevertheless, a state official, when asked what effect that agency would have on the courses offered, curtly replied "none," because the federal government refused to take a forthright stand. Reluctantly, Bell concluded that legal action might be necessary.[13]

In October, Executive Secretary Bell began focusing on the Local Advisory Committee (LAC). Its appointees, chosen from business and labor groups, could approve or reject training courses suggested by the State Employment Service. Blacks should have representation on the LAC, Bell thought. Indeed, USOE commissioner Studebaker had so stated. Thus excluded, blacks had no official status with defense training authorities. They should be appointed either to the committee or to a Negro subcommittee created to advise on training.[14] That Bell expected this proposal to be taken seriously seems doubtful. By pursuing this unending, tedious, and frustrating process of arranging meetings, making statements, and registering complaints, the AUL had been putting together a detailed and carefully conceived written record that might be useful now that federal laws and regulations against discrimination existed.

By February of 1942, in the midst of the unprecedented war emergency, Executive Secretary Bell recommenced his battle with the Atlanta public school system. Meeting with Assistant Superintendent H. Reid Hunter, he learned that officials in Washington had rejected two of the local defense courses for Negroes, laundry and institutional cooking, as failing to meet training standards. In fact, Bell may have been relieved that the Washington bureaucracy saw through this blatant, local distortion of the national program. But Assistant Superintendent Hunter continued to justify the courses as "Secondary Job Training" for blacks who would replace white workers going into war production. Hunter *did* seem receptive to Bell's suggestion for a Negro advisory committee to the LAC and promised to call its chairman, E. S. Papy.[15]

William Bell then asked Hunter to get training started at Washington High in sheet metal, machine shop, arc welding, and other bona fide, war-related pursuits, not an unreasonable request considering the war emergency. Hunter countered that the school had no equipment, but Bell knew that additional supplies would be available from the federal government. Hunter still foresaw great difficulty in getting the material, and, besides, white Tech High, Atlanta's elite public boys' school, also lacked equipment. He advised Bell to approach the National Youth Administration, which ran a daytime training program at the black Clark College, for help. Perhaps night school work could be offered there.[16] In effect, Bell and the AUL still faced a blank wall.

Seasoned from years of struggle in the Atlanta job market, and acutely aware of the prejudices of the defense program's local and state administrators, the AUL seemed eager early in 1942 to fight for jobs at the Bell Aircraft Corporation. Organizing the Council on Defense Training for Negroes (CDT), comprised of leaders from the colleges, the business community, the civil service, and civic organizations, the AUL began a campaign for aircraft training programs. Meeting with the Local Advisory Committee's E. S. Papy on February 26, council members cited the injustices already perpetrated. Training classes had been announced for Georgia Tech, four Fulton County high schools, and nine Atlanta schools, besides a special twenty-four-hour training center run by Fulton County. Not one Negro school had been listed, nor were any plans revealed to train blacks. When questioned, Papy agreed that blacks should receive consideration. He advised them to outline the situation in writing to Atlanta superintendent Willis Sutton, who would present it to the LAC.[17]

Although this task may have seemed like one more meaningless hurdle contrived to frustrate and delay, the CDT prepared a list of ten "facts" with cogent arguments based on economic and social considerations. If Bell Aircraft really intended to exhaust the local labor force before recruiting outside, it could not ignore African Americans, who comprised half of the untapped supply. The alternative would involve "vicious social results." The housing and health problems resulting from a large in-migration of workers would strain local resources, while the increasing crime rate would threaten law and order.[18]

On the other hand, trained and working black Atlantans would spend their money to the benefit of the local economy. Outsiders, lacking local interests, would either save their money or send it home. After the war, departing migrants would take their skills with them. Thus, investing in skilled local blacks would pay dividends by providing a reservoir of trained labor for industrial development. Negroes, moreover, were the historic artisans of the South, and southern tradition supported their training. Bell Aircraft's announcement that 80 percent of the production jobs involved semi-skilled and unskilled mechanical tasks reinforced the CDT's arguments. These were the work categories "done almost exclusively by Negroes."[19]

The CDT met on March 12 with M. D. Mobley, the state director of vocational training. Mobley, like the other officials, claimed that he possessed little power, denied responsibility, and mentioned others that the group should contact, such as Major Leonard Kline, Bell Aircraft's director of training, and the United States Employment Service. Since the USES recommended the training programs, "Negro inclusion should begin there." Of course, the LAC would have to be involved, and it was "meeting at that very time." Its decisions probably would be presented next week to the State Advisory Committee in Macon. Mobley suggested that the group prepare their case in writing for its chairman. Mobley himself was "bound to follow the recommendations of the local school systems and the State Advisory Committee."[20]

But the CDT refused to let the evasive director bow out so easily. They pressed him about the federal funds that passed through his office. Was the money to be handled without discrimination? "Yes," Mobley answered, and he wanted the state department of education to abide by the law. The group suggested that this goal could be accomplished "only if he disapproved local plans." Would Mobley send memoranda reminding local school systems to distribute the funds without discrimination? They repeated this question three times before Mobley replied that "he would see." He did not "like to set many things down on paper."[21]

Changing the subject, Mobley tried to return the focus to the United States Employment Service, known as the State Employment Service until its nationalization in December of 1941. Since the USES recommended and referred persons for training, it should request specific programs for blacks. This obligation, Mobley believed, absolved the state department of vocational education of any blame for refusing to do so. At the same time, Mobley conceded that Negroes faced a vicious circle. Without training they could not get jobs, but they needed job prospects in order to get training. That situation could be solved, the CDT countered, by enforcement of the federal policy that required training even when no jobs were available, but Mobley remained immovable.[22]

Trying again to shift responsibility, Mobley labeled Bell Aircraft's recently announced plan to hire blacks as "the crux of the matter." For the second time, he referred the group to Major Leonard Kline. But the CDT members had heard enough. Distrustful of both Papy and Mobley, and doubting both men's statements about the importance and power of the local and state advisory committees, they wired USOE commissioner Studebaker and asked if these two committees could make binding recommendations upon local school authorities, especially if federal policy regarding discrimination had been violated.[23]

Meanwhile, officials at the FEPC headquarters and the War Production Board (WPB) knew about the CDT's activity. The FEPC's John Beecher was "very much impressed by the calibre of the local [Atlanta] Negro leadership, by their grasp of the situation, [and] by their collective determination not to be appeased by cloudy promises or by token concessions." By late February, Beecher's field reports, along with those of the WPB's Cy Record, aroused concern. Shortly, the WPB's Sidney Hillman contacted the Bell Aircraft president.[24]

President Lawrence Bell assured Hillman that company personnel had approached vocational schools on training workers of both races, although the exact jobs for Negroes remained undetermined. But he was "sure that, with due consideration to the traditions of the South concerning the employment of white and colored workers and to your wishes for training and employment of colored workers . . . a suitable arrangement can be worked out which will employ Negroes for some specific jobs in this factory."[25] Of course, this vague statement had little meaning, and presented in the context of southern traditions, it could mean jobs with mops and brooms instead of aircraft tools.

Bell Aircraft also contacted the AUL. Works manager Lester Benson wanted to correct the misunderstanding over organizing the new plant and selecting employees. Actually, little had been done except the completion of grading contracts by the U.S. Army. Building contracts would follow, but no preliminary design had been approved. Consequently, hiring could not begin for a good many months. "You can rest assured that Negro labor will be given proper consideration and that the whole subject will be treated sympathetically and with foresight," Benson wrote.[26]

Benson also relayed other interesting news. The aircraft training program was beyond the scope of Bell Aircraft's direction. It would be carried out through local and state vocational departments in cooperation with the local schools. Of course, the company would report the type and kind of machines used by workers in the plant, but future employees would be referred for training by the USES.[27] If Benson himself was not trying to shift responsibility, this information revealed how evasive and deceitful Georgia public officials had been in dealing with the AUL.

Certainly, the AUL leaders knew how formidable the local USES could be, particularly with its biased staff inherited from the old State Employment Service. But the agency might be persuaded to deal fairly with Atlanta blacks. Its new national director, Colonel Frank McSherry, had earlier promised the National Negro Congress that federalization of the USES would insure the adoption of a uniform policy toward the full integration of all workers. He urged unemployed people to make use of defense training. Indeed, they should register at the USES whether or not they wanted to join the program.[28]

Armed with this knowledge, the CDT visited the new manager of the Atlanta USES, Frank A. Dolan. To their surprise, Dolan provided new, encouraging information. The Bell Aircraft program no longer would be handled by the USES. Bell's Major Kline had just returned from Washington with the power to act in a special capacity out of the office of Donald Nelson, head of the WPB. Kline would decide the training to be inaugurated and the referrals. Dolan also reported that the local white schools tentatively accepted as training sites would be replaced by one large center, a policy later modified. But the USES would refer trainees under Kline's direction. On departing, the group asked Dolan to provide a more dignified entrance for black patrons, who had to approach the USES segregated entrance through a back alley. They also wanted Dolan to employ Negro personnel, a practice abandoned when the state took over that office several years earlier.[29]

As the word spread that blacks would work in the new bomber plant, Georgia's race-baiting governor, Eugene Talmadge, who shortly would face a reelection campaign, got involved. Speaking at Atlanta's Capital City Club, Talmadge warned that it would be unwise for a northern industrialist moving to Georgia to equalize wages between the races. Negroes were not used to the same pay as whites, and they should receive less because of their lower standard of living and low intelligence. Indeed, the war could be won without Negro help. Talmadge also expressed his opposition to the training program at Tuskegee College for black flying cadets. Officials at the NAACP's national headquarters immediately responded to these insults. "We want to direct your attention to remarks reported to have been made by Governor Eugene Talmadge," they informed the WPB's Donald

Nelson. "This Association believes that the War Production Board ought to take a hand if such a policy is in truth to be instituted."[30]

Although encouraged by the news that the WPB and Bell Aircraft had taken control of the training program, AUL leaders apparently took nothing for granted. Shortly, they initiated a campaign to put pressure on the Atlanta board of education. On March 11, the *Daily World* announced a citywide drive to register "technically-minded men and women" for training at Washington High to fill skilled and semiskilled jobs at the bomber plant with salaries as high as thirty-three dollars per week. Executive Secretary William Y. Bell believed that more than two thousand would respond. When the drive ended two weeks later, more than six thousand had signed up, although the overly enthusiastic *Daily World* reported ten thousand.[31] Nevertheless, the drive showed that large numbers of black workers wanted training and jobs in the new aircraft plant.

The AUL kept the FEPC informed of the registration drive and the negative activities of Georgia officials. A weak federal agency operating out of the executive office without a congressional mandate, the FEPC could take little direct action. Through a defense housing agent in Buffalo, however, the FEPC warned Bell Aircraft that its request for a substantial housing project at the Marietta site might not be considered without a promise to train and hire Negroes. The FEPC also made other approaches to Bell Bomber through the War Department.[32]

Soon John Beecher, preparing for an FEPC hearing in Birmingham on discrimination in defense training, issued a dire warning. If the company selected only whites to go to Buffalo for preliminary training, if local officials placed all of the new equipment in previously selected white schools, and if white training got under way ahead of Negro training, "the familiar pattern of discrimination will have been well-established and will become confirmed." He suggested that it is best to correct the problem "while it is shaping, not after its crystallization." From his visits to Atlanta, Beecher saw a "viciously discriminatory situation" developing in regard to Bell Aircraft. "It can be corrected, but time is short and correction will take strong action from all government agencies."[33]

On March 30, five days after Beecher expressed these views, Bell Aircraft broke ground for the new plant. Some six thousand construction workers, half of them unskilled, would participate in this phase of the project. The company targeted November 1 for the partial beginning of production, with the intention of completing part of the facility on December 1, 1942, and the remainder on February 1, 1943.[34] How production could begin so soon remained unexplained.

Beecher's call for "strong action from all government agencies," made privately to his Washington superior, would have elicited little support in much of the Washington bureaucracy. Officials in the United States Office of Education, particularly, either refused or avoided taking a stand. Responding to repeated messages from the AUL, Commissioner Studebaker blandly suggested appeals to state and local school authorities. Indeed, he remained so aloof that the FEPC held a USOE hearing in April. At that event, Studebaker professed to be unaware "of a single case of discrimination or alleged discrimination," and he had little patience with those who "cling slavishly to the idea that all" employees in a factory should be recruited locally. While previously the USOE had used economic persuasion in dispersing federal funds, Studebaker admitted that such leverage had never been used to correct discriminatory behavior. The USES's General Frank McSherry, recently promoted from colonel, remained equally unenthusiastic despite earlier promises to the National Negro Congress. He advised the AUL to contact the regional Labor Supply Committee.[35]

Not surprisingly, state appointees in the National Youth Administration and the USES, and state education officials, noting indifference in Washington and defiance in the governor's office, continued their opposition. Even if programs for blacks were set up, they would countenance no training unless an employer requested "Negro personnel." As the impasse continued, the *Daily World* reported "seething unrest" among the area's 100,000 blacks and a flood of letters to local officials demanding action. The National Urban League (NUL) used what clout it had in Washington. Bell Aircraft's promises to hire Negroes were too general for the intelligent planning of training, NUL staffer Franklin Nichols wrote to the WPB's Donald Nelson. Training should begin even without specific information from the company on the types of jobs available.[36]

Action from Washington finally proved decisive. Two days after Commissioner Studebaker's embarrassing testimony at the FEPC hearing, the USOE acted. "We are required to instruct you that training courses for Negroes must be established on the same basis as for whites," L. S. Hawkins, director of the Office of Vocational Training for Defense Workers, informed Georgia's M. D. Mobley on April 15. "Complete plans and submit necessary requisitions for equipment immediately." At FEPC headquarters, Executive Secretary Lawrence Cramer justifiably claimed credit for the action. The committee's investigations and the USOE hearing brought results, he wrote.[37]

In Atlanta, Director M. D. Mobley immediately conferred with his staff and with representatives of the Atlanta public school system. Booker T. Washington Senior High, serving the whole metro area, would offer training to any Negro referred by the USES. The courses, the same as for whites, included aircraft riveting, sheet metal, fabrication, and subassembly. The proposal would be submitted to the Local Advisory Committee at the earliest possible date. But Mobley tried to shield his office from any local repercussions. He demanded from Washington a statement in writing to the effect that local authorities "need not be concerned as to where and when these men will be employed."[38]

While other groups had provided vital support, the victory really belonged to the Atlanta Urban League. Yet it was barely a beginning. The AUL dealt with white officials who grew up in a segregated society and believed that legally mandated separate schools, among other restrictions, provided the foundation of the southern Jim Crow system. Not only that, as state and local officials, they had the power and the political motivation to remain unyielding. In the murky and byzantine arena of southern segregation politics, numerous opportunities still existed for hostile Georgia officials to sabotage the Bell Aircraft training program for blacks. The CDT continued to monitor every detail.

The CDT next met with Atlanta Schools assistant superintendent Hunter, who announced that the program would accommodate sixty to seventy black trainees. They would undergo the basic, two-month aircraft construction course required of 90 percent of all participants. But Hunter remained vague about the additional courses specified in the USOE's instructions. At the same time, training the three Negro instructors, each responsible for twenty to twenty-five students, might be extremely difficult. Hunter could not say whether Bell Aircraft personnel would participate. The situation had become even more complicated because of the large contingent of white Atlantans already in Buffalo for ten weeks of training.[39]

Hunter also professed to have no knowledge of the compensation to be paid black instructors. In the Atlanta school system, blacks traditionally received less money for performing the same tasks as whites, and a recent campaign for equal pay had failed. Furthermore, Hunter complained, a call for blacks to take instructor training had attracted half a dozen respondents, none of whom he deemed qualified. The CDT members promised to recruit competent applicants, but over a month passed before Hunter provided enough information to advertise the positions. Finally, a mid-May notice in the *Daily World* announced the pay scale at $350 a month, equal to whites.[40]

Hunter set a $6,000 program funding limit because of insufficient space at Washington High. When the CDT protested such a small allocation, Hunter countered that financing would be based on "need." Since neither Bell Aircraft nor the USES had issued any statements on that subject, "need" would be determined by the Atlanta school system.[41] It became clear that Georgia officials would scrutinize every sentence and clause in the instructions from Washington for omissions or phraseology that might be used as an excuse to relieve them of their obligations.

Having learned from Assistant Superintendent Hunter the details of the defense training proposal, the CDT met with state education officials on May 1. This acrimonious session revealed white officials to be more determined than ever to block the program. Director Mobley began by announcing that the $6,000 in funding specified by Assistant Superintendent Hunter would be reduced. The allocation constituted 30 percent of the total, although the figures stated—$15,000 for whites and $5,000 for blacks—amounted to considerably less. Special Agent J. B. Yingling, of the USOE's Defense Training Division, made another startling statement. Blacks referred for training as instructors must have experience in all of the details of airplane construction and some knowledge of inspection. Then, having established nearly impossible obstacles, Yingling challenged the CDT to find competent persons for referral.[42]

A vigorous protest followed. Did the thirty-one whites who went to Buffalo for training have comparable background experience? Special Supervisor Richard Whitehead of the Georgia Defense Training Division admitted that they did not. Asked if black instructors could pick up this detailed knowledge in the training process rather than having to know it at the time of admittance to the program, Yingling, after a pause, replied "yes." But he insisted that persons referred for instructor training must have worked in aircraft production or have attended technical school. The CDT also challenged this statement. It penalized blacks for having no aircraft experience, a result of being excluded from technical training in Georgia's segregated schools. Yingling replied that they must get their training in Negro schools.[43]

Next, the CDT asked if any more people would be sent to Buffalo for training. Supervisor Whitehead responded with a resounding "no," because of the expense. In the future all instructors would receive training locally. For this task, Whitehead had planned to seek two or three of the most capable whites trained in Buffalo, but Director Mobley ruled the proposal as contrary to state law. Special Agent Yingling then explained that the Negro instructors would have to be trained by blacks in their own schools, because the Georgia Constitution prohibited race mixing. CDT members vigorously objected on the grounds that federal antidiscrimination laws were being violated. Mobley then allowed that the state of Georgia did not have to take federal defense training funds, although it intended to do so for reasons of patriotism.[44]

CDT members then stated the obvious. If black instructors were not to be trained by whites in Atlanta, and if they could not learn the work in Buffalo, there would be no instructors and no training program. The state officials agreed: there would be no black instructors unless a local school system authorized a plan that violated state law. Several times the CDT members asked Special Agent Yingling if the state vocational education system, as custodian of federal funds and agent of the USOE, was not compelled to set up training programs without discrimination. State and local laws must be obeyed, Yingling replied, and federal procedure must conform to state and local legal practices. While the USOE made policy, it could not enforce it. Indeed, the USOE lacked the power even to see that Negroes were trained, although that agency could withhold funds if dissatisfied with local procedures. At the same time, Yingling vowed that his office would continue to approve training for whites whether or not blacks received it. On that matter, he claimed to speak for officials in the USOE's Washington office, including both Director Hawkins and Commissioner Studebaker.[45]

After this hostile encounter, the CDT took their grievances to Commissioner Studebaker, but copies of all their correspondence went to the FEPC. The CDT dealt first with Director Mobley's misinterpretation of Georgia's laws and constitution. While one statute *did* prohibit the payment of compensation to any teacher giving instruction to white and black students in the same school, no law controlling the racial identity of teachers for African Americans existed. Shortly thereafter, AUL executive secretary William Bell so informed Commissioner Studebaker.[46]

Next, Executive Secretary Bell turned to the funding issue. Although gratified that Director Mobley earmarked between $5,000 and $6,000 for the black program, he wrote, that sum represented only 9 percent of the $60,000 requested for additional equipment. Set up on an equitable basis in proportion to the blacks available for training, the amount for Atlanta alone would be closer to 40 percent. Under Mobley's proposal, only 1,200 Negroes per year would receive training, making a total of less than 2,000 by December of 1943, when the plant was scheduled to employ between 25,000 and 40,000. Unless changed, the plan, by including only a small fraction of the available Negro labor supply, would be inequitable.[47]

AUL executive secretary Bell also reminded Studebaker that the plan included only aircraft training. Blacks presently received absolutely no defense training for jobs in other war industries. Finally, the commissioner should be aware that the USOE's field and special agents needed particular instructions on the meaning of the nondiscrimination clause and on the USOE's resolve to enforce it. William Bell singled out Special Agent J. B. Yingling as a prime target. By advising state officials that local school systems could practice discrimination, Yingling effectively had sabotaged much of the good that Commissioner Studebaker had done.[48]

Undoubtedly, the AUL's aggressive challenges, along with FEPC support, made it more difficult for southern officials to engage in future, unchallenged discriminatory behavior in administering the training program. On May 13, a WPB official warned USOE director Hawkins that labor supply reports from Atlanta indicated serious shortages of workers unless African Americans were included, and he urged their training for employment at Bell Aircraft. Not surprisingly, Hawkins stoutly defended the errant Georgia officials. Both the Local Advisory Committee and state vocational education appointees had approved training, he noted. While black instructors must be knowledgeable in the work they taught, they would be trained by qualified whites brought in from other states if none were available in Georgia. Furthermore, nearly ten thousand dollars in equipment for Negro schools, not six thousand dollars as stated, had been authorized. School officials were sincere in their plans to train Negroes, Hawkins wrote, and he hoped local black leaders would cooperate in every way possible.[49]

By mid-June, USES agent James H. McGinnis provided a clearer picture of the area's available manpower resources. The USES files for Atlanta carried 27,052 registrants (12,421 white men, 6,201 white women, 6,494 black men, and 1,944 black women). During the previous March, the USES also had assessed the labor supply within a thirty-five-mile radius of Marietta, involving counties that comprised about 21 percent of the state's population. A total of 34,082 people registered, including 24,061 men and 10,021 women. In this labor market, 77 percent were Caucasian (53 percent men, 24 percent women), and 23 percent were African American (18 percent men, 5 percent women). About 3,000 other workers remained unregistered. The June high school graduation augmented this supply by 5,500, including 4,800 whites (2,300 men, 2,500 women) and 661 blacks (241 men, 420 women). This labor pool provided enough workers for the plant's construction and the initial production requirements.[50]

When production began in November, McGinnis continued, Bell Aircraft would be the principal source of new employment, initially involving 12,000 workers. The date of projected peak employment, at 40,000, remained unknown. The plant force would include riveters (33 percent), fabricators (25 percent), assembly line workers (25 percent), and machine shop operators (16 percent). Two months later, McGinnis could make better estimates on the labor supply. The three Atlanta and Fulton County schools remaining in the program would be turning out white trainees at the rate of 2,000 per month. Presently, however, trainees remained reluctant to enroll because production would not begin for an estimated six to eight months. Indeed, at the time of McGinnis's report, only 3 percent of the plant had been constructed.[51]

McGinnis had no projections on black trainees, and he expressed anger over the slow progress in establishing that program. "Despite a specific USOE directive to the state director of vocational education [M. D. Mobley] to set up such courses on an equitable basis," nothing yet had been done. Continuous but nearly futile efforts to establish these facilities met "with various and sundry excuses and obstacles thrown in the way" even though the Atlanta Urban League had registered African Americans desiring training, some 2,000 in Atlanta alone.[52]

Meanwhile, the FEPC, on June 19, called upon Director Mobley to explain publicly his handling of defense training for African Americans. Summoned to testify at the Birmingham hearing, Mobley demonstrated either contempt for the proceedings or utter incompetence, and perhaps both. When questioned by the committee, which included two African Americans appointed by the president, he hedged and dodged repeatedly. He had not brought the information the FEPC requested because it took too long to prepare. He had no knowledge of the situation in each locality and claimed familiarity only with the state as a whole. He lacked information on the racial breakdown of trainees by centers because the committee had not asked for it. He could provide no detail on the courses offered because he interpreted the FEPC letter as not having requested it, although he could supply such information. Mobley *could* state that the Bell Aircraft program had been approved at a cost of $9,933, but it was not yet under way. He then recited the titles of courses offered but professed not to know the number available to Negroes.[53]

Despite pressure at the Birmingham hearing, implementation of the training program continued at the same slow pace. Not until late July did the Atlanta school system send a representative to Baltimore to procure teaching materials. Submitting the required duplicate requests for a priority rating on equipment also seemed to take an inordinate amount of time. Eventually, a special USOE representative conferred with officials of the Freeport State School of Aviation on Long Island about teaching materials and training in aircraft sheet metal.[54]

With all the delays, it was early November 1942 before four blacks from Atlanta began their instructor training, but they went to Long Island rather than Buffalo. Ever suspicious of Georgia education officials, G. James Fleming, a black FEPC examiner working on the case, wondered "if this difference in training background may arise later to disqualify Negro workers for some types of jobs" at the Marietta plant. "Will it be possible to say that Negroes do not have the kind of training needed by their local plant?"[55]

Nevertheless, on November 16, 1942, training in aircraft construction began at Washington High. Out of the 50 individuals requisitioned at the USES, 46 reported, including 42 women and 4 men. The final enrollment of 26 for that session included 24 women and 2 men. The attrition rate surely disappointed, when only 11 women and 2 men finished. Of the 50 trainees selected for the next session on December 9, only 13 women and 5 men reported. Yet training officials remained optimistic. White recruits showed a similar lack of interest, and the USES expected that pattern to continue until Bell Aircraft actually started hiring. In addition, trainees as yet received no pay, while blacks also were offered no daytime classes.[56]

As time would reveal, the Bell Aircraft training program attracted large numbers of women of both races. But among African Americans, women apparently constituted the majority of trainees and skilled employees. In January 1943, a total of 70 African American women took training, including 24 in riveting, 22 in assembly, and 26 in fabrication. Only 2 male riveters participated, although 20 others enrolled in automotive mechanics. The reason for the gender disparity in favor of black females remains unknown, although the overwhelming preference of early male trainees for auto mechanics instead of aircraft assembly may provide a partial answer, along with the draft.

The preponderance of skilled black women apparently continued in the workplace. Among 100 Bell skilled race workers studied after the war (40 men and 60 women), female workers greatly outnumbered males in three tasks, including assemblers, riveters, and drill press operators. In this group, only women worked as stack drill operators. Whether these jobs had been labeled as "women's work" is not known. All of the routers and circular saw operators clearly were men. Despite the preponderance of black women, however, by January 1944 women of both races comprised only 35 percent of the total Bell workforce, with 43 percent expected within six months.[57]

By the end of January 1943, 60 black workers per month were being trained, making a total of 200 up to that time. Indeed, Cy Record of the War Manpower Commission's (WMC's) predicted that blacks would comprise between 25 and 30 percent of the total personnel when the plant reached peak employment. But such optimism proved unrealistic. Although more than 1,000 nonwhites worked at Bell Aircraft by December, only slightly more than 2,200 African Americans could be counted a year later, less than 9 percent of the plant's then peak employment of 25,840.[58]

The implementation of the Bell Aircraft training program for black Atlantans received widespread national coverage in major African American newspapers. It began only after nine months of struggle, the *Pittsburgh Courier* reported, and it provided the first such training in the South. The paper gave credit for this achievement to the Atlanta Urban League, the FEPC, and particularly to Executive Secretary William Y. Bell. The influential *Norfolk Journal and Guide* also celebrated the event.[59] It was a significant accomplishment, considering the fact that the aircraft industry, both nationally and in the South, had been a serious offender in terms of employment discrimination. But a stable employment environment did not yet exist. Undoubtedly, neither the members of the CDT nor the hundreds of African Americans who worked at Bell Aircraft could have envisioned the trouble that lay ahead.

As African Americans completed training and took up job assignments at Bell Aircraft, racism and discrimination immediately became serious problems. Although concerned, the AUL increasingly referred problems to the FEPC, which in November 1943 opened its Region 7 office in Atlanta.

The new regional director, A. Bruce Hunt, soon reported alarming news to Washington headquarters. "There is serious racial prejudice within the Bell plant, so serious that rivets and other dangerous articles have been thrown by whites at Negroes while at work because the whites objected to Negroes coming into certain departments."[60]

Later, Hunt learned that white workers went to Negro job locations in a violent, threatening manner, but no injuries were reported. They received no reprimands for this behavior. In addition, a National Labor Relations Board (NLRB) election between the International Association of Machinists (IAM-AFL) and the United Aircraft Workers (UAW-CIO) contributed to the hostility. "I am sorry to see the IAM stoop to racial prejudice as a campaign argument," Hunt added.[61]

Complaints began arriving at the Atlanta FEPC office. Among the plant's several segregated cafeterias, the black area was so far from the workplace that one employee had been discharged for being late from lunch. Others cited discriminatory work assignments and an inability to get jobs for which they were qualified. Few received positions above general laborer. A Bell manager also refused to hire a Jewish applicant. By the end of February, the FEPC had twelve such complaints, with more to come in March. The new charges included refusal to train and hire, wage differentials, discriminatory classification, and newspaper advertisements specifying race. At the plant, the two resident Army Air Force officers refused to confer with FEPC investigators or admit them on the grounds to interview employees, claiming that a clearance from Washington was needed. At the same time, Bell's industrial relations manager insisted that the cases be handled by the sympathetic and accommodating WMC-USES, not the FEPC, and he refused to provide information relative to the complaints.[62]

Over the next three months, FEPC investigators found most of the complaints to be justified. An ad in the *Atlanta Journal* for white men mentioned draftsmen, cafeteria supervisors, and radio installers and operators, with newly completed housing available for them near the plant. Black men read about openings for laborers, janitors, porters, and metal cleaners. An examination of Bell Aircraft's work orders at the Atlanta USES also revealed widespread discrimination. While the company requested 364 white workers to fill some seventy-two types of positions, only 63 black men were needed for three types of positions, and 2 black women for one type of position. While the various positions remained unidentified, the work assigned to Caucasians obviously involved skills, while blacks were assigned lower-paying service-area jobs.[63]

The Atlanta USES duly explained the program of nondiscrimination to Bell Aircraft, the FEPC was told, and asked the company to stop submitting discriminatory orders. In return, the USES claimed to have received willing cooperation, but FEPC regional director Hunt remained skeptical. "The truth is that the employer has not changed its employment policies and that the USES has continued to make referrals in accordance with those policies," he reported to headquarters.[64]

Some of the rejected black applicants cited unusually strong credentials. George H. Andrews, a Morehouse College graduate with vocational training in electrical engineering at Tuskegee, had served as a vocational instructor in radio and electrical work for the Civilian Conservation Corps, had taught mathematics at Atlanta's Washington High, and had given courses in radio theory, construction, and code at Bethune-Cookman College until enrollment dropped in April of 1944. Seeing a newspaper advertisement from Bell Aircraft, he wrote the division manager stating his qualifications and race. Upon receiving an application with the suggestion he call at the Atlanta office, Andrews went to Marietta and took tests, which he passed. His white interviewer then offered him a laborer's job. Andrews mentioned a recent ad in the *Atlanta Constitution* for radio mechanics, but the interviewer refused him the job and rejected his request to see someone else.[65]

An Atlanta riveter, Elijah W. Thompson, worked at Detroit's Briggs Aircraft for fourteen months. Unable to find accommodations for his family, he wrote Bell Aircraft requesting employment. In reply, the company made no commitment but enclosed an application form, which Thompson filled out and returned. Told at the company's Marietta office that he needed a release from Briggs Aircraft, Thompson went back to Detroit, resigned his job, and received the release. At the company's Marietta office, however, a Bell official refused to hire him. Thompson then went to the Atlanta USES and talked to another Bell interviewer, describing his experience and qualifications. He learned that Bell had no skilled or unskilled openings, but the company would notify him if something came up.[66]

Bell's vice president of personnel, retired naval captain H. E. Collins, admitted refusing employment to skilled blacks for fear of work stoppages by whites. Earlier, Collins had conferred with the AUL and promised to set up segregated job opportunities, but A. Bruce Hunt rejected the agreement. "They apparently have decided it cannot be done otherwise," Hunt wrote Washington, but he disagreed. "We think the better procedure is to place a few well-chosen and qualified Negroes into skilled jobs until the whites have accepted them"; then others could be added. "This idea is consistent with the practice which now exists since there are few, if any, production departments in which Negroes are not employed." Indeed, blacks already worked "with whites throughout the production building . . . coming in close contact with whites, although they work in lesser jobs." Captain Collins agreed to consider Hunt's strategy, which, in effect, amounted to gradual integration.[67]

In their skepticism, Bell officials could cite, besides southern tradition, at least one other reason to fear the kind of workplace that Hunt proposed. A year earlier, white workers had rioted at a Mobile shipyard after a few black welders, at FEPC insistence, worked just one integrated night shift. The violence ended only after the arrival of federal troops. Surely, Hunt knew of such risks. On the other hand, the war emergency had not turned Atlanta into a congested, seething boomtown like Mobile, with housing and urban support services strained far beyond capacity and endurance. Nor apparently was Bell Aircraft, unlike Mobile's Alabama Dry Dock and Shipbuilding Company, guided by a management that despised the New Deal and precipitously, without preparation, integrated its welders to foment trouble.[68]

Nevertheless, Bell chose the apparently safe course, and nothing came of Hunt's proposal. By this time, the FEPC had twenty-three cases pending against the company, twenty-one involving race. In exasperation, Hunt requested the local WMC to deny Bell Aircraft the services of the USES in recruiting workers outside the local employment area in any occupations not open to all qualified applicants. When the WMC refused, Hunt appealed to Washington.[69]

Bell Aircraft had engaged extensively in outside recruitment, and plant officials really may have feared negative WMC action as a result of their racial policies. Shortly, Bell's announcement that a segregated work area for blacks would be established seemed to indicate such concern. The separate facility would be used for assembly and subassembly work in skilled and semiskilled classifications. The company also would cooperate with Washington High's training program, paying unskilled trainees sixty-five cents per hour. The decision to segregate came after the WMC requested that everything possible be done to employ black workers, company officials stated. But in return, they expected clearance "to those areas where there is available a labor supply" suitable to their needs.[70]

Suspicious and dissatisfied, Regional Director Hunt warned the WMC that his office, uninformed about the segregation move, could not judge whether Bell's plans conformed with the antidiscrimination policy. He still believed that the company and the FEPC should work together toward compliance. In the meantime, Hunt refused to withdraw the request for restrictions on Bell's outside recruitment. Nevertheless, just as Bell Aircraft's treatment of black workers clearly violated administration policy, so did Hunt also tread on shaky ground. The executive order creating the FEPC gave that agency power to investigate discrimination, but it had authority to deal with segregation only when that practice resulted in discrimination. In insisting on the slow integration of the workplace, Hunt may have exceeded the FEPC's mandate. The situation had become even more complicated because Bell purported to be using segregation as a means of avoiding job discrimination.[71]

Hunt also had become deeply concerned about lagging war production. "There are hundreds of skilled jobs open at the Bell plant," he told union members at a gathering of UAW Local 10. Hunt knew, but refrained from reminding them, that their union avidly recruited blacks and promised full union membership. Local 10 then went on narrowly to defeat the segregated IAM and win exclusive bargaining rights at Bell with the aid of Negro votes in a close election. "Those of us close to the local employment situation know that white persons are not available in large enough numbers to meet" Bell's employment needs, and Hunt predicted that "more and more skilled jobs at Bell will be filled by qualified Negroes." He knew that "some of you at first would be inclined to oppose the hir[ing] or upgrading of Negroes," and some "may object to closer association at work." Hunt told the group that "the present need for war production, and the strength and morale of your union today, as well as in times of peace, transcend in importance the feelings you have." The members should "look again at the problem of race relations . . . and cast aside your prejudices in favor of the interests of your Nation and your union."[72]

Local 10's contract with Bell Aircraft, completed at the end of July 1943, surely disappointed Hunt. The negotiators seemingly concentrated on two issues, union security and wages. While the contract forbade racial discrimination in advancement, seniority, wages, and layoffs, it accepted Bell's insistence upon segregation in the main plant, which the leaders of Local 10 also believed to be necessary. A union official claimed that black workers themselves agreed to segregation. To assure the preservation of segregation, however, the contract also specified that laid-off workers of one race would not be transferred to departments staffed by workers of another race.[73]

As Local 10 accepted segregation in the workplace and adopted a policy of no interracial transfers, its leaders pursued questionable internal policies in dealing with minorities. With little more than 50 percent of Bell employees organized, Local 10 faced daunting challenges. Initial attempts to set up interracial meetings allegedly failed because of black reluctance to participate. The regional director then called shift or departmental meetings made up mainly of blacks to encourage them to become more active and also to pay their dues. Typical of UAW practices during organizational campaigns, meetings of ethnic or language groups had become acceptable and well established. Nevertheless, such meetings in Local 10 continued for nearly two years and ended only after the pointed disapproval of the UAW's Fair Practice Committee. The extent of black participation remains unknown, although one integrated local meeting at Atlanta's CIO building was disrupted when an international representative, without consulting the regional director, requested the African Americans to sit in the back of the hall. This violation of UAW policy brought the perpetrator a reprimand and a warning that it should never happen again.[74]

Bell Aircraft's segregated facility for skilled and semiskilled blacks, known as Department 86, attracted mostly female riveters, drillers, and assembly workers. A small operation, it reportedly could accommodate only 260. Blacks also had jobs in Department 51, apparently as helpers. With these openings filled, however, Bell refused to hire blacks except in the service occupations available in Department 29. Meanwhile, during the fall of 1944 and the following spring, company ads in the "white" columns of Atlanta's newspapers touted "HUNDREDS OF JOBS! Jobs for skilled or unskilled—all important jobs building the big B-29 bombers that take the war right back over the Jap's own bases. Every Bell worker is proud of the potent weapon he produced in the South's greatest aviation plant." As Department 86 filled, the company began curtailing the training program. Yet while the number of trainees at the white schools declined, Negro applicants at Washington High were being turned away.[75]

In February 1945, the remaining two instructors at Washington High offered courses only in blueprint reading, drilling, and riveting to just twenty-four trainees. According to one observer, "under such a program . . . it is obvious that the School is doomed to a sure and slow death." Meanwhile, job prospects for blacks at Bell Aircraft continued to dwindle. "The situation is having a negative effect on the morale of Atlanta Negroes," an investigator reported to the local WMC. Hundreds of men and women wanted work but could not find jobs "even though daily they hear public announcements requesting such workers." The problem became especially acute as the Congress debated a "work or fight" bill, which would draft men without war-related jobs into the armed forces. The effect of such legislation on minorities, refused employment because of discrimination, could be devastating.[76]

Faced with scores of complaints, the FEPC continued to conduct investigations, to urge the WMC and the USES to put pressure on Bell, and to hold conferences with company officials, all with only limited success. Although FEPC agents finally received clearance to enter the plant, severely restricted mobility therein seriously hampered their activity. Meanwhile, the WMC, backed by Washington, flatly refused to suspend Bell's outside recruiting.[77]

A January conference between the FEPC's new regional director, Witherspoon Dodge, and Bell's industrial relations manager, Joseph Daugherty, accomplished nothing. While promising that the plant's laborers and janitors would be trained and upgraded, Daugherty also said that no more openings existed in the departments in which blacks could be considered for employment. Amidst such contradictory pronouncements, he declined to name those departments but admitted that certain other departments turned away blacks. When asked for a breakdown of the classifications in which white employees worked, in which whites and blacks worked together, and in which blacks worked alone, with the total number in each classification, Daugherty said that such figures would have to come from the army's area commanding officer. In a final, meaningless statement, Daugherty said Bell would hire and train as many Negroes as possible while keeping in mind "how many people we can get and still keep things running smoothly."[78]

Two and a half months later, in a final meeting with Witherspoon Dodge, Bell's plant manager, native Mariettan James Carmichael, refused to consider working blacks and whites "side by side" because it violated company policy. Curiously, in a state with rigid segregation laws, a white establishment demanding their strict enforcement, hostile officials doggedly refusing to train blacks, and a former governor spouting racial hatred, Carmichael blamed the racism at the plant on "lower type" whites, the "undeveloped hill-billies of Georgia with deeply entrenched prejudice." Integration would close the plant down, even produce a race riot. He could not jeopardize production for a few skilled workers.[79]

Nevertheless, Bell Aircraft *did* plan a wider diversification of jobs for African Americans within its segregated facilities. In fact, Carmichael believed that the company, with fifteen Negro job classifications, had done more in creating employment, providing toilets, arranging eating places, and furnishing other unnamed amenities than any other plant in the South. Black workers at the segregated facility, mostly women, received eighty cents per hour and worked a nine-hour day, with time and a half for overtime. Washington High would be kept open, he promised, although fewer employees from both races would be needed as the war came to an end.[80]

After this March conference, Regional Director Dodge spent much of his time before the FEPC regional office closed that fall trying to negotiate satisfactory adjustments of the numerous discrimination cases filed against Bell Aircraft and other war contractors in the Atlanta area. Most of this effort ended in failure. With the war ending, Bell announced general cutbacks, while Dodge, in one of his last reports, referred to the unsatisfactory conditions there. Thus the great bomber manufacturer ended World War II guilty of discriminatory behavior in its race relations.[81]

The struggle for defense and wartime training by Atlanta blacks initially revolved around the hitherto unappreciated efforts of the Atlanta Urban League and several capable community leaders who realized that the instruction offered in the nation's defense program could be crucial for the advancement of the race. In this effort, AUL executive secretary William Y. Bell stood out despite a leadership style that displayed unfortunate paternalistic and autocratic tendencies. In his handling of defense training, he emerged as one of the more capable black leaders in the area and perhaps even in the region. He challenged recalcitrant public officials with unusual skill and fortitude. William Bell also kept a detailed record of the AUL's encounters with public officials, an account that later became indispensable both to his organization and to the historian. His activity may well have laid the groundwork for the expanded role that the AUL, under other leadership, later would assume. It included a campaign to improve Atlanta's black schools, a voter registration drive immediately after the war, and, like its parent, the National Urban League, a focus on improved housing for African Americans.[82]

While Atlanta's black workers could look to the AUL and other indigenous organizations for support, the organized labor movement proved less dependable. The UAW-CIO's Local 10 surely appreciated black union members' votes, which were crucial in its victory at the plant. Yet in becoming an accomplice to Bell Aircraft's decision to set up a segregated workplace, Local 10 exhibited greater concern for the prejudices of its more numerous white members than the economic well-being of minorities. Its meetings, too long segregated, mimicked the practices of its defeated AFL rival. Had the IAM-AFL organized the Bell Aircraft plant, however, it remains problematic whether many or any skilled black men and women would have worked there despite the AUL's efforts in getting training for them.

Thus CIO unions in the aircraft industry, despite all of their shortcomings, *did* make a difference, in Atlanta and sometimes elsewhere in the South. At the North American Aviation plant near Dallas, Local 645 (United Aircraft Workers–CIO) at the end of 1943 had 1,900 paid-up black unionists. These workers comprised 15 percent of its membership and 7.6 percent of the labor force in a plant that at the time employed more than 25,000. In this endeavor, blacks had received strong support from the Dallas Negro Chamber of Commerce. About a year later, the North American Aviation workforce had increased to 34,621, including 2,250 nonwhites. By then they comprised 6.5 percent of the total, indicating a stagnant growth rate in their employment. Nevertheless, FEPC investigators during this period found union officers and stewards to be helpful and cooperative in handling the grievances of these workers, including Mexican Americans who faced their own problems of job discrimination. Meanwhile, the company had set up a program to train and employ skilled black women.[83]

A different story unfolded a few miles away at Consolidated Vultee Aircraft's Fort Worth facility. Black employees, denied membership in the International Association of Machinists (IAM-AFL), belonged to a segregated Negro local. In 1944, its president faced dismissal for attempting to get upgrading for himself and others who worked with him as janitors. This decision was reversed only after strong representations from the FEPC and the Fort Worth Negro Welfare Council. Meanwhile, charges had been filed against the IAM for preventing such upgrading in Fort Worth and in other facilities across the nation. In a plant with 24,693 workers, only 931 were nonwhite in May of 1945, and a paltry 90 to 100 of these worked in skilled jobs. While blacks fared decidedly better in the Marietta and Dallas aircraft plants organized by the UAW-CIO, that union's record still left much to be desired.[84] It provided for some CIO unions an ambiguous legacy in race relations in the postwar period.

While the unions often remained unreliable allies, the AUL's activity illustrated that African American organizations had their own agenda well before a government agency such as the FEPC came into existence. At the same time, a city like Atlanta, often branded with the "epithet" Yankee or northern city, provided the AUL with a hopeful, although not always hospitable, setting for its activity. Atlanta's selection in 1913 as a Federal Reserve banking center for the Southeast bolstered the city's regional importance and brought in outside influences. Other federal agencies followed. By the early 1920s, Atlanta's large and active black population, with a focused leadership, had made its presence felt in Atlanta politics. In 1923, the AUL began receiving regular financial support from the Community Chest.

A strong union presence also developed in Atlanta, first in the printing and construction trades. Then, in 1937, the CIO union at the city's Lakewood automobile assembly plant participated in the famous sit-down strikes. As the defense program got under way, the CIO obtained a foothold in other war plants such as Firestone, in addition to Bell Aircraft. Nevertheless, the fact that these forces may have made the AUL's task less difficult in no way detracts from the resolve and perseverance that its leaders displayed in their struggle for defense training.

Like black groups in other urban areas, the AUL assisted the FEPC in fighting job discrimination, and it used that agency's limited power whenever possible.[85] Meanwhile, the FEPC made a difference in the economic advancement made by black workers during the war decade.[86] A significant government presence, it provided resources hitherto unavailable to African Americans, including trained and dedicated investigators, legal and other professional expertise, and contacts with government agencies involved with wartime employment. The FEPC also insisted that blacks work at their highest skills, and it relentlessly pursued this goal until its demise in June of 1946.

Bell Aircraft, in its token compliance with the FEPC agenda, denied perhaps hundreds of skilled blacks better jobs and higher living standards. Yet those whom Bell Aircraft accepted *did* receive wages equal to whites, inconceivable in the prewar Deep South. Blacks also could apply to a Bell counselor of their own race for the same rationed necessities granted to whites, including help in applying for gasoline, tires, and other items important to their employment. That the Bell Bomber plant became important in "getting an economic base for the blacks of the city," as a black Bell counselor later believed, remains doubtful.[87] Located outside the city and away from the area's major black community, the government-owned plant closed when the national emergency ended, to be reopened later by a different proprietor during the Korean War.

Notes

1. George B. Tindall, *The Emergence of the New South, 1913–1945* (Baton Rouge, La., 1967), 694–702; Herbert R. Northrup, *The Negro in the Aerospace Industry* (Philadelphia, 1968), 20.

2. *Atlanta Journal*, 23, 24 Feb. 1942. For insight as to the political maneuvering that brought Bell Aircraft to Marietta, see Jean Edward Smith, *Lucius D. Clay: An American Life* (New York, 1990), 91–93.

3. Locality Analysis, Bureau of Program Requirements, War Manpower Commission, June 1943, and Reports on War Production Centers, 14 Feb. 1944, Reports, Analysis, Compilations, Atlanta folder, Region VII, War Manpower Commission, Record Group (RG) 211, Federal Records Center, East Point, Georgia, hereinafter cited FRCEP; John Beecher to Lawrence Cramer, 28 Feb. 1942, Central Files, Reports 1-1, Records of the Fair Employment Practice Committee, RG 228, National Archives, Reel (R) 48, Headquarters Records (HR), hereinafter cited R48HR.

4. *Atlanta Journal*, 23, 24 Feb. 1942.

5. E. A. Adams to Cy W. Record, 16 Mar. 1942, Division of Field Operations (DFO), Office Files of John Beecher, Bell Aircraft, Atlanta folder, RG 228, R78HR; John Beecher to Lawrence Cramer, 28 Feb. 1942, Central Files, Reports 1-1, RG 228, R48HR.

6. Atlanta Urban League, Semi-Annual Report (1940), pp. 3, 8, box 4, folder 13, Robert Woodruff Library, Atlanta University; Jesse T. Moore, *Search for Equality: The National Urban League, 1910–1961* (University Park, Pa., 1981), 90; Paul D. Moreno, *From Direct Action to Affirmative Action: Fair Employment Law and Policy in America, 1933–1972* (Baton Rouge, La., 1997), 58; Clarence Stone, *Regime Politics: Governing Atlanta, 1946–1988* (Lawrence, Kans., 1989), 33.

7. Willis A. Sutton to Almita S. Robinson, 6 Aug. 1940, Central Files, Vocational Education, RG 228, R35HR; Merl E. Reed, *Seedtime for the Modern Civil Rights Movement: The President's Committee on Fair Employment Practice, 1941–1946* (Baton Rouge, La., 1991), 175–76; Ronald H. Bayor, *Race and the Shaping of Twentieth-Century Atlanta* (Chapel Hill, 1996), 106–7.

8. Chronology of Efforts to Have Defense Training Extended to Negroes in Atlanta, typescript, carbon, n.d., unauthored [AUL], Legal Division, Office Files of Frank D. Reeves, Defense Training Program, RG 228, R7HR.

9. Ibid.; *Atlanta Daily World*, 2 Jan. 1942, p. 2.

10. Chronology of Efforts to Have Defense Training Extended to Negroes in Atlanta.

11. Ibid.

12. *Atlanta Daily World*, 1 Feb. 1942, p. 4.

13. William Y. Bell to J. L. LeFlore, 23 June 1941, H. Reid Hunter to W. Y. Bell, 30 Sept. 1941, Central Files, Vocational Training, RG 228, R35HR.

14. Chronology of Efforts to Have Defense Training Extended to Negroes in Atlanta.

15. Ibid.

16. Ibid.

17. Ibid.

18. Ibid.

19. Ibid.

20. Ibid.

21. Ibid.

22. Ibid.

23. Ibid.; Dr. William Dean to John Studebaker, 13 Mar. 1942, Central Files, Vocational Education, RG 228, R35HR.

24. John Beecher to Lawrence Cramer, 28 Feb. 1942, Central Files, Reports 1-1, John Beecher, R48RH, 25 Mar. 1942, DFO, Office Files of John Beecher, Bell Aircraft, Atlanta folder, R78HR.

25. Lawrence D. Bell to Sidney Hillman, 10 Mar. 1942, Atlanta folder, R78HR.

26. Lester Benson to William Y. Bell, 13 Mar. 1942, Legal Division, Office Files of Frank D. Reeves, Defense Training Program, RG 228, R7HR.

27. Ibid.

28. *Atlanta Daily World*, 30 Jan. 1942, p. 1.

29. Chronology of Efforts to Have Defense Training Extended to Negroes in Atlanta.

30. *Pittsburgh Courier*, 21 Mar. 1942, p. 4; Roy Wilkins to Donald M. Nelson, 20 Mar. 1942, Administrative Division, Hearings, Alabama, RG 228, FRCEP.

31. *Atlanta Daily World*, 11, 12, 19 Mar. 1942; William Y. Bell to Lawrence Cramer, 27 Mar. 1942, Legal Division, Office Files of Frank D. Reeves, Defense Training Program, R7HR; Lester Brooks, *Blacks in the City: A History of the National Urban League* (Boston, 1971), 307.

32. William Y. Bell to George M. Johnson, 23 Mar. 1942, Legal Division, Office Files of Frank D. Reeves, Defense Training Program, R7HR; Lawrence Cramer to John Beecher, 24 Mar. 1942, Central Files, Public Relations 5, Cramer, R45HR.

33. John Beecher to Lawrence Cramer, 25 Mar. 1942, DFO, Office Files of John Beecher, Bell Aircraft, Atlanta folder, R78HR.

34. Report of James McGinnis, 12 June 1942, summary, typescript, Central Files, Reports, A–C, General, RG 228, R47HR.

35. Telegram, John W. Studebaker to Dr. William Dean, 24 Mar. 1942, Central Files, Vocational Training, RG 228, R35HR; testimony of John W. Studebaker, Hear-

ing on Discrimination in Defense Training, 13 Apr. 1942, RG 228, R15HR; Frank J. McSherry to Subcommittee of the Council for Defense Training for Negroes, 26 Mar. 1942, DFO, Office Files of John Beecher, Bell Aircraft, Atlanta folder, RG 228, R78HR; Reed, *Seedtime*, 185–86.

36. *Atlanta Daily World*, 24, 29 Mar. 1942; Franklin O. Nichols to Donald M. Nelson, 30 Mar. 1942, Central Files, Public Relations 5, National, RG 228, R45HR.

37. L. S. Hawkins to M. D. Mobley, 15 Apr. 1942, DFO, Office Files of John Beecher, Bell Aircraft, Atlanta folder, RG 228, R78HR; Lawrence Cramer to Earl B. Dickerson, 30 Apr. 1942, Central Files, Public Relations 5, RG 228, R45HR.

38. M. D. Mobley to L. S. Hawkins, 16 Apr. 1942, Central Files, Vocational Training, RG 228, R35HR.

39. AUL Council on Defense Training for Negroes, Conference with Dr. H. Reid Hunter, n.d. [soon after 15 Apr. 1942], DFO, Office Files of John Beecher, Bell Aircraft, Atlanta folder, RG 228, R78HR.

40. Ibid.; *Atlanta Daily World*, 20 May 1942, p. 1.

41. Council on Defense Training for Negroes (CDT), Conference with Dr. H. Reid Hunter, n.d. [soon after 15 Apr. 1942], DFO, Office Files of John Beecher, Bell Aircraft, Atlanta folder, RG 228, R78HR.

42. Abstract of Conference, Subcommittee of the AUL Council with state education officials, 1 May 1942, DFO, Office Files of John Beecher, Bell Aircraft, Atlanta folder, RG 228, R78HR.

43. Ibid.; Outline of Training for Bell Aircraft Workers, May 1942, Training, Georgia folder, Divisional Records-Training, RG 211, FRCEP.

44. Abstract of Conference, Subcommittee of the AUL Council with state education officials, 1 May 1942.

45. Ibid.

46. A. T. Walden to Council on Defense Training for Negroes, 7 May 1942, DFO, Office Files of John Beecher, Bell Aircraft, Atlanta folder, RG 228, R78HR.

47. William Y. Bell to John Studebaker, 9 May 1942, DFO, Office Files of John Beecher, Bell Aircraft, Atlanta folder, RG 228, R78HR.

48. Ibid.

49. Lieutenant Colonel N. A. Burnell II to L. S. Hawkins, 13 May 1942, Central Files, Vocational Education, RG 228, R35HR; Hawkins to Burnell, 22 May 1942, DFO, Office Files of John Beecher, Bell Aircraft, Atlanta folder, RG 228, R78HR.

50. Report of James H. McGinnis, 12 June 1942, summary, typescript, Central Files, Reports, A–C, General, RG 228, R47HR.

51. James H. McGinnis to B. F. Ashe, 20 Aug. 1942, Reports, Analysis, Compilations, Georgia, Region 7, Atlanta folder, RG 211, FRCEP.

52. Ibid.

53. Testimony of M. D. Mobley, transcript 2, 19 June 1942, Legal Division, Birmingham Hearing, RG 228, R17HR.

54. Memorandum to L. S. Hawkins, 23 Jan. 1943, Legal Division, Office Files of Frank D. Reeves, form letters, etc., RG 228, R7HR.

55. G. James Fleming to William Y. Bell, 9 Nov. 1942, Miscellaneous folder II, RG 228, Reel 3 (R3), Field Records (FR), hereinafter cited R3FR.

56. Memorandum to L. S. Hawkins, 23 Jan. 1943, Legal Division, Office Files of Frank D. Reeves, form letters, etc., RG 228, R7HR. For profiles of skilled black Bell workers, see Mildred Boyd Turner, "A Study of One Hundred Skilled Negro Workers at Bell Aircraft Corporation and the Problems Encountered in Adapting to a Peacetime Economy" (M.A. thesis, Atlanta University, 1946).

57. Reports on War Production Centers, Region 7, Atlanta folder, Atlanta-Marietta, 14 Feb. 1944, Reports, Analysis, Compilations, J. R. Womack to J. E. McDaniel, 29 Jan. 1943, Negro Training, Regional and State Office Training Material, Region 7, Georgia folder, RG 211, FRCEP; Turner, "One Hundred Skilled Negro Workers," 33.

58. Clarence Mitchell to George M. Johnson, 29 Mar. 1943, Office Files of Joy P. Davis, RG 228, R73HR; Atlanta Industry, 28 Dec. 1944, Division of Reports and Analysis, WMC, Atlanta folder, RG 211, FRCEP.

59. *Pittsburgh Courier*, 5 Dec. 1942, p. 24; *Norfolk Journal and Guide*, 5 Dec. 1942, Central Files, Publications 3, Weekly Releases on Negro Newspapers, RG 228, R47HR.

60. Telegram, Grace T. Hamilton to George M. Johnson, n.d. [Summer 1943] Central Files, Vocational Education, RG 228, R35HR; A. Bruce Hunt to Will Maslow, 19 Feb. 1944, Bell Aircraft, RG 228, FRCEP.

61. *Journal of Labor*, 14 May, 29 Oct., 5 Nov. 1943; oral interview with Jacob Henderson, p. 8, Georgia Government Documentation Project, Special Collections, Pullen Library, Georgia State University; A. Bruce Hunt to Will Maslow, 19 Feb. 1944, Memorandum, James H. Tipton to A. Bruce Hunt, 18 Apr. 1944, Bell Aircraft, RG 228, FRCEP. At that time, material on the local CIO unions also appeared in an FEPC folder entitled Automobile, Aircraft, and Agricultural Implement Workers of America (AAAIWA). See Cases 7UR520 and 7UR82, RG 228, FRCEP.

62. A. Bruce Hunt to Clarence M. Mitchell, 24 Feb. 1944, Hunt to Major E. J. Bennett Jr., 26 Feb. 1944, James H. Tipton to Bryant H. Prentice, 18, 31 Mar. 1944, Prentice to Tipton, 3 Apr. 1944, Bell Aircraft, RG 228, FRCEP.

63. *Atlanta Journal*, 2 Jan. 1944, Minority Discrimination Case Files, Bell Aircraft folder, RG 211; A. Bruce Hunt to Will Maslow, 18 Apr. 1944, Bell Aircraft, RG 228, FRCEP.

64. A. Bruce Hunt to Will Maslow, 18 Apr. 1944, Bell Aircraft, RG 228, FRCEP.

65. Complaint of George Hulen Andrews, 24 Apr. 1944, Bell Aircraft folder, Case 7BR618, RG 228, R82FR.

66. Complaint of Elijah W. Thompson, 9 May 1944, Bell Aircraft folder, Case 7BR618, RG 228, R82FR.

67. A. Bruce Hunt to Will Maslow, 4 May 1944; Hunt to Emanuel Bloch, 29 June 1944, Bell Aircraft, RG 228, FRCEP.

68. Bruce Nelson, "Organized Labor and the Struggle for Black Equality in Mobile during World War II," *Journal of American History* 80 (Dec. 1993): 952, 956, 967, 978–82; Merl E. Reed, "The FEPC, the Black Worker, and the Southern Shipyards," *South Atlantic Quarterly* 74 (Autumn 1975): 454–57.

69. A. Bruce Hunt to Frank A. Constangy, 6 May 1944, telegram, A. Bruce Hunt to Will Maslow, 3 July 1944, Bell Aircraft, RG 228, FRCEP.

70. Thomas Quigley to B. F. Ashe, 20 Feb. 1943, Division Records—Training, Georgia folder, RG 211; Bryant H. Prentice to Dillard B. Lassiter, 6 July 1944, Bell Aircraft, RG 228, FRCEP.

71. A. Bruce Hunt to Dillard B. Lassiter, 19 July 1944, Bell Aircraft, RG 228, FRCEP; Merl E. Reed, "Pennsylvania's Black Workers, the Defense Industries, and the Federal Agencies, 1941–1945," *Labor History* 27 (1986): 366–73; Reed, *Seedtime*, 119, 121.

72. Clarence Mitchell to George M. Johnson, 29 Mar. 1943, Office Files of Joy P. Davis, R73HR; FEPC Region 7 Press Release, 11 July 1944, Bell Aircraft, RG 228, FRCEP; *Pittsburgh Courier*, 29 July 1944, p. 15.

73. Memorandum of telephone conversation, A. Bruce Hunt and UAW Regional Director Starling, 29 July 1944, Bell Aircraft, RG 228, FRCEP.

74. George W. Crockett, Jr. to George L-P. Weaver, 13 Sept. 1945, Crockett to Witherspoon Dodge, 5 Feb. 1945, Bell Aircraft folder, Case 7UR520, RG 228, R82FR.

75. John Hope II to Witherspoon Dodge, 1 Jan. 1945, Bell Aircraft, RG 228, FRCEP; *Atlanta Journal*, 10 Sept. 1944, *Atlanta Constitution*, 5 Apr. 1945.

76. Memorandum, William Shell to Dillard B. Lassiter, 13 Feb. 1945, Bell Aircraft, RG 228, FRCEP.

77. Memorandum for Truman K. Gibson, Jr., 13 Sept. 1944, A. Bruce Hunt to Clarence Mitchell, 27 Sept. 1944, Bell Aircraft, RG 228, FRCEP.

78. Resume of conference with Joseph Daugherty, 18 Jan. 1945, Bell Aircraft RG 228, FRCEP.

79. Memorandum [handwritten] on conference with James Carmichael, 1 March 1945, Bell Aircraft, RG 228, FRCEP.

80. Ibid.

81. Witherspoon Dodge to File, 18 July 1945, Dodge to Eugene Davidson, 5 Sept. 1945, Bell Aircraft, RG 228, FRCEP.

82. After winning the struggle for black training, William Bell took a temporary appointment with the local United Service Organization until being named as head of the National Urban League's Field Office in Atlanta. Lorraine Nelson Spritzer and Jean B. Bergmark, *Grace Towns Hamilton and the Politics of Southern Change* (Athens, Ga., 1997), 82, 88, 93, 105, 149; Moore, *Search for Equality*, 103.

83. Excerpt from Weekly Report, 4 Dec. 1943, Office Files of George M. Johnson,

Field Reports, 6HR; typescript (confidential) for Mr. Ross, WILL folder, Office files of Malcolm Ross, 3HR; Leonard Brin to R. J. Thomas, 13 May 1944, 10BR156, Documents file, 1HR; Final Disposition Report (FDR), 26 Feb. 1944, 10BR8, FDR 4 Jan. 1944, 10BR72, FDR 27 Nov. 1944, 10BA73, 99FR. On the role of CIO unions in two southern shipyards, see Nelson, "Organized Labor and Black Equality in Mobile," 955, and Alex Lichtenstein's essay in this volume.

84. Clarence M. Mitchell to George M. Johnson, 8 Jan. 1945, Office Files of George M. Johnson, Clarence Mitchell folder, 3HR; FDR, 2 Aug. 1944, 10BR336, FDR, 22 May 1945, 13BR461, 97FR.

85. See August Meier and Elliott Rudwick, *Black Detroit and the Rise of the UAW* (New York, 1979), 112–13, 173. For a more critical view of the AUL's role, see Karen Ferguson, "The Politics of Exclusion: Wartime Industrialization, Civil Rights Mobilization, and Black Politics in Atlanta, 1942–1946," in Philip Scranton, ed., *The Second Wave: Southern Industrialization from the 1940s to the 1970s* (Athens, Ga., 2001).

86. For a statistical analysis of black gains during this period, see William J. Collins, "Race, Occupational Mobility, and Government Intervention in the World War II Era" (Working Paper #98–204, Department of Economics and Business Administration, Vanderbilt University, July 1998), in possession of the author.

87. Oral interview with Jacob Henderson, 8 May 1989, Georgia Government Documentation Project, SCGSU; Clifford M. Kuhn, Harlon E. Joye, and E. Bernard West, *Living Atlanta: An Oral History of the City, 1914–1948* (Athens, Ga., 1990), 364.

Exclusion, Fair Employment, or Interracial Unionism: Race Relations in Florida's Shipyards during World War II

Alex Lichtenstein

In 1943 William Kitchen, a black shipyard worker and war veteran living in Jacksonville, Florida, notified the Fair Employment Practice Committee (FEPC), established by President Roosevelt's executive order two years before, of serious wage discrimination. Black workers at Gibbs Gas Engine shipyard received only sixty cents per hour, "the lowest common labor price," for the same skilled grinding work on ships' hulls done by whites for $1.20 per hour. Kitchen informed the FEPC, however, that "we are in the knowledge of an election to be held in the yard in the near future via C.I.O." He asked this new federal agency to await the outcome of the union election before taking action on his case. "I feel we will be given better consideration through the union," Kitchen wrote optimistically, "if not I shall notify your office and ask that you take steps for us."[1]

The union eagerly anticipated by Kitchen, the Industrial Union of Marine and Shipbuilding Workers of America (IUMSWA), was a typical example of the mass production industrial unions built in the core of the nation's economy by the breakaway Congress of Industrial Organizations (CIO) during labor's radical upsurge of the 1930s.[2] IUMSWA subsequently lost the election at Gibbs, in part because of accusations by the company-loyal workers that this CIO affiliate was "building a nigger union."[3] The FEPC, failing in repeated attempts to reconnect with Kitchen, closed his case without taking action.[4]

This brief glimpse into the effort of one black worker to challenge the racial division of labor in Florida's wartime shipyards reveals the strategies available to the tens of thousands of African Americans who took advantage of the unprecedented opportunity to break into the primary sector of the industrial labor market opened up by World War II. Overnight, Florida's shipbuilding industry created a huge unmet demand for skilled and semi-skilled workers in Tampa, Jacksonville, Miami, and Panama City, a demand that black workers proved eager to meet. Yet as Kitchen's complaint suggests, black shipyard workers typically received the traditional pay scale of "common labor" regardless of the tasks they took up in the yards or the skills they had recently acquired under the auspices of government training programs. Moreover, the numerous complaints filed by Florida shipyard workers with the FEPC Region 7 office in Atlanta indicate that despite the wartime need for their labor, black workers in Florida often were denied access to shipyard work altogether.

Civil rights historian Harvard Sitkoff has recently argued that World War II marked a period of quiescence among African Americans.[5] Yet when it came to matters of job discrimination, the wartime labor regime made it possible for blacks directly to challenge the racial division of labor—even in southern war plants—in ways they had rarely dared before. Though initiated by New Deal legislation such as the Wagner Act, the federal power to shape labor relations, collective bargaining, and contractual shop-floor matters greatly expanded in the wartime state. Both the number of agencies with such a mandate and the scope of their power increased dramatically after the nation's entry into the war. As Melvyn Dubofsky notes, "management and labor bargained under the shadow of coercive state power" during the war.[6] This proved especially true in industries dependent on government contracts like shipbuilding, the heart of the CIO's drive and the focus of FEPC investigations in Florida between 1942 and 1945; and it worked to the advantage of African Americans.

At the same time, the flooding of black workers into the industrial workplace in numbers unprecedented since World War I dramatically reshaped the nature of working-class race relations. Most notoriously, the influx of black workers, the increasingly integrated shop floor, the congested housing markets and urban space, and the demands by blacks for equal treatment in these areas generated enormous racial conflict. This racial recomposition of the industrial workforce, and the hate strikes and racial pogroms it often generated, represented a distinct challenge to the nascent CIO; but it also offered a powerful opportunity for CIO unions to put their professed interracialism into practice. Hence the third important aspect of the wartime labor regime: This was the moment when, in concert with the state, the CIO could consolidate its gains in the core of the American economy by embracing the democratic promises of the fight against fascism and, by implication, racism. For both the labor movement and those concerned with the advance of a civil rights agenda, the war provided a golden opportunity to transform their place in the American political economy and society. Especially in the South, these changes—expanding state intervention in the economy, dramatic expansion and recomposition of the industrial workforce, and a novel context for working-class race relations—opened up fissures in a social order devoted to white supremacy. Into this breach stepped black workers like William Kitchen, wielding two new weapons against ubiquitous workplace discrimination: the state and the union.[7]

At the urging of local civil rights organizations like the National Association for the Advancement of Colored People (NAACP) and A. Philip Randolph's March on Washington Movement (MOWM), black workers who were denied shipyard employment or Jim-Crowed into unskilled positions would contact the FEPC, one of the earliest instances of state intervention in labor relations on behalf of black workers.[8] This wartime federal agency sought to combat racial discrimination in hiring, promotion, and job classification in all industries with war contracts. The agency's voluminous records demonstrate that FEPC investigators pursued discriminatory employers, unions, and even other government agencies like the U.S. Employment Service (USES) with equal vigor in every region of the country, including Region 7, the Southeast. If ever the black worker had an ally in the struggle to gain full rights as an employee and as a union member, the FEPC was it.[9] Despite its noble intentions, however, FEPC efforts to ensure racial equality in the labor market had no enforcement capability: the committee could issue findings but had no power to order compliance. Moreover, the admirable racial liberalism of the FEPC should be weighed against the other alternative available to African Americans in their struggle for racial justice in the wartime industrial workplace: the new industrial unions spawned during the 1930s. CIO affiliates like IUMSWA entered the South for the first time after 1941, and African Americans usually provided the initial spark for the organization of unions in the war plants of a region implacably hostile to an interracial labor movement.[10]

In Florida, both the FEPC and the CIO competed vigorously with more-established American Federation of Labor (AFL) metal trades unions to put their stamp on shipyard race relations during the war. These lily-white

AFL unions, especially the International Brotherhood of Boilermakers, Iron Shipbuilders and Helpers Union (known as the Boilermakers), found themselves strengthened during the war by closed-shop agreements negotiated under government oversight; and they controlled access to skilled positions in many Florida shipyards. In yards with large numbers of black workers, the Boilermakers sometimes established black auxiliaries. Supervised by the white local, these organizations had no voice at conventions, no independent business agent, and no grievance committee of their own, and they could be fined for "creating a disturbance at meetings." Indeed, their not-so-hidden purpose was to ensure that black workers never moved beyond unskilled categories of labor in the shipyards.[11]

Much of the FEPC's efforts in Florida went into investigating the Boilermakers and preparing hearings—never to be held—about that union's discriminatory practices. When pressed by FEPC investigators or the War Manpower Commission (WMC), management in Florida's shipyards insisted that they would gladly hire blacks into skilled positions if only the AFL would let them. Yet upon closer examination it appears that many shipyards happily relied upon the skills black workers brought with them to the yards but continued to pay them as unskilled laborers. Indeed, William Kitchen's "common labor" job had initially been done by whites; they had walked off the job when the company would not increase their pay rate from $1.08 to $1.20 per hour. William Kitchen had then been hired at half that rate. "I grit my teeth and go on," he told the FEPC, "but it doesn't get any better, and I know it is because I am colored. I would be getting more if I was white, but white or colored this work must be done."[12] Ultimately, the CIO, not the FEPC, proved more adept at challenging this state of affairs.

The struggle to shape shipyard race relations in four Florida cities during the war—Tampa, Panama City, Jacksonville, and Miami—had very different outcomes. In Tampa, where the notoriously racist Boilermakers union retained an iron grip on employment in the city's two large shipyards, black workers had almost no access to that line of work. There, the FEPC pursued a vigorous campaign to provide blacks with access to training and skilled positions, often in concert with local black protest organizations, but to no avail. In Panama City, black entry into skilled positions provoked physical attack by members of the Boilermakers, something the FEPC proved helpless to prevent or punish. By contrast, in Jacksonville and Miami, where the CIO battled fiercely against the AFL to organize the shipyards, black workers played an important role in the fledgling IUMSWA, and thus looked to the CIO union for racial justice. Led in Florida by a communist organizer named Charles Smolikoff, IUMSWA successfully organized several yards in these cities against violent company and AFL opposition. In these workplaces, organized black workers relied on the union to seek equal pay and access to skilled jobs, with a modicum of success. For its part, the CIO union had to negotiate the delicate terrain of race, pragmatically balancing the need to defend the interests of its loyal black membership with the need to continue recruiting whites, who remained a significant majority in the industry.

Tampa

Nowhere in Florida is the history of trade unions as vehicles of racial exclusion borne out more forcefully than in the Tampa Shipbuilding Company (TASCO) yards.[13] By the time World War II had begun, the all-white AFL Boilermakers union completely controlled access to skilled and semiskilled work at TASCO. African Americans found themselves almost entirely shut out from employment for the duration, despite the best efforts of the NAACP, local black activists in the MOWM, and FEPC investigators.[14]

Lily-white union employment at TASCO represented a certain irony, for during the 1930s six hundred black workers had been well established in several skill levels in this major Gulf Coast shipyard.[15] However, when the Boilermakers won union recognition in 1939, they secured a closed-shop agreement excluding black workers from all but the most menial work. With the advent of AFL hegemony in the yard, five hundred black workers were laid off, with the remaining one hundred demoted in their job classifications, even as black shipyard employment rapidly expanded elsewhere in the South. A. Philip Randolph noted the case of a skilled black hoisting engineer who found himself picking up trash in the TASCO yard after the AFL victory there.[16] When black workers objected to the union's policies, they received visits from the local Klan, which many suspected was closely allied with the city's central labor council and leading corrupt politicians.[17]

To add insult to injury, during the war the Boilermakers retained their closed shop in Tampa with the aid of the Office of Production Management, which sought stabilization agreements in defense industries. As Robert Weaver noted bitterly at the close of the war, when forced to choose between stabilization of industrial relations in collusion with exclusionary unions and an ostensible commitment to nondiscriminatory employment, the federal government often capitulated to the racism of the AFL unions.[18]

When blacks applied for work at TASCO, the company turned them away for lack of a union card; when they visited the office of the Boilermakers to obtain one, they were told to secure employment first. Faced with this catch-22, black workers in Tampa, at the urging of locals of the NAACP, the MOWM, the Urban League, and the Brotherhood of Sleeping Car Porters (BSCP), sought redress from the FEPC.[19] But when FEPC investigators visited Tampa and confronted Joe Ray, the Boilermakers' Tampa business agent, he informed them that most of the whites at TASCO "also had their wives, daughters and sweethearts working there" and "they wouldn't stand to have no niggers doing any kind of work but labor or helper work."[20] Apparently mistaking him for a white man, Ray told John Hope II, the dignified and light-skinned son of the president of Atlanta University, that he "had nothing against niggers as long as they stayed in their place." In his report, and elsewhere, the aptly named Hope expressed the optimistic opinion that it was Ray's own anti-Negro sentiments that shaped union policy and that the rank and file might actually have a different opinion about an integrated yard.[21]

The FEPC eventually *did* docket a handful of individual cases against the AFL union and TASCO, and by 1945 Region 7 investigators began preparing a series of hearings on discrimination in Tampa's shipbuilding industry. But before these hearings could be held, conservatives in Congress terminated the committee. From the initial complaints of the NAACP, filed in 1939, until the close of the war six years later, the white wall of skilled shipyard work in Tampa had never been breached. TASCO and the USES recruited white workers from beyond the Tampa Bay area, while not one of the 250 African Americans who received WMC-sponsored training as welders and electricians in a local vocational school found work in Tampa's shipbuilding industry.[22] "They say this is our war," complained a black worker at TASCO, "but it is a white man war and we dont have any write to be empler [*sic*] in the yard."[23] Even TASCO's president insisted that if skilled blacks were hired, they would still have to be segregated: "You can't have a nigger giving orders to a white man," he reminded John Hope II. "He would be a dead nigger in five minutes." By February 1945, with 9,500 workers in TASCO's yards, only 580 were black.[24]

Panama City

When confronted by FEPC investigators who stated their intention to expose in public hearings the exclusionary practices of Tampa's

Boilermakers union, the AFL representative to the War Production Board warned—or threatened—that this action would cause a race riot in the shipyards. This did not appear to be an idle threat, as such violence had already occurred in a Panama City shipyard only six months before. On September 14, 1944, at a predetermined signal, hundreds of white workers wielding "monkey wrenches, iron bars, hammers, sticks, blackjacks, and other weapons" had descended upon two dozen blacks in the Wainwright shipyard and driven them from the yard.[25]

In this instance, even black shipyard workers' nominal status as auxiliary members of the Boilermakers union failed to protect them from their union brothers' wrath when they intruded on whites' claimed territory of skilled job classifications. The attack at Wainwright was widely understood to be at the instigation of the Boilermakers union itself, whose members "objected to Negroes doing white men's work," even though the upgraded workers were members of the AFL union's auxiliary.[26]

The spark for this racial attack was the training of a handful of black shipyard workers at Wainwright as riveters, a skilled classification from which they had been previously excluded. For months the WMC had recognized the critical shortage of skilled workers at Wainwright, a major Gulf Coast yard employing more than ten thousand, but had only reluctantly embraced the idea that African Americans could fill this gap. Eighteen months before the attack, the WMC had noted that "Negroes are not used in skilled trades . . . due to the fact that the majority of workers on the yard are southerners and would not work with Negroes if they were placed on the same level."[27] At WMC's urging, the J. A. Jones Shipbuilding Company, which ran the Wainwright yard, had set up training programs for its white workers. Under pressure from FEPC investigators, who suspected that the WMC and the USES were deliberately refusing to train and place blacks for work at Wainwright, the company relented and began to recruit blacks for training as well.[28] Faced with the inevitability of black entry into the realm of skilled shipyard trades, the Boilermakers union successfully reasserted the color line by force, driving blacks permanently from skilled positions in the Wainwright yard.[29]

Most of the elements of this incident are sadly familiar. By 1944, Panama City was "vibrant with hostility towards negroes" in the words of an FEPC investigator. A Florida panhandle town of thirteen thousand, Panama City had swelled to forty thousand during the war years, and the number of workers in the shipyard alone nearly equaled the city's entire prewar population. Between April 1943 and September 1944, the proportion of white women working in the yard went from 12 to 20 percent, the highest proportion in any Florida shipyard, adding another potential flash point to race relations. The local NAACP chapter, established a mere month before the attack at Wainwright, had initially alerted the FEPC to the shipyard riot. But when Leonard Brin, a white investigator, finally got to town—*more than six weeks later*—no one in the cautious black community would even admit to him the organization's existence.[30]

The Boilermakers were responsible for barring black workers from skilled classifications, even though these workers belonged to the AFL union's auxiliary; and while the J. A. Jones Company professed a desire to train, upgrade, and hire skilled blacks in the yard, it did so (as in a similar yard in Brunswick, Georgia) in part because black workers drew less pay than their white counterparts, even in skilled classifications. Discrimination in job placement not only stemmed from union and company intransigence but depended on collusion with local officials of the War Manpower Commission and the USES. Faced with such an array of powerful foes, the FEPC itself had helped create the conditions leading to the riot by pressing for the training of black workers without preparing management or white workers for the results. Finally, while a belated FEPC investigation uncovered the Boilermakers as the culprit, "the union would do nothing about it, and neither in the end could the FEPC, with its limited authority, limited budget, and limited public respect in the South," FEPC Region 7 director Witherspoon Dodge admitted years later.[31]

Jacksonville

At first glance, the wartime situation for black workers in Jacksonville, at the time Florida's largest city, with a population of 250,000 (35 percent black), looked much the same. African Americans seeking employment at St. John's shipyard, by far the largest in the city, with more than 10,000 workers, faced the same problem as their Tampa and Panama City counterparts. According to John Hope II, in Jacksonville, too, "the failure of the Boilermakers' union to admit Negroes to membership" excluded blacks from skilled work at St. John's.[32] But in Jacksonville, IUMSWA Local 32 had a toehold in the shipbuilding industry; and the industrial union movement provided the city's growing African American working class with a new set of possibilities. Indeed, while the CIO deliberately made feints in the direction of the St. John's yard in order to distract their bitter rivals in the metal trades AFL unions, they were busy organizing the city's smaller shipyards—Merrill-Stevens and Gibbs Gas Engine. Black and white IUMSWA organizers, some of them members of the Communist Party, endured frequent beatings in 1942 and 1943, from both AFL members and company stooges, as they sought to build a CIO union in these yards.[33]

St. John's was an entirely new yard, established for the war. Many of the white, building trades workers who constructed the yard subsequently worked there, creating a solid constituency for the AFL's exclusionary unions. FEPC investigations of St. John's revealed that, as in Tampa, "the closed shop contract . . . has become a convenient device behind which the yard may legally refuse to employ any worker because he is not a member of the union, and by means of which the [Boilermakers] union aids and abets discrimination."[34] Further investigation revealed that African American welders who had worked in other Jacksonville shipyards as long ago as World War I were classified as unskilled helpers at St. John's and paid accordingly. These men resisted incorporation into the Boilermakers' auxiliary, preferring their segregated Laborers' Union Local, over which they maintained full control. The black leader of this local, however, suggested that rank-and-file whites at St. John's were willing to countenance black skilled workers, but the Boilermakers' leadership would not hear of it.[35]

Meanwhile, as war contracts swelled their existing repair and ship construction jobs in 1941 and 1942, both Gibbs and Merrill-Stevens already had contingents of black workers, some working side by side with whites without conflict, a racial peace attributed by FEPC investigators to the absence of AFL metal trades unions in these yards. Merrill-Stevens in particular had employed black workers "in many capacities throughout its history," some for as long as thirty-five years, and 250 of its 700 employees were black. FEPC investigator John Beecher reported in 1942 that blacks at Merrill-Stevens worked as blacksmith foremen (over an all-black gang, of course), blacksmiths, crane men, riggers, and painters, among other skilled categories. These workers formed the core of the CIO drive in Jacksonville.[36]

IUMSWA's Local 32 in Jacksonville had its roots in a small group of black workers employed by the United Fruit Company to work on its freight boats. In late 1939 these men wrote the international to complain that their business agent doubled as a foreman and was "serving the co. instead of the union." "Send an organizer down here and build this organization *up* as the port here has possibilities," they implored. At Gibbs Gas Engine, across the river from the huge St. John's installation, CIO organizers began to meet with black and white workers separately in October 1943. Black organizer E. D. Koelman made house-to-house visits to African American workers and addressed community gatherings. White organizers did the same with white workers at Gibbs. After a few weeks, the organizers called a mass meeting, something of a misnomer, since whites and blacks attended separately—fifteen of the former and sixty of the latter.[37]

This strategy reflected the IUMSWA organizers' recognition of the immense obstacles facing interracial unionism in Jacksonville's shipyards. "A unique problem for CIO organizers in this territory," wrote IUMSWA regional director William Smith in November 1943, "is that southern negroes are generally much more receptive to our program than southern whites." The danger was that successful recruitment of black members would result in an all-black local—"large in membership, but completely ineffective in terms of collective bargaining, because such a local will inevitably be boycotted by the whites" according to Smith.[38] Given that blacks made up only 10 to 15 percent of the entire shipyard labor force in Jacksonville, this fear was legitimate, and it dictated the IUMSWA's pragmatic approach to what the Left called the "Negro Question." Organizers hoped to bring blacks and whites into the local separately and then gradually encourage them to work together. At Gibbs, where only 6 percent of the workers were black, the CIO went down to defeat; but at Merrill-Stevens, with blacks making up nearly one-fourth of production workers, IUMSWA Local 32 won an election in July 1943 by a slim margin of 81 votes.[39] AFL metal trades leaders pledged to "move their men out of the yards if they lost the election" to the CIO, the War Manpower Commission reported. But they did not make good on the threat.[40]

Such a delicate situation required compromises—or in William Smith's euphemism, "precautionary measures"—which did not always sit well with blacks, especially E. D. Koelman, a well-respected figure in Jacksonville's African American community. Koelman served as president of the Negro Chamber of Commerce, even while working on the CIO payroll as an organizer among black workers. When Local 32 refused to appoint a black vice president, Koelman objected, claiming that organizers "began to promise and spread racial discrimination within the newly formed local with a hope of winning the white worker." Koelman wrote to the international and threatened to "expose these acts of discrimination by the CIO."[41]

Regional director Smith retorted that the election of a black official at this stage of the union's development would "prove disastrous to Local 32," and he insisted that the building of the local must "take precedence over the granting of a rather dubious advance in prestige for a colored member." Significantly, the black rank and file appeared to agree with Smith: after he urged them "not [to] isolate yourselves by alienating the white membership," they voted to withdraw their candidate for vice president and bide their time until the union was on a surer footing.[42]

In his defense against charges of racism, Smith recounted Local 32's record on behalf of its black members. It included the incorporation of black shop stewards into an integrated executive board; black representation on grievance, negotiating, and labor-management committees; training programs for African American blacksmiths, riggers, and blueprint readers; and an integrated union hall (though it appears that meetings were still held separately) —all firsts in the state, and a marked contrast to blacks' status when members of segregated AFL auxiliary unions.[43] Another IUMSWA organizer charged that Koelman, who had lived in Jacksonville for eighteen years, maintained close ties with city officials, had run gambling houses, and had "joined and helped the CIO only to further the cause of Koelman and become a leader of the Negro people."[44] Communist IUMSWA organizer Charles Smolikoff noted that, contrary to Koelman's approach, "the only degree to which we can advance Negro rights is the degree to which we consolidate the whites into the CIO . . . so that both negro and white can fight together."[45] This interracial program, Smolikoff insisted, required the development of genuine black rank-and-file leadership, something deliberately neglected by Koelman in an effort to enhance his own standing. Nevertheless, Smolikoff admitted the justice of the black workers' desire for a vice president, since they constituted 80 percent of the local's membership at the time.[46]

Another "precautionary measure" taken by Local 32 involved collusion with the Jacksonville-area United States Employment Service in placing discriminatory orders for skilled labor. By this sleight of hand, IUMSWA could appear to maintain a commitment to black workers and still recruit whites. FEPC field examiner Leonard Brin reported discovering more than forty white electricians and welders hired to Merrill-Stevens through the CIO's advertising these jobs, with racial specifications, in the Jacksonville press.[47] This may well have been hypocrisy for an interracial union, as Brin charged; but it also proved a clever way to preserve an interracial union, since it brought in dues-paying white members who might otherwise be reluctant to join the CIO.[48] At the same time, the IUMSWA brought complaints of racial discrimination against black workers at Merrill-Stevens to the

FEPC, a maneuver understood by management as an effort to "enhance [the union's] power with the negroes."[49]

By 1944, Merrill-Stevens employed two thousand workers in Jacksonville, one-fourth of them black—but only fifty black workers were classified above laborers, according to the CIO.[50] Smolikoff repeatedly pressed the FEPC office in Atlanta to investigate discriminatory wages, improper job classifications, and lack of upgrades suffered by black employees at Merrill-Stevens. Indeed, at one point he warned the FEPC that he had to step in to prevent a wildcat strike of black workers over these issues. Upon its investigation, the FEPC discovered that the Merrill-Stevens shipyard "appears to utilize Negroes at their maximum skills, but classifies and compensates them as laborers and semi-skilled workers," a tactic in which the USES colluded. Nevertheless, the agency informed the CIO union that it did not "anticipate early and effective action in clearing up what appears to be the discriminatory practices at the Merrill-Stevens yard." The FEPC's small staff had its hands full, Region 7 director A. Bruce Hunt claimed, with complaints brought against Florida branches of the USES.[51]

Still, in its efforts to represent the race-specific grievances of its African American members, Local 32 had other avenues open to it. Because IUMSWA had won a collective bargaining agreement with Merrill-Stevens, labor relations at the shipyard were governed by the National War Labor Board (NWLB), the wartime federal agency that adjudicated union-management disputes in defense plants. In a case brought before the War Labor Board, IUMSWA charged that four separate semiskilled labor classifications in the yard had been lumped by the company under the rubric of "laborers" and "helpers" and thus paid at rates incommensurate with the actual labor done by black workers. "There seems to be no other [reason] than . . . the workers' color for the company to insist [on] classifying [them] as mere helpers," claimed Local 32 in its complaint to the board.[52] Unlike individual cases filed with the FEPC, this grievance could be made collectively, as would potential redress. Moreover, the union threatened to make the issue bargainable as part of upcoming contract negotiations. Finally, unlike the FEPC, which depended on moral suasion, the NWLB had the legal power to compel Merrill-Stevens to upgrade its black workers, and the company did so only several months after IUMSWA brought the complaint, instating premium pay or upgrades for more than sixty black workers at Merrill-Stevens.[53] This advocacy on behalf of black workers at Merrill-Stevens was followed by another election in the yard, which the CIO won handily by nearly five hundred votes. In other words, white workers continued to support IUMSWA even while it helped advance blacks into skilled positions.[54]

Miami

Charles Smolikoff, the leading CIO and Communist Party figure in the Miami area throughout the 1940s, used much the same strategy to advance the interests of black shipyard workers in that city as well. Born and raised in Brooklyn, Smolikoff moved to Miami in 1937 for his health even though he was only twenty-one years old. Upon his arrival in Florida he immediately helped organize a movement to support the Spanish Republic's fight against Franco. Subsequently, he organized a south Florida chapter of the American Peace Movement, a Communist Party front that soon outlived its usefulness when the Nazis invaded the Soviet Union in June 1941.[55] Then, in 1942, at the behest of Florida Communist Party leader Alex Trainor, Smolikoff began trade union agitation among Miami's growing numbers of wartime shipyard workers. Working as a volunteer, he distributed leaflets and the IUMSWA's *Shipyard Worker*, met (separately) with black and white workers, and even prepared an NLRB case for the union, all the while keeping his political affiliation clandestine. At the end of 1942 a visiting IUMSWA organizer praised his work and especially commended his understanding of the "Southern approach, Negro problem and white workers angle." Smolikoff, this organizer claimed, "is respected by the negroes and whites alike in Miami."[56]

Smolikoff and IUMSWA Florida regional director William Smith quickly discovered that many of the workers at the Miami Shipbuilding Corporation, busy building subchasers on six ways, appeared eager to join the CIO. After only a few months they had already collected initiation fees from 450 workers and had signed cards from an additional 350. Smith reported that they could count on "a solid bloc of some 100 votes" from two-thirds of the yard's small contingent of black workers, all of whom the company classified as laborers. Foremen at Miami Shipbuilding continued to pressure white workers to join AFL unions, but many of them would take an AFL button even while they joined the CIO.[57] On Memorial Day, 1943, IUMSWA won an NLRB election at the Miami Shipbuilding yard, 562 to 207 (for the AFL). "Not once during the course of the campaign," declared IUMSWA organizer Jerry Lee, "did the racial issue threaten to create dissension or disunity."[58]

By June 1943, Smolikoff had helped the newly chartered IUMSWA Local

59, the first CIO union in Miami, win a contract with the Miami Shipbuilding Corporation. Before long, Smolikoff brought black workers' classification complaints before the NWLB. When the company had provided the union with a list of job classifications during contract negotiations, Smolikoff claimed, they had "lumped together" four distinct kinds of semiskilled work performed by blacks, "because all were Negro workers, into the general inapplicable heading of 'laborers.'" When challenged by the union, the company "promoted" twenty-two black workers to the grade of "helper" and continued to pay them a maximum of 75¢ an hour. This group of "helpers" lifted boats into dry docks, scraped, sanded, and painted hulls, relaunched boats, and operated a towboat, operations that commanded pay scales ranging from 85¢ to a $1.10 when done by whites in other shipyards around the state.

In contrast to employers in Jacksonville and Tampa, employers in Miami could not blame the color line on intransigent white workers represented by AFL metal trades unions. In Miami the company itself proved so resistant to reclassification, "solely because of the color line," that they asked blacks to conduct the laborious and inefficient labor of scraping wooden hulls by hand rather than use disk sanders, which would require a rate of $1.10 per hour and open the door to steel-hull sanding as a reclassified skill as well. Moreover, the black worker who had operated the towboat, a job that "requires consummate skill," was removed from the job when the union brought the case before the NWLB because "the Company refuses to even discuss the matter."[59] Eventually Miami Shipbuilding must have shown some inclination to bend, however, since IUMSWA dropped its claim before the NWLB when the union decided to address the issue as part of its contract negotiations in May 1944. Meanwhile Smolikoff, by now IUMSWA's Florida regional director, complained to the international that in Jacksonville "we have hundreds of vicious cases of discriminatory practices of every kind against the Negroes [at Merrill-Stevens], which FEPC has been unable to get to for months now."[60]

Conclusion

What can one make of this complex and diverse set of race relations in wartime southern shipyards? Much of the writing on the FEPC, an important and understudied administrative arm of the state, has focused on its effectiveness—or lack thereof. Most historians have concluded that while well intentioned, without any enforcement capability the FEPC was administratively toothless and politically vulnerable during its brief tenure. Checked at every turn by intransigent AFL unions, indifferent employers, hostile representatives of local, state, and even federal agencies, and violently repressive local communities, FEPC proved nearly helpless to enact substantive change, especially in Region 7, the Southeast. John Egerton, for instance, in his compendium of southern dissent during the 1940s, *Speak Now against the Day*, concludes simply—and somewhat unfairly—that "Blasted by southern whites for doing too much and by blacks for doing too little, the FEPC in reality didn't do much at all."[61]

Obviously the many fruitless cases brought by the FEPC in Florida confirm a rather critical view of the agency's record. Nevertheless, the Region 7 FEPC papers reflect well on the intentions of southern liberals, black and white, who staffed the agency and traveled around the South challenging employers, union leaders, and even other government officials to live up to the democratic premises of the war.[62] FEPC staff members also put interracialism into practice in their own organization, insisting, for example, that the bathroom they used in Atlanta's federal building be used by both black and white employees. But the focus on *results* in the historiography ignores the long-term significance of the FEPC's *strategy* and approach to ameliorating workplace racism. Here indeed one can detect the "seedtime for the modern civil rights movement," in Merl Reed's evocative phrase. In particular, at least in the South, the FEPC proved a working laboratory for an emergent coalition of liberal white southerners like Witherspoon Dodge (a Methodist minister and teacher from Jacksonville, and a onetime Textile Workers organizer, who went on to work with CIO-PAC and the Southern Conference for Human Welfare after the war) and A. Bruce Hunt, their black counterparts like John Hope II, and grassroots civil rights organizations, often rooted in beleaguered middle-class black communities.[63] In order to combat racial discrimination in employment, this coalition worked closely with—and within—the federal government. This proved an ineffective strategy.

While there is no reason to challenge the orthodoxy that civil rights in the South required federal intervention for success—indeed, the CIO looked to the War Labor Board to combat discrimination—the history of the FEPC suggests that in the area of employment discrimination, an interracial liberal coalition wedded to federal administrative power led the challenge to racism down a distinctive path with important consequences. It is in the crucible of wartime industrial race relations that one can see the forging of a strategy to combat employment discrimination pioneered by an interracial liberal civil rights coalition allied with federal administrative power. This approach can be contrasted to its forgotten, more effective alternative: a militant interracial industrial unionism born in the workplace itself. Black shipyard workers in Florida did best when they helped to organize and joined the CIO union in the yards. Not only did they gain protected access to shipyard labor that the USES seemed unwilling to provide (despite government-sponsored training!), but union grievance procedures, contractual negotiations (including nondiscrimination clauses), and federal mediation requests won blacks the classification upgrades they sought far more readily than did appeals to the overtaxed and weak FEPC. Despite occasional capitulation to the racial mores of its white constituency (and one can interpret this as pragmatic, if distasteful), given the alternatives, the Florida IUMSWA proved an excellent antidiscrimination weapon in the hands of its black members.

Of course, one should not paper over the flaws in the interracialism of the CIO, which was frequently compromised in the face of white intransigence and black resignation. When Smolikoff discussed what he wryly called "L'Affaire Koelman" with Local 32's black constituency, many confessed to him that they were just "yassuhing" white organizers and still genuinely felt shortchanged by IUMSWA in the matter of a vice president, something Smolikoff later remedied.[64] While far better than the AFL and its auxiliaries, the CIO and its affiliates were hardly perfect on race.[65] Nevertheless, the state and the union should be regarded as new antidiscriminatory tools placed in the hands of black workers during the war, and thus weighed by their possibilities, their promise, and their long-term trajectories, as well as by their immediate results.

The weight of history shows the union as a potentially more versatile and long-lived weapon for black workers than the FEPC, which remained limited in its scope. Hampered by bureaucratic structures, and highly individualistic in the grievances it aired and the results it gained, the FEPC's mandate applied only to defense plants. Indeed, Congress terminated the politically vulnerable agency at the close of the war on the eve of a major hearing on discrimination in southern shipyards, a project that had soaked up months of investigative effort and delayed the disposition of many complaints, while failing to budge the Boilermakers' racial policy an inch. In contrast, by its very nature, the CIO stretched its power to organize black workers beyond war plants and beyond the war, and it incorporated the African American working class into a collective endeavor that both provided what labor historians have called "industrial citizenship" and engaged black and white workers in interracial practice. By 1945, as the FEPC found itself unable to hold hearings, Charles Smolikoff could boast that IUMSWA Local 32 in Jacksonville had advanced to mixed membership meetings, and that the union had elected a black vice president and three other blacks to the executive board.[66] Meanwhile, in Miami, where the CIO made the greatest inroads in Florida, and where black workers used the power of the union to obtain upgrades as they had in Jacksonville, the struggle for racial justice did not come to a close in 1945 with the shutting down of the shipyards. Instead, it shifted to new terrain, at the Miami airport, where hundreds of laid-off shipyard workers took jobs at the end of the war and organized another CIO union with the promise of the chance to break the skill barrier for black workers.

Unlike the FEPC, to which individual complaints were brought, often brokered by the black middle class, the CIO relied on the power and loyalty of black workers themselves. Their complaints about discrimination in the shipyards carried weight because of their ability to enforce their demands collectively. Finally, at crucial moments, the CIO could encourage interracial solidarity, while the FEPC usually threatened to set the interests of black workers against white. Recent work has argued that during the 1940s CIO unions—including the IUMSWA in Mobile—distanced themselves from, rather than embraced, the struggle for racial equality.[67] But the evidence from Florida's shipyards suggests that interracial industrial unions, even with minority black membership, may have proved the most effective vehicle for the aspirations of black workers during the war. Certainly William Kitchen's willingness to turn to the CIO before the FEPC calls for investigating the wartime roots of this path not taken.

Notes

1. William E. Kitchen to President's Committee on Fair Employment Practice, Nov. 8, 1943, and Jan. 20, 1944, Field Records (FR), Closed Cases, Region 7, Gibbs Gas Engine, microfilm, Roll 83, FEPC Records, Center for Research Libraries (CRL), Chicago.

2. For a recent history of the IUMSWA see David Palmer, *Organizing the Shipyards: Union Strategy in Three Northeast Ports, 1933–1945* (Ithaca: Cornell University

Press, 1998). See also Bruce Nelson, "Organized Labor and the Struggle for Black Equality in Mobile during World War II," *Journal of American History* 80 (Dec. 1993): 952–88, for a critical account of IUMSWA's civil rights record in a large southern shipyard.

3. Report by Charles Smolikoff, Apr. 10, 1944, series 2, subseries 4, box 18, Florida Organizers' Reports, Industrial Union of Marine and Shipbuilding Workers of America papers, University of Maryland Libraries, College Park, Maryland (IUMSWA papers).

4. A. Bruce Hunt to William E. Kitchen, June 24, 1944; Aug. 15, 1944; Final Determination Report, Aug. 3, 1944, FR, Closed Cases, Region 7, Gibbs Gas Engine, Roll 83, FEPC Records, CRL.

5. Harvard Sitkoff, "African American Militancy in the World War II South: Another Perspective," in *Remaking Dixie: The Impact of World War II on the American South*, ed. Neil R. McMillen (Jackson: University Press of Mississippi, 1997).

6. Melvyn Dubofsky, *The State and Labor in Modern America* (Chapel Hill: University of North Carolina Press, 1994), 185.

7. A great deal of material documenting these wartime developments can be found in Charles S. Johnson's indispensable digest, *A Monthly Summary of Events and Trends in Race Relations*, which appeared monthly between 1942 and 1948. See also Jessie Parkhurst Guzman, Vera Chandler Foster, and W. Hardin Hughes, eds., *Negro Year Book* (Tuskegee: Tuskegee Institute, 1948), esp. 134–52, 232–57; Pete Daniel, "Going among Strangers: Southern Reactions to World War Two," *Journal of American History* 77 (Dec. 1990): 886–911.

8. For a history of government attacks on employment discrimination, mostly held to be ineffective interference with market mechanisms, see Paul Moreno, *From Direct Action to Affirmative Action: Fair Employment Law and Policy in America, 1933–1972* (Baton Rouge: Louisiana State University Press, 1997).

9. The single most important and comprehensive study of the FEPC remains Merl E. Reed, *Seedtime for the Modern Civil Rights Movement: The President's Committee on Fair Employment Practice* (Baton Rouge: Louisiana State University Press, 1991), which provides a detailed administrative history of the agency but does not delve much into its social history or that of the workers who appealed to it. For a brief sketch of the FEPC's place in the evolution of antidiscrimination law, followed by a series of case studies of its practice, see Herbert Hill, *Black Labor and the American Legal System: Race, Work, and the Law* (Madison: University of Wisconsin Press, 1985), 173–382. For an account by a onetime chairman of the FEPC, see Malcolm Ross, *All Manner of Men: The Racial Crisis in American Life* (New York: Reynal and Hitchcock, 1948). Merl E. Reed does address the plight of black workers in southern shipyards in "The FEPC, the Black Worker, and the Southern Shipyards," *South Atlantic Quarterly* 74 (Autumn 1975): 446–67, but the CIO does not play an important role in his account.

10. Robert Korstad and Nelson Lichtenstein, "Opportunities Found and Lost:

Labor, Radicals, and the Early Civil Rights Movement," *Journal of American History* 75 (Dec. 1988): 786–811; Michael K. Honey, *Southern Labor and Black Civil Rights: Organizing Memphis Workers* (Urbana: University of Illinois Press, 1993).

11. Herbert R. Northrup, *Organized Labor and the Negro* (New York: Harper and Brothers, 1944), 214; Herbert Hill, "The Shipbuilding Industry and the International Brotherhood of Boilermakers," in Hill, *Black Labor and the American Legal System*, 185–208; John Hope II to Witherspoon Dodge, Report, Apr. 1, 1945, FR, Region 7, Closed Cases, St. John's Shipyard, Roll 85, FEPC Records, CRL.

12. William E. Kitchen to War Labor Board, July 12, 1943; Kitchen to FEPC, Nov. 8, 1943, FR, Region 7, Closed Cases, Gibbs Gas Engine, Roll 83, FEPC Records, CRL.

13. This is a view associated with Herbert Hill, who insists that unions have always served as vehicles for racial exclusion and never as arenas of interracial possibility. Hill's briefs against the labor movement's racial practices, combined with detailed recent case studies, have swayed many scholars who began their careers with the belief that a racially progressive thread could be found in the history of labor in the Knights of Labor, the Industrial Workers of the World, the Communists, and the CIO. Herbert Hill, "Myth-Making as Labor History: Herbert Gutman and the United Mine Workers of America," *International Journal of Politics, Culture, and Society* 2 (Winter 1988): 132–200; Herbert Hill, "The Problem of Race in American History," *Reviews in American History* 24 (June 1996): 189–208; Herbert Hill, "Lichtenstein's Fictions: Meany, Reuther, and the 1964 Civil Rights Act," *New Politics* 7 (Summer 1998); Bruce Nelson, "Class, Race, and Democracy in the CIO: The 'New' Labor History Meets the Wages of Whiteness," *International Review of Social History* 41 (Dec. 1996): 351–74; Bruce Nelson, "'CIO Meant One Thing for the Whites and Another Thing for Us': Steelworkers and Civil Rights, 1936–1974," in *Southern Labor in Transition, 1940–1995*, ed. Robert H. Zieger (Knoxville: University of Tennessee Press, 1997), 113–45. A good summary of this literature is found in Eric Arnesen, "Up from Exclusion: Black and White Workers, Race, and the State of Labor History," *Reviews in American History* 26 (Mar. 1998): 146–74; for a good survey of the black experience in the CIO's southern unions see Rick Halpern, "Organized Labor, Black Workers, and the Twentieth Century South: The Emerging Revision," in *Race and Class in the American South since 1890*, ed. Melvyn Stokes and Rick Halpern (Oxford: Berg Publishers, 1994), 43–76.

14. Memorandum, Tampa Labor Situation, Oct. 8, 1940, NAACP Papers, microfilm Series 13A, "The NAACP and Labor, 1940–1955," reel 11, frames 276–78.

15. American Federation of Labor, *Report of the Proceedings of the Annual Convention, 1940* (Washington, D.C.: AFL, 1940), 509.

16. American Federation of Labor, *Report of the Proceedings of the Annual Convention, 1941* (Washington: AFL, 1941), 478; Anonymous letter to NAACP, Jan. 27, 1943, NAACP Papers, microfilm Series 13A, "The NAACP and Labor," reel 11, frame 293.

17. Oliver Maxwell to Walter White, Aug. 14, 1939, Lucy Mason Papers, microfilm reel 62, Perkins Library, Duke University, Durham, N.C.

18. Robert C. Weaver, *Negro Labor: A National Problem* (New York: Harcourt, Brace and Co., 1946), 35.

19. AFL, *Proceedings, 1941*, 478.

20. Leonard Brin to A. Bruce Hunt, Sept. 14, 1944, FR, Region 7, Administrative Files, Brin folder, Roll 80, FEPC Records, CRL.

21. John Hope II to Witherspoon Dodge, Apr. 10, 1945, FR, Region 7, Closed Cases, Tampa Shipbuilding Co. (TASCO), Roll 85, FEPC Records, CRL; Hope II to Dodge, Mar. 30, 1945; Apr. 1, 1945, FR, St. John's Shipyard, Roll 85, FEPC Records, CRL.

22. Witherspoon Dodge to Clarence Mitchell, Jan. 6, 1945, Headquarters Records, Central Files, Tension Area Reports, Region 7, Roll 63, FEPC Records, CRL; A. Bruce Hunt to Frank Constangy, July 7, 1944, FR, Region 7, Closed Cases, U.S. Employment Service, Tampa, Roll 85, FEPC Records, CRL; Leonard Brin to Witherspoon Dodge, Mar. 8, 1945, FR, Region 7, Closed Cases, TASCO, Roll 85, FEPC Records, CRL.

23. Robert Evans to Secretary of the Navy, Apr. 30, 1943, FR, Closed Cases, TASCO, Roll 85, FEPC Records, CRL.

24. John Hope II to Witherspoon Dodge, Apr. 11, 1945; Witherspoon Dodge to Clarence Mitchell, Apr. 3, 1945, Final Disposition Report, FR, Region 7, Closed Cases, TASCO, Roll 85, FEPC Records, CRL.

25. Eugene Davidson to Clarence Mitchell, Mar. 27, 1945; John Hope II to Witherspoon Dodge, Apr. 10, 1945; Witherspoon Dodge to Clarence Mitchell, Mar. 12, 1945, FR, Region 7, Closed Cases, TASCO, Roll 85, FEPC Records, CRL; Witherspoon Dodge to Leonard Brin, Nov. 4, 1944, FR, Region 7, Closed Cases, J. A. Jones Construction Co. (Panama City), Roll 84, FEPC Records, CRL.

26. Bay County (Fla.) Chapter of the NAACP to John Hope II, Sept. 14, 1944, Sept. 26, 1944; Witherspoon Dodge to Leonard Brin, Nov. 4, 1944; Brin to Dodge, Nov. 16, 1944, all in FR, J. A. Jones, Roll 84, FEPC Records, CRL.

27. "Labor Market Development Reports," Panama City, Apr. 15, 1943, War Manpower Commission Reports, box 4, folder 20, Florida Industrial Commission Records, RG389, Florida Library and State Archives, Tallahassee, 18.

28. Witherspoon Dodge, in cooperation with Clair Cook, *Southern Rebel in Reverse: The Autobiography of an Idol-Shaker* (New York: American Press, 1961), 149–50; John Hope II to Will Maslow, "Weekly Report," Sept. 16, 1944, Sept. 23, 1944, Headquarters Records, Central Files, Roll 52, FEPC Records, CRL.

29. Witherspoon Dodge to Will Maslow, Weekly Report, Dec. 16, 1944, Headquarters Records, Central Files, Roll 52, FEPC Records, CRL, 3–4; Leonard Brin to Witherspoon Dodge, Nov. 16, 1944; "Report by Dr. Witherspoon Dodge on Boilermakers Union, A.F. of L., Panama City, Fla.," FR, Closed Cases, J. A. Jones (Panama City), Roll 84, FEPC Records, CRL.

30. Ella Baker to E. C. Edwards, 18 Aug. 1944, Bay County (Fla.) Branch Files, 1944–45, Part 2:C, Branch Files, 1940–55, NAACP Papers, Manuscripts Division, Li-

brary of Congress, Washington, D.C.; Brin to Dodge, Nov. 16, 1944, FEPC Records; "Labor Market Development Reports," Panama City, Oct. 15, 1943, War Manpower Commission Reports, box 4, folder 20, Florida Industrial Commission Records, RG389, FLSA, 20. On race and gender in wartime shipyards see Eileen Boris, "'You Wouldn't Want One of 'Em Dancing with Your Wife': Racialized Bodies on the Job in World War II," *American Quarterly* 50 (Mar. 1998): 77–108; Katherine Archibald, *Wartime Shipyard: A Study in Social Disunity*, with a new introduction by Eric Arnesen and Alex Lichtenstein (1947; rpt., Berkeley: University of California Press, forthcoming).

31. Brin to Dodge, Nov. 16, 1944, FEPC Records; "Report by Dr. Witherspoon Dodge on Boilermakers Union"; John Hope II to A. Bruce Hunt, Feb. 25, 1944; George D. McKay to Witherspoon Dodge, Dec. 5, 1944, FR, Region 7, Closed Cases, J. A. Jones (Brunswick), Roll 84, FEPC Records, CRL; Dodge, *Southern Rebel in Reverse*, 150.

32. Council of Social Agencies, *Jacksonville Looks at Its Negro Community* (Jacksonville: The Council, 1946), 61–74; Jacksonville Chamber of Commerce, Industrial Division, *Economic Survey of Jacksonville, Florida* (Jacksonville: Chamber of Commerce, 1945); Samuel Harper, "Negro Labor in Jacksonville," *Crisis*, Jan. 1942, 11, 13, 18; Witherspoon Dodge to Will Maslow, Weekly Report, Mar. 31, 1945, Headquarters Records, Central Files, Roll 52, FEPC Records, CRL.

33. Report by Charles Smolikoff, Apr. 22, 1944; Report of beatings in Jacksonville, Fla., Mar. 13, 1943; both in "Florida Organizer Reports," series 2, subseries 4, folder 18, Florida Organizers' Reports, IUMSWA papers.

34. Leonard Brin to Witherspoon Dodge, Nov. 4, 1944, FR, Region 7, Active Cases, St. John's Shipyard, Roll 81, FEPC Records, CRL.

35. John Hope II to Witherspoon Dodge, Apr. 11, 1945, FEPC Records.

36. "Report of Shipbuilding Activities in Jacksonville," Apr. 7, 1942; "Outlook for Training and Employment of Negroes in Florida Shipyards," with attached Memorandum, Cy Record to Robert Weaver, May 7, 1942, Headquarters Records, Office Files of John Beecher, Jacksonville folder, Roll 77, FEPC Records, CRL.

37. Petition to Philip Van Gelder, Dec. 12, 1939, series 5, box 77, Local 32 correspondence, IUMSWA papers; Organizer Reports, Gibbs Gas Engine, series 2, subseries 4, box 15, IUMSWA papers.

38. William Smith to Thomas Gallagher, Nov. 18, 1943, series 5, box 77, Local 32 correspondence, IUMSWA papers.

39. Charles Smolikoff to Thomas Gallagher, Apr. 10, 1944, series 2, subseries 4, box 18, IUMSWA papers.

40. "Labor Market Development Report," Jacksonville, July 15, 1943, War Manpower Commission Reports, box 1, folder 26, Florida Industrial Commission Records, RG389, FLSA.

41. E. D. Koelman to George Weaver, Nov. 15, 1943, series 5, box 77, Local 32 correspondence, IUMSWA papers.

42. William Smith to Thomas Gallagher, Nov. 18, 1943, series 5, box 77, Local 32 correspondence, IUMSWA papers.

43. Ibid.

44. Affidavit of Charles Mathias, series 5, box 77, Local 32 correspondence, IUMSWA papers.

45. Charles Smolikoff to Thomas Gallagher, Dec. 27, 1943, series 2, subseries 4, box 12, Organizers' Reports, Charles N. Smolikoff folder, IUMSWA papers.

46. Smolikoff to Gallagher, Dec. 27, 1943.

47. A. Bruce Hunt to Will Maslow, "Weekly Report," Sept. 2, 1944, Headquarters Records, Central Files, Weekly Reports, Roll 52, FEPC Records, CRL.

48. Leonard Brin to A. Bruce Hunt, Sept. 4, 1944, FR, Administrative Files, Region 7, Brin folder, Roll 80, FEPC Records, CRL.

49. Witherspoon Dodge to John Hope II, Dec. 9, 1944, FR, Administrative Files, Region 7, Field Reports folder, Roll 80, FEPC records, CRL.

50. Clarence Mitchell to Malcolm Ross, July 10, 1944, FR, Region 7, Closed Cases, Merrill-Stevens Dry Dock, Roll 84, FEPC records, CRL.

51. Charles Smolikoff to A. Bruce Hunt, July 2, 1944, and Aug. 17, 1944; A. Bruce Hunt to Harvey Baker, Sept. 28, 1944, FR, Region 7, Closed Cases, Merrill-Stevens Dry Dock, Roll 84, FEPC records, CRL; A. Bruce Hunt to Will Maslow, "Weekly Report," Sept. 2, 1944, FEPC records.

52. E. C. Holman to Wallace Miller, Mar. 22, 1944, series 6, subseries 4, box 15 (National War Labor Board, Merrill-Stevens Dry Dock and Repair Co., Case No. 111–1687 HO), IUMSWA papers.

53. Report and Recommendations of Hearings Officer, May 11, 1944; Directive Order, Oct. 9, 1944, series 6, subseries 4, box 15 (National War Labor Board, Merrill-Stevens Dry Dock and Repair Co., Case No. 111– 6186 HO), IUMSWA papers.

54. Charles Smolikoff to Thomas Gallagher, June 9, 1944; "Report: Merrill Stevens—Jacksonville"; "Election Results, Held June 15th [1944]," all in series 2, subseries 4, box 16, Organizers' Reports, Merrill-Stevens Dry Dock and Repair, IUMSWA papers.

55. Smolikoff's background is pieced together from the *Miami Herald*, Dec. 26, 1944, 8-B; John Steedman, ed., *Who's Who in Labor* (New York: Dryden Press, 1946), 334; "Smolikoff Identified as a Key Man for Reds," *Miami Daily News*, Mar. 1, 1948, p. 1; author's interview with Berthe Small (Smolikoff), Dec. 8, 1995, tape and transcript in author's possession; "Survey Report of Miami Florida," n.d. (c. Dec. 1942), series 6, subseries 3, box 6, Miami Shipbuilding Corp. folder, IUMSWA papers.

56. Alexander Trainor to Charles Smolikoff, June 8, 1942, reprinted in the *Miami Daily News*, Feb. 25, 1948 (probably acquired by the FBI, which had a "highly confidential source" with access to Trainor's correspondence, "Communist Infiltration of Transport Workers Union of America," Miami Report #100-7319-241, Dec. 31, 1943, Federal Bureau of Investigation—Freedom of Information Act request, in author's possession); "Survey Report of Miami Florida," IUMSWA papers.

57. William Smith, "Greater Miami Area Report," May 8, 1943; William Smith to Thomas Gallagher, April 9, 1943, series 2, subseries 4, box 18, Florida Organizers' Reports, IUMSWA papers.

58. *Shipyard Worker,* June 4, 1943, p. 6.

59. In Re: Case No. 25-1226D, Miami Shipbuilding Corp. and IUMSWA Local 59, Mar. 1944; Charles Smolikoff to W. A. McAllister, Feb. 16, 1944, series 6, subseries 4, box 15 (National War Labor Board—Miami Shipbuilding Corp.), IUMSWA papers.

60. Charles Smolikoff to Michael Ross, July 3, 1944, series 2, subseries 4, box 16, Organizers' Reports, Merrill-Stevens, IUMSWA papers.

61. John Egerton, *Speak Now against the Day: The Generation before the Civil Rights Movement in the South* (New York: Knopf, 1994), 217.

62. I am far more optimistic, for instance, than Dan Kryder, who sees the FEPC's feebleness as a reflection of the Roosevelt administration's subordination of progressive social policy to the necessity of warmaking. See Daniel Kryder, "The American State and the Management of Race Conflict in the Workplace and the Army," *Polity* 26 (Summer 1994): 601–34.

63. Dodge, *Southern Rebel in Reverse*; Egerton, *Speak Now against the Day*; Reed, *Seedtime for the Modern Civil Rights Movement.*

64. Charles Smolikoff to Thomas Gallagher, Dec. 27, 1943, IUMSWA papers.

65. For an array of views on this question, see Honey, *Southern Labor and Black Civil Rights*; Rick Halpern, *Down on the Killing Floor: Black and White Workers in Chicago's Packinghouses, 1904–1954* (Urbana: University of Illinois Press, 1997); Roger Horowitz, *"Negro and White, Unite and Fight!": A Social History of Industrial Unionism in Meatpacking* (Urbana: University of Illinois Press, 1997); Nelson, "Class, Race, and Democracy in the CIO"; Korstad and Lichtenstein, "Opportunities Found and Lost"; Michael Goldfield, "Race and the CIO: The Possibilities for Racial Egalitarianism during the 1930s and 1940s," and responses by Gary Gerstle, Robert Korstad, Marshall F. Stevenson, and Judith Stein, *International Labor and Working Class History* 44 (Fall 1993): 1–63; Kevin Boyle, "'There Are No Union Sorrows That the Union Can't Heal': The Struggle for Racial Equality in the United Automobile Workers, 1940–1960," *Labor History* 36 (Winter 1995): 5–23; Robert H. Zieger, *The CIO, 1935–1955* (Chapel Hill: University of North Carolina Press, 1995), 155–61, 345–49.

66. Charles Smolikoff to Lucy Mason, May 31, 1945, box 4, Lucy Mason papers, Perkins Library, Duke University, Durham, N.C.

67. Nelson, "Organized Labor and the Struggle for Black Equality in Mobile during World War II"; Nelson, "Class, Race, and Democracy in the CIO"; Robert J. Norrell, "Caste in Steel: Jim Crow Careers in Birmingham, Alabama," *Journal of American History* 73 (Dec. 1986): 669–94; Alan Draper, "The New Southern Labor History Revisited: The Success of the Mine, Mill and Smelters Workers Union in Birmingham, 1934–1938," *Journal of Southern History* 62 (Feb. 1996): 87–108, are four of the more critical assessments of the CIO record on race relations.

A Venture into Unplowed Fields: Daniel Powell and CIO Political Action in the Postwar South

Robert H. Zieger

Throughout the late 1940s and early 1950s, the Congress of Industrial Organizations' Southern Political Action Committee (PAC) director Daniel Powell and his associates pursued a distinctive southern strategy. Of course, it was not the "southern strategy" promoted in the 1960s by leaders of the emerging Republican Party in the wake of the Voting Rights Act of 1965, which used black enfranchisement as a means of encouraging the racialization of the Democrats and recruitment of working-class whites into the GOP. Nor was it the "southern strategy" urged in the 1940s by Popular Front liberals, who foregrounded questions of racial justice. These men and women sought to use the CIO as the entering wedge for a militant, black-led confrontation with the racial oppression and economic exploitation that characterized the South. Rather, the "southern strategy" of Powell and the CIO leadership focused on economic concerns and tied advances in civil rights specifically to the role that a politically enfranchised and economically vibrant black community could play in furthering a liberal political and economic agenda. It entailed securing the loyalty of white workers through concentration on economic issues, cautious support for suffrage expansion as the central civil rights concern, and cooperation with non-CIO laborites and with race and liberal organizations that shared the CIO's anticommunist perspective.[1]

In the decade after his early 1946 appointment as CIO PAC's southern regional director, Daniel Powell worked tirelessly to bring this version of liberal politics to southern working people. Operating within the context of liberal-labor anticommunism, Powell attempted to foster a humane civic consciousness in a postwar South in which racial tensions and powerful economic forces joined to pose frustrating and at times overwhelming obstacles. This was a turbulent and unsettled time, for economic, legal, and demographic changes during the New Deal–World War II years encouraged hopes that biracial working-class liberalism could transform the South even as it triggered powerful forces of race-charged reaction.

The CIO's political presence in the postwar South has generated historiographical controversy. Scholars such as Michael Honey, Michael Goldfield, Numan Bartley, Nelson Lichtenstein, Robert Korstad, and Patricia Sullivan have perceived a window of opportunity for labor-led progressive politics in the immediate wake of World War II. New union footholds in war-engorged southern industry, Supreme Court decisions promising to expand the black electorate, and the Popular Front ideology of progressive unity, these scholars argue, held promise for a class-based resurgence of Populist-era southern liberalism. The emergence of southern politicians who welcomed labor support, and quietly accepted or encouraged the expansion of the black electorate, betokened bright promise for a rapidly industrializing South. Governors Ellis Arnall in Georgia and Jim Folsom in Alabama, senators such as Alabama's Lister Hill, Florida's Claude Pepper, and North Carolina's Frank Graham, as well as labor-backed congressmen such as Estes Kefauver in Tennessee, Henderson L. Lanham in Georgia, and Carl Elliott and Albert Rains in Alabama brought fresh hope, as did the emergence of an expanding black electorate. Participation in National Labor Relations Board elections helped energize working-class black activists, who used their union base to reinvigorate somnolent civil rights organizations. Supreme Court decisions undermined the white primary, encouraging a surge in black registration. With both of the national labor federations planning postwar organizing drives in Dixie, progressive-minded southerners saw the immediate postwar period, in the retrospective words of one, as "a kind of lovely moment . . . when everything seemed to be working."[2]

Alas for these hopes, sweet prospects soon soured. The CIO's widely publicized drive to organize the South quickly fizzled. Determined employer counterattacks, union-splitting conflicts over the role of communists and their allies in the postwar labor movement, and fierce resistance to black political participation soon stalled the liberal-labor advance.

While acknowledging the resurgent power of countervailing forces of racism, reaction, and retreat, recent historians, echoing in many cases the views of contemporary activists, lay the blame for liberal setback squarely on the shoulders of the leadership of the CIO and their allies. They charge that top CIO officials, succumbing to anticommunist hysteria, drew back from assertive support for racial equality, cut or weakened ties with progressive labor support organizations such as Tennessee's Highlander Folk School, excluded Popular Front–oriented militants from key roles, and bowed to the anticommunist priorities of political and cultural elites. Rather than building on the proven militancy of black workers, directors of the CIO's Southern Organizing Campaign (SOC) poured their limited resources into the lily-white textile industry and excluded proven radical organizers. While paying lip service to racial justice, CIO leaders such as SOC director Van Bitter placed the highest priority on recruiting whites, accepting without serious objection the need to marginalize the concerns of black workers and citizens. Concludes Michael Honey, "The new cold war atmosphere," as exemplified by the passage in June 1947 of the Taft-Hartley Act, "set the stage for the final dissolution of the left-center alliance in the CIO and the demobilization of the southern organizing drive."[3]

When Powell was appointed Southern PAC director in February 1946, however, Popular Front unity and labor-liberal political advance seemed likely to continue. In the 1944 elections, the fledgling CIO PAC had gained a reputation for vigor and effectiveness and was widely credited with the retirement or defeat of such right-wing legislators as Texas congressman Martin Dies and Missouri senator Bennett Clark. Serving as Southern PAC director was George Mitchell, on loan from the progressive Southern Conference for Human Welfare, which in turn had close ties with such pro-Soviet CIO affiliates as the Food and Tobacco Workers and the Mine, Mill, and Smelter Workers, both of which had a significant southern membership. Echoing the wartime rhetoric of unity, PAC activists in cities such as Memphis and Winston-Salem, in which these unions had a strong presence, worked effectively to expand the black electorate and to forge black-CIO political ties.[4]

In fact, however, the entire CIO PAC operation rested on shaky foundations. Without the stimulus of war and the presence of FDR on the ticket, enthusiasm was hard to generate. PAC founder Sidney Hillman died in July 1946, leaving PAC's future direction uncertain. PAC contributions to candidates, by law separate from union dues, proved difficult to collect, and PAC organizations, particularly in the only partially organized southern states, quickly began to deteriorate. As early as January 1945, Mitchell was complaining that "the CIO Political Action Committee [in the South] has only two paid employees," while CIO regional director Paul Christopher discovered in July of that year that in South Carolina "our entire . . . structure will have to be completely rebuilt. . . . there is nothing left of last year's organization." In New Orleans, Miami, and Memphis, growing tensions between political activists from pro-Soviet CIO affiliates and anticommunists increasingly impeded unified political efforts.[5]

Even when PAC operated effectively, as it did in the key 1946 Georgia primary, the results were both encouraging and bitterly disappointing. Indeed, this contest illustrated both the promise and defeat of liberal hopes. With Georgia's white primary invalidated, 135,000 black voters, along with the determined support of labor and civic reform groups, seemingly stood poised to deliver a crushing blow to Georgia's notorious Eugene Talmadge in his quest for a third (nonconsecutive) gubernatorial term. Supporting mildly progressive racial moderate James V. Carmichael, Peach State liberals and laborites hailed the July 17 primary as the dawning of a new day in southern politics. When the votes were counted, they could indeed take heart in the returns. Carmichael gained a popular vote margin of 16,000 over Talmadge, garnering 45 percent of the vote in a four-man race. But owing to Georgia's county unit system of weighing the popular vote, Talmadge won the election. Although Carmichael swept to a plurality of more than 37,000 votes in Fulton County (Atlanta), his opponent captured 105 of Georgia's 159 counties and claimed victory with 242 county unit votes versus Carmichael's 146. Moreover, many of Talmadge's narrow victories in rural counties resulted from a de facto purge of black registrants, augmented by unpunished violence and fraud, that sharply reduced the anticipated black vote and tipped the balance against Carmichael. Thus, despite the favorable auguries, reaction had triumphed once again, as the promising liberal regime of Governor Ellis Arnall soon gave way to a new round of race-based reaction in one of the South's seemingly most cosmopolitan states.[6] A CIO-led drive in Tennessee to oust veteran incumbent archconservative Kenneth McKellar fell victim to unpunished voting irregularities in Memphis, an industrial union stronghold, while in Alabama the election of a surprisingly prolabor congressional delegation was accompanied by the success, in a statewide referendum, of a blatantly discriminatory measure designed to curtail voting by blacks and lower-income whites.[7]

In key respects, then, Powell was stepping into an uncertain and fluctuating situation. Adding to his difficulties was the structural position of CIO PAC. With Hillman in the vanguard, CIO leaders had created it in 1943 and 1944 as a means of reversing the declining liberal-labor political fortunes, which had been ebbing since the failure of the Roosevelt Purge in the 1938 Democratic primary elections. PAC was primarily dedicated to the reelection of Franklin Roosevelt. While the CIO generated elaborate plans for PAC's organic relationship to the national CIO and to both the affiliated unions and state and local bodies, actually, in the immediate wake of their impressive wartime electoral efforts, PAC's future remained cloudy. Funding of laborite political action, restricted by the terms of the Smith-Connally Act and under litigation, was shaky. The CIO's state and local organizations, especially in states (including most of those in the South) with small or recent influxes of industrial union members, struggled to survive. For many CIO activists, the very creation of PAC and the hectic activity it conducted in 1944 served as a surrogate for the aggressive collective bargaining and organizing that they considered the central concerns of unions in the United States but that the exigencies of wartime labor relations had temporarily marginalized. The end of the war turned attention once again to collective bargaining and organizing. With the great strike wave of 1945–46 and the Southern Organizing Campaign, many activists believed that the CIO was at last returning to its proper role as a labor organization. Thus SOC directives stressed that the postwar effort to unionize the South was "to be purely an organizational campaign," with "no extra curricular activities—no politics—no PAC—no FEPC" (that is, no agitation in favor of an expanded Fair Employment Practice Committee, a CIO political goal). Yet at the same time, CIO leaders such as Director of Organization Allan Haywood stressed "the absolutely essential need of increasing the activity of southern workers in line with the program of the CIO Political Action Committee."[8]

At the time of his appointment, Powell was thirty-five years old. He grew up in Wilson and Goldsboro, North Carolina, where he graduated from high school. While attending Presbyterian Junior College in Maxton and the University of North Carolina, he became a reporter for several North Carolina newspapers. Moving to Memphis in 1936, Powell worked for the next six years in the advertising business, first as a solicitor for the *Memphis Press-Scimitar* and then as a salesman for an agency that provided business forms and program layouts for banks, schools, and businesses. In 1942 he entered the United States Army Air Force and served on a B-24 crew before receiving a medical discharge early in 1945. After a stint with the Office of Price Administration in Tennessee, he began working with CIO PAC in December, replacing regional director Paul Christopher, who had become acting Southern PAC director after the departure of George Mitchell earlier that year.[9]

Over the course of his career in the CIO and AFL-CIO, Powell participated in a variety of liberal organizations. A Unitarian-Universalist, he belonged to the American Humanist Association, the Center for the Study of Democratic Institutions, and the National Association for the Advancement of Colored People (NAACP). He served as vice president of the Tennessee Civil Liberties Union and of the Memphis Chapter of the United Nations Association. In later years he was a member of the Tennessee Advisory Committee to the United States Commission on Civil Rights. While retaining cordial personal relations with Popular Front progressives, he never doubted the basic legitimacy of American cold war policies and the need to limit pro Soviet elements in the CIO. Indeed, to men such as Powell and his immediate predecessor as Southern PAC director, Paul Christopher, anticommunism was simply a given, an essential component of any effective liberal politics. As a civil libertarian, Powell deplored McCarthyism and red-baiting. At the same time, he believed that the events of the 1930s and 1940s had proved that the Soviet regime posed a serious threat to liberal values and that laborites and other progressives who regularly apologized for the USSR or chose to work in friendly cooperation with communists were mistaken at best, and often downright pernicious. For Powell and others sharing his views, Popular Front unity provided no firm basis for postwar liberal advance in the South, for it rested on false premises. Unlike those in the labor movement such as the CIO's secretary-treasurer James B. Carey and West Tennessee regional director "Red" Copeland, Powell rarely highlighted the issue of communism within the CIO, nor did he fall into the trap of equating passionate concern for racial justice with de facto pro-Soviet sympathies, as Copeland frequently did. At the same time, he believed that the price of continued cooperation with pro-Soviet elements within the CIO was public opprobrium and practical ineffectiveness, however much Popular Front activists might proclaim common commitment to racial justice, expansion of labor rights, and democratic advance.[10]

Idealistic and committed to bringing positive social change to his native region, Powell registered no dissent from the prevailing liberal anticommunist consensus. During his service with CIO PAC, he, his wife, Rachel, and their two young children lived in a modest one-family house in a segregated Memphis subdivision. Until the last two years of the CIO's separate existence, officials such as Powell had no medical insurance or pension plan. Hired in 1945 at a salary of thirty-six hundred dollars a year, Powell struggled to support his family, often needing advances on his pay to meet unexpected medical or personal emergencies. Because his territory embraced the vast southeastern section of the United States, Powell was endlessly on the road, typically logging more than fifty thousand miles a year driving to union meetings, voter registration drives, and conferences with state and local CIO officers and representatives of other liberal groups. In those days, when long-distance telephone communication was usually reserved for emergencies, letters from home were cherished. "Monday night," reported Rachel in a typical mid-1950s letter, "[daughter] Pam said isn't it quiet around here without Daddy, and then they both said they wished you had a job and stayed in town all the time. . . . I miss you too." In 1952, a Memphis newspaper printed a picture of Powell in an advertisement in which he endorsed Prestone Motor Oil and was described as an "Enthusiastic Memphis Businessman."[11]

In attempting to implement the CIO's postwar political program, Powell and his coworkers faced a wide range of frustrations. Some, such as the structural and financial relationship between PAC and other CIO activities, were inherent in the complex federal structure of both the labor movement and the United States political system. Financial uncertainties and confusions exemplified these problems: in theory, funding of PAC candidate-support activities derived from money that union members contributed voluntarily, apart from union dues. The typical one dollar contribution was then divided up, with fifty cents going to national CIO PAC, whose headquarters were in Washington. The remaining half-dollar was in turn divided, half going to the member's international union's political action organization and the rest remaining with the local union, which in turn contributed to the political action campaign of the city or district body to which the local belonged. Even on a flowchart, these arrangements were complicated; in practical reality, the system was prone to multiple breakdowns. Moreover, the movement of funds out of a district or out of a state often bred local resentment and suspicion, especially since key elements in the national, and even statewide, CIO agendas, especially those relating to race, clashed with the political preferences of large numbers of white workers. Adding to the confusion was the fact that many local unions failed to join their city or district industrial union councils, which provided the basic institutional framework and, usually, the office space and facilities on which political action committees relied.[12]

Complicating these structural and financial conflicts were turf battles over union jobs and political priorities between the international unions with strength in a given state or district. For at least the first few years of Powell's tenure, for example, in Alabama the industrial union council, and, by extension, the state political action apparatus, was all but paralyzed by incessant rivalry between the United Steelworkers and the clothing and textile unions.[13] Structural confusion and internal rivalries in turn made even more difficult the always-problematic effort to collect PAC money from rank-and-file unionists, who often seemed either indifferent to the CIO's political efforts or downright hostile to its liberal agenda. The political action arms of the national CIO and of the politically active industrial unions, such as the United Automobile Workers and United Steelworkers, had great difficulty in building and sustaining a system of grassroots financial support for their political programs even in northern states. In the South as late as the mid-1950s, despite years of exhortation by Powell and his coworkers, fewer than half of the CIO members were registered to vote.[14] Collecting PAC dollars from those who were registered proved time-consuming and discouraging, especially as during this period of heightened civil rights agitation, large numbers of southern CIO members flatly rejected their national organization's highly visible position in behalf of African American rights.[15]

Nor did the frustrations stop with factors internal to the labor movement. Voter registration and qualification procedures in the southern states were often arcane, complex, and subject to manipulation by entrenched urban machines and courthouse rings. Powell spent much of his time and energy tracking the ever-changing rules and procedures in his eleven-state region, supporting efforts to eliminate or moderate poll taxes, seeing to it that local union political operatives kept abreast of the often lengthy lead times between registration and voting, and generally monitoring and working within a system whose very purpose was to limit and discourage autonomous political activism, especially among blacks, but also among the lower-income whites who formed the heart of southern CIO membership. Labor lobbyists spent an enormous amount of time and scarce political capital in southern legislatures fighting right-to-work initiatives, responding to absurd charges of communist influence, and attempting to beat back nuisance measures that imposed heavy registration and licensing fees on union and civil rights organizers.[16]

Of course, in seeking to build a postwar political presence in the South,

Powell and other PAC operatives were not without allies. In particular, as he quickly realized, African American voters, or potential voters, represented a powerful force for modern liberalism in Dixie. And through the 1940s, black political participation had been rising as the courts struck down some of the more blatantly discriminatory methods of disfranchisement. Throughout the first postwar decade, Powell worked closely with black community leaders and trade unionists to register voters, pay poll taxes, and mobilize the black electorate behind desirable (or, often, the least objectionable) candidates. Yet Powell feared that militant appeals in behalf of civil rights would alienate white workers and that a political strategy focusing largely on bread-and-butter issues had the greatest chance of success in furthering the liberal-labor agenda. Highlighting the moral evil of segregation, union leaders held, would only isolate white workers and encourage defensiveness among them, playing into the hands of racist demagogues.[17] Thus, Powell believed, support for the aspirations of African Americans had to be pressed quietly and cautiously. This perceived need for caution necessitated that he and his operatives cultivate the established, often entrenched, local black leadership rather than reach out to militant, younger black activists. Especially in these years before the rise of a vocal, community-based civil rights crusade, Powell, following the priorities of southern CIO union leaders and national CIO policy, hewed close to the established black power structure, stressing gradualism and civility rather than the kinds of conflict and confrontation that had been so evident in the origins of the CIO in the 1930s and that would come to characterize the emerging civil rights movement of the later 1950s and 1960s. The expansion of the number of southern black voters from 170,000 in 1940 to more than 1,000,000 by 1952 provided some support for these cautious judgments.[18]

Other trade unionists also provided potential allies. Affiliates of the American Federation of Labor and lodges of the politically influential Railroad Brotherhoods were well established in the southern states and could offer support for political objectives important to the CIO. Indeed, in the 1950s AFL membership far outpaced that of the CIO in the South, as the older federation, with almost a million southern members, represented nearly three times as many workers as did the CIO. But as in the North, cross-union cooperation was not easy to achieve. Although the AFL had broadened its membership base since the 1930s, its most influential affiliates and its best-established local unions were in the construction and urban transit trades. Concerns of AFL unionists in the South tended to be parochial and localistic, stressing matters such as building codes, safety ordinances, and other directly job-related issues. AFL and CIO members did share common concerns about workers' compensation programs, union security issues, funding for public facilities such as schools and hospitals, and other practical matters. But AFL construction unions, along with the Railroad Brotherhoods, had long records of racial exclusion. During the 1950s they were actively fighting efforts on the part of the federal government and civil rights groups to break racially defined control of jobs in their trades. Entrenched railroad and craft unionists, however much they may have agreed with their CIO counterparts on a wide range of economic and governmental issues, were often chary about involvement with an organization they deemed leftist. "You apparently will not get it into your head," wrote a Democratic political broker in Virginia to the PAC's state director during the 1950 primary season, "that the other labor groups in the Sixth District are afraid of the CIO." To the extent that CIO political operations involved coalition with civil rights groups, AFL-CIO cooperation remained fragile and usually required that joint campaigns remain confined to narrow definitions of labor's interests. Powell and his colleagues had to negotiate and police carefully balanced interlabor electoral coalitions. Moreover, there were many examples of open (and influential) AFL support for candidates whose racial views were anathema to the CIO.[19]

Indeed, during these years racial matters permeated CIO southern political efforts. Convenors of every state convention or political action workshop had to calculate the precise degree and character of black participation. Failure to involve black unionists and activists, of course, would break faith with civil rights groups and contribute to the demobilization of African American voters, liberalism's most faithful and consistent constituency in the postwar South. Inclusion of too many blacks, or black speakers who were other than modest, deferential, and moderate, could lay bare the fierce racial feelings that lay just beneath the surface of southern industrial life. Moreover, those making arrangements for meetings had to steer between rigid observance of the white South's closely monitored segregationist requirements and the sensibilities of their own members, black and white. The CIO official in charge of arrangements for a political action meeting to be held at the Wade Hampton Hotel in Spartanburg, South Carolina, reported that "[t]he colored delegates will . . . be asked not to loiter around in the lobby, or in other words will be asked to go directly to the

conference room." In Georgia, PAC director Dave Burgess reported that
south Georgia locals of the important Communications Workers of America initially refused "to come to an inter-racial meeting," largely, he added,
"because of their understandable race prejudice."[20]

State CIO conventions and PAC meetings generally avoided overt and
provocative statements on civil rights. Invariably, delegates adopted resolu-
tions and policy declarations that condemned communism and broadly
endorsed civic equality in language that carefully avoided specific criticism
of southern racial attitudes and customs. Powell and other southern CIO
operatives soft-pedaled the more vigorous denunciations of southern racial
practices emanating from the national CIO and its liberal allies and urged
national leaders to treat racial issues gingerly when they addressed southern workers. Thus, for example, at a 1953 North Carolina meeting, in his
brief remarks touching on race, CIO secretary-treasurer James B. Carey,
chairman of the CIO Committee Against Racial Discrimination, stressed
that "the evils of minority persecution . . . are daily ammunition for the pro-
pagandists behind the Iron Curtain." That same year at a Georgia convention, new CIO president Walter Reuther briefly touched on the same
theme. In a lengthy speech that discussed housing, Social Security, au-
tomation, minimum wage, taxation, the cost of living, and a wide variety of
other foreign and domestic issues, he devoted but a single, elliptical paragraph to race. Acknowledging that "we have double standards of citizenship, and we know that problem is acute in the southern part of our country," he reminded his listeners that "half the people in the world are dark
skinned." Americans could no longer "permit the Communists to exploit"
the racial situation in the United States in their diabolical attempt "to win
over hundreds of millions of people in Asia, and to mobilize those people
against a free world."[21]

Widespread voter suspicion of organized labor also limited the scope of
the CIO's southern strategy. Its operatives were constantly in the position
of raising funds, mobilizing voters, and generating support for candidates
who begged them to remain in the background. Thus, in the spring of 1946,
young Florida congressional aspirant George Smathers approached national PAC leaders asking for support. PAC assistant national director Tilford Dudley recalled that Smathers pledged that he "would be friendly to
organized labor and to the negro people." He was eager for CIO help but
equally insistent that there be no public announcement of it. Indeed, "he
even suggested that it would be wise for our canvassers not to identify them-

selves as CIO members." Powell characteristically coupled pledges of support for friendly politicians with assurances of discretion in public statements. In 1949, CIO operatives were outraged when Francis Pickens Miller, the gubernatorial candidate whom they were quietly backing in a futile effort to unseat the candidate of the Byrd machine, dramatically returned CIO financial contributions and used the occasion of a statewide radio broadcast—paid for in part by PAC—to deny that he had CIO support. Furious, Dudley castigated the candidate's aide, declaring, "When you lead people out on a limb and then saw that limb off, those people are bound to be angry." Nonetheless, PAC continued to support Miller.[22]

If their racial appeals were muted and their support for candidates low-keyed, CIO spokesmen in the South did conduct a certain populistic, class-based discourse in their efforts to sustain a liberal-labor movement. They implored southern CIO members to contribute to PAC fund-raising, stressing the practical benefits to be gained from political action and the dangers of ruling-class domination of legislatures, governorships, and congressional delegations. Lack of effective political action, declaimed a Georgia CIO leader in 1949, had put into power "the willing tools of Industry," and the hard-working union member found his most basic rights hostage to "his most vicious enemies," the lackeys of the big corporations. Especially after the Republican national victories in 1952, in which the Eisenhower ticket made substantial inroads into the South, PAC representatives warned that, in the words of Georgia Industrial Union Council president W. H. Crawford, "All over this state . . . the big money boys are pouring money like water into the hands of the Republican Committee." A union member who failed to contribute to PAC was failing his brothers and sisters and permitting big business to take back in the political arena what unions had gained in collective bargaining. Southern PAC officials were fond of quoting National Director Jack Kroll to the effect that "'any union member who fails to register and vote . . . is just as bad as the scab who crosses your picket line.'"[23]

Powell and his operatives worked endlessly with local unionists to compile elaborate card files, their chief means of tracking grassroots support. Frequent two- and three-day PAC workshops and seminars combined an emphasis on nuts-and-bolts techniques of political recruitment and organization with detailed exhortation and instruction on issues such as taxation, workers' compensation, and labor legislation. At these gatherings in particular, Powell and those who worked with him in the Southern PAC effort exhibited an earnest civic idealism and a faith in the ability of education and training to create a smooth-running and powerful liberal-labor political presence. CIO leaders directed attention to the class bases of American politics and the dangers of permitting business a free hand in the legislative arena. Even so, these gatherings relied less on exhortation and fiery rhetoric than on sober, carefully planned instruction in the practical techniques of political organization and the functioning of the political system. These PAC gatherings did not entirely ignore race issues, usually including some resolution or statement favoring equal rights and criticizing franchise restrictions. But such expressions invariably were linked to an essentially class-centered analysis, implicitly encouraging union members to turn away from racial fears and resentments and to focus instead on the machinations of big business and its political henchmen, and such expressions were usually advanced within the anticommunist idiom common to liberals in the 1950s.[24]

The experience of the CIO's Textile Workers in one Georgia community exhibited both the benefits and limitations of this approach. Throughout the postwar period, Textile Workers Union of America (TWUA) Local 689 represented workers at the Celanese Corporation's plant in Rome, Georgia, and remained a union bastion in the nonunion territory of northern Georgia. Through bitter experience with hostile employers, an antagonistic local media, and anti-union public authorities, Local 689's members learned the value of political action, a labor activity stressed incessantly by its New York–based parent union. Creating an effective local PAC, the local leadership worked hard, and successfully, to elect friendly city, county, and judicial officials. By 1950, more than 70 percent of the age-eligible residents in areas with large numbers of Celanese workers were voting, up from 19 percent in 1942. They were instrumental in the surprising success of district congressman Henderson L. Lanham, one of a handful of southern Democrats who voted to uphold President Truman's veto of the Taft-Hartley Act in 1947. Indeed, Local 689 and its vigorous political action program were bright spots in TWUA's otherwise gloomy postwar experience in the South.

But Local 689's members did not follow the whole TWUA and CIO agendas. Textile Workers officials learned to be silent on racial issues and to encourage the membership to stay focused on economic and law-enforcement concerns. Perhaps most dismaying to national union leaders was the fact that through the 1950s, Local 689 members overwhelmingly flocked to the banners of race-baiting Herman Talmadge in his gubernatorial and senatorial campaigns. They supported him despite his poor labor record and despite the bitterness that his father, Eugene, had engendered among Georgia laborites. Fully capable of shrewd and effective political action, these white Georgia unionists had a clear agenda of their own, one that combined effective marshaling of influence in behalf of laborite goals in the local community and support for the racial and political status quo in the broader arena.[25]

Of all the episodes involving the CIO's political operations in the South, the events surrounding the 1950 primary elections were the most disappointing. As the new decade dawned, liberals had reason to be pleased with Dixie's senatorial contingent. In Alabama, Lister Hill and John Sparkman had defied the Dixiecrats to remain loyal to the national party, consistently supporting the Truman administration. In Tennessee, ebullient Estes Kefauver had routed the Crump machine's candidate and captured a Senate seat in 1948. Florida's Claude Pepper, in the upper chamber since 1936, was a strong economic liberal, and in the spring of 1949, University of North Carolina president Frank Porter Graham, an ardent New Dealer with close ties to organized labor, had been appointed to fill a vacant seat. With populist liberals holding governorships in Alabama and North Carolina, there seemed hope that PAC's "southern strategy" was paying dividends. Thus, an enthusiastic PAC activist in North Carolina reported, after labor-backed Kerr Scott had defeated an old-guard Democrat in the Tarheel State's 1948 gubernatorial primary, "this latest triumph of . . . labor over a machine candidate is proof positive that Labor is a political force to be reckoned with from now on."[26]

In the 1950 Florida Democratic primary, however, Pepper, seeking a third full term, faced a stiff challenge from his former protégé, a young lawyer named George Smathers. Kroll, Powell, and other PAC operatives worked hard for Pepper's reelection, frequently prodding the senator's campaign staff. Kroll poured thousands of scarce national PAC dollars into Pepper's coffers, while Powell spent much of his time during the early spring in Florida in an unusually bitter campaign characterized by red-baiting and personal attacks. With relatively few CIO members in the Sunshine State, PAC concentrated on African Americans. "The CIO is doing everything in its power to help Claude get re-elected," Powell declared from Miami.

Actually, Florida observers faulted PAC for being too open, too visible, and too closely identified with efforts to mobilize black voters. Certainly

Smathers played the issue for all it was worth, producing correspondence between George Weaver, an African American national CIO official, and Kroll that, in Smathers's words, "blue printed CIO's plan of campaign to take the Senate seat away from the people of Florida." When Smathers rode to victory by a wide margin, editorialists and pundits portrayed the results as a sharp rebuke to the CIO and its efforts to energize the black electorate.[27]

In North Carolina, where Graham was running for election to a full term, election results were even more devastating. Here, things had started out well. In the balloting on May 27, the articulate and popular Graham outpolled several challengers in the first round of the Democratic primary, nearly capturing a majority and thus gaining the nomination outright. Graham successfully withstood criticism of his New Dealish liberalism and his association with organized labor; even McCarthyite attacks on his character and associations failed to rally the electorate against him. Graham's victory left him but fifty-six hundred votes short of a clear majority, and labor operatives expected his chief opponent, conservative Democrat Willis Smith, to concede a second primary runoff contest.[28]

But disaster soon befell the complacent Graham. Early in June, as Smith contemplated withdrawal, the United States Supreme Court handed down a triad of explosive decisions undermining segregation. The most far-reaching, *Sweatt v. Painter*, a Texas case, struck at the roots of the "separate but equal" doctrine by requiring that the University of Texas Law School admit a black applicant, despite the state's creation of a separate, segregated law school. These decisions held immediate implications for states such as North Carolina. More to the point, they buoyed conservative Democrats' hopes since Graham privately endorsed these decisions and was already suspect because of his implicit association with the advanced racial agendas of his allies in the liberal community, the Truman administration, and the labor movement.

After some hesitation, Smith forced the runoff. Almost overnight, the race issue, hitherto hovering on the margins, took center stage. Graham spent the last weeks of the increasingly sordid campaign denying that he favored race mixing, intermarriage, and creation of an FEPC that would cost white workers their jobs and put black foremen in charge of white women workers. In a record runoff turnout on June 27, Smith narrowly defeated Graham by a vote of 281,000 to 262,000. Lacking sophisticated polling techniques, laborites and political analysts alike pointed to the impact of the race issue on blue-collar voters as the key to Smith's upset victory. According to one Graham supporter, "Lots of laboring people with whom I talked told me that they had much rather work for lower wages than to have their children going to school with Negroes." An editorial writer for the *Raleigh News and Observer*, which had supported Graham enthusiastically, declared that "the Negro issue played a predominating role. . . . If the working people had not been so susceptible to the cry of 'Nigger,'" he charged, "Senator Graham would undoubtedly have won by a very large margin." Political scientist Samuel Lubell agreed: "The fact is . . . ," he declared, ". . . the Graham supporters really had nothing with which to fight the racial issue."[29]

The defeats of Pepper and Graham challenged the CIO commitment to a class-based attack on the South's old order. The notion of an increasingly progressive South, undergoing gradual change on the basis of common class interests of black and white working people, was hard to sustain as racial issues became central. "The defeat of Claude Pepper . . . ," declared the executive board of the Florida State Industrial Union Council, ". . . was a blow not only against organized labor, but a body blow against mankind." Almost four years after the North Carolina election, a Textile Workers' political operative told the state's PAC representatives that "one of the most tragic . . . one of the most obscene things to happen in American life in the last decade was the tragic defeat of Dr. Frank Graham."[30]

Powell and other PAC functionaries pored over the details of the two campaigns, looking for ways in which to present their message better and to rekindle the liberal-labor project. But in truth, there was little that men such as Powell *could* do once highly charged racial issues began to dominate public discourse. CIO PAC continued to preach its "economics first" doctrine and to attempt to marginalize divisive racial issues in the service of a class-based coalition. PAC continued to hold seminars and workshops designed to bring civic activism to southern workers. Powell and his colleagues kept up the tough, slogging effort to collect PAC dollars from workers who remained suspicious at best of the CIO's national agenda. But, as Powell later observed, "The introduction of the race issue by those who desired to maintain the status quo in the South . . . frustrated . . . efforts to focus the attention of the voters on the authentic issues[,] . . . the economic and social conditions of the South and its people." A "southern strategy" predicated on interracial cooperation on the grounds of economic mutual self-interest could achieve limited electoral success even as black political participation expanded, but it faced more problematic prospects once black militancy, controversial court decisions, and working-class backlash shifted the ground of southern politics.[31]

Were there viable alternatives to the CIO PAC strategy Powell sought to implement? Critics on the left have held that a forthright confrontation of the race issue, predicated on the reality of blacks' support for industrial unionism and progressive politics, would have enabled the CIO to sustain its fighting edge into the 1950s. It was the ardent anticommunism, these critics have argued, that turned the industrial union federation away from the race-based militancy that alone could have saved it from the doldrums into which it allegedly fell in the final years of its separate existence. Moreover, aggressive CIO championing of the more assertive elements in the emerging civil rights movement would have provided a laborite presence within the movement, linking rather than severing the moral and economic dimensions of the crusade for racial justice.[32]

Of course, this was not Powell's judgment. Proud of his achievement in rebuilding PAC in the late 1940s, he never doubted the appropriateness of the anticommunist liberalism that he and his colleagues advanced. Powell's anticommunism was not primarily a defensive stance designed to appease the American power structure; rather, it was part of a coherent worldview that saw the Soviet Union as an enemy of liberal values and saw those in the United States and in the labor movement who collaborated with communists as misguided ethically and futile practically. Equally inconceivable, however, was the option of abandoning the PAC's commitment to racial justice, however circumspect its spokesmen believed the CIO needed to be in articulating labor's views in the South. "Union members," Powell observed in 1976, "are a cross section of the community, [and in the 1950s] we had Klansmen, White Citizen Council members, and unorganized racists in our local unions." Powell and his coworkers could not hide from the CIO's southern members the organization's endorsement of FEPC and other civil rights measures, its cooperation with the National Association for the Advancement of Colored People, and its approval of explosive Supreme Court decisions regarding segregation. They could only hammer away at economic issues and attempt to place in the foreground the practical political and financial benefits of changing racial patterns.[33]

Though Powell's end-of-career assessment of his and PAC's work stressed the CIO's earnest efforts and pointed with pride to its occasional successes in the South, implicitly he highlighted the modesty of the resources at

hand and the marginality of the CIO's role. With CIO membership a frac-
tion of that of the AFL and the brotherhoods, with a white working class always prone to racialist political priorities, and with powerful entrenched
white elites determined to maintain the racial and economic status quo,
the boundaries within which Powell and his colleagues worked were sharp
and sturdy. A PAC operation that foregrounded race and radicalism was
doomed to failure and courted destruction. Congratulating Powell on his
new position in February 1946, PAC founder and director Sidney Hillman
observed that political "work in the South is . . . a venture into unplowed
fields," but even the experienced and astute Hillman underestimated just
how rocky and inhospitable those fields could be.[34]

Notes

1. Assumptions are rife but detailed studies few when it comes to the labor politics of the first postwar decade in the South. All students start with V. O. Key (with
Alexander Heard), *Southern Politics in State and Nation* (New York: Knopf, 1950), who
predicted a major expansion of labor influence but who in fact dealt only fleetingly
with organized labor's actual political activities (673–74). Numan V. Bartley, *The New
South, 1945–1980* (Baton Rouge: Louisiana State University Press, 1995), 38–73,
presents a provocative but, I think, skewed overview featuring the CIO. Most significant historical accounts focus on the post-*Brown* period. See, for example, Alan
Draper, *Conflict of Interests: Organized Labor and the Civil Rights Movement in the South,
1954–1958* (Ithaca: ILR Press, 1994); Robert J. Norrell, "Labor Trouble: George
Wallace and Labor Politics in Alabama," in *Organized Labor in the Twentieth-Century
South*, ed. Robert H. Zieger (Knoxville: University of Tennessee Press, 1991), 250–
72; Robert S. McElvaine, "Claude Ramsay, Organized Labor, and the Civil Rights
Movement in Mississippi, 1959–1966," in *Southern Workers and Their Unions, 1880–
1975*, ed. Merl E. Reed, Leslie S. Hough, and Gary M Fink (Westport: Greenwood
Press, 1981), 109–37; Claude Ramsay, "Comment," ibid., 139–42; Patrick J. Maney,
"Hale Boggs, Organized Labor, and the Politics of Race in South Louisiana," in
Southern Labor in Transition, 1940–1995, ed. Robert H. Zieger (Knoxville: University
of Tennessee Press, 1997), 230–50. James Caldwell Foster, *The Union Politic: The CIO
Political Action Committee* (Columbia: University of Missouri Press, 1975), has little
material on the South. Daniel Powell and the CIO make cameo appearances in
many of the biographies of and monographs about southern political figures cited
in the notes below, but neither has received sustained treatment.

2. Bartley, *New South*, 38–73, quote p. 38. Virginia Van der Veer Hamilton, *Lister
Hill: Statesman from the South* (Chapel Hill: University of North Carolina Press, 1987),
144–46. Key, *Southern Politics in State and Nation*, 673–74, posits a trajectory of labor-

led liberal transformation of southern politics. Other recent works stressing the hopeful possibilities of 1945–46 include Robert Korstad and Nelson Lichtenstein, "Opportunities Found and Lost: Labor, Radicals, and the Early Civil Rights Movement," *Journal of American History* 75, no. 3 (Dec. 1988): 786–811; Michael K. Honey, *Southern Labor and Black Civil Rights: Organizing Memphis Workers* (Urbana and Chicago: University of Illinois Press, 1993); Michael Goldfield, "Race and the CIO: The Possibilities for Racial Egalitarianism during the 1930s and 1940s," *International Labor and Working-Class History* 44 (Fall 1993): 1–32; Patricia Sullivan, *Days of Hope: Race and Democracy in the New Deal Era* (Chapel Hill: University of North Carolina Press, 1996), 193–220; and Wayne Flynt, "The Flowering of Alabama Liberalism: Politics and Society during the 1940s and 1950s," in William Warren Rogers et al., *Alabama: The History of a Deep South State* (Tuscaloosa: University of Alabama Press, 1994) 524–44. For a different perspective, see Robert J. Norrell, "Labor at the Ballot Box: Alabama Politics from the New Deal to the Dixiecrat Movement," *Journal of Southern History* 57, no. 2 (May 1991): 201–34. On the white primary and related issues, see H. D. Price, *The Negro and Southern Politics: A Chapter of Florida History* (New York: New York University Press, 1957), 26–58, and Key, *Southern Politics in State and Nation*, 624–28.

3. Honey, *Southern Labor and Black Civil Rights*, 214–75, quote 237. See also Sullivan, *Days of Hope*, 208–10, 235, 250–51.

4. Mitchell's reports to Sidney Hillman throughout the 1944 campaign are found in AFL-CIO Region 8, 1933–1969, Papers (Christopher Papers), Southern Labor Archives, Georgia State University (SLAGSU henceforth), Box 1876. See, for example, Mitchell to Hillman, Nov. 1, 1944, Folder 1. For evidence of assertive CIO pursuit of black registration and voting, see flyer, Roosevelt Victory Rally, 1944, ibid., Folder 12. Foster, *Union Politic*, 16–48, however, casts doubt on the CIO's impact in congressional races, as does Dennis K. McDaniel, "The C.I.O. Political Action Committee and Congressman Martin Dies' Departure from Congress: Labor's Inflated Claims," *East Texas Historical Journal* 32 (Fall 1993): 48–56. On Memphis, see Honey, *Southern Labor and Black Civil Rights*, 233–34; on Winston-Salem, see Larry J. Griffin and Robert R. Korstad, "Class as Race and Gender: Making and Breaking a Labor Union in the Jim Crow South," *Social Science History* 19, no. 4 (Winter 1995): 425–54.

5. Mitchell to J. N. Dunivin, Jan. 11, 1945, and Paul Christopher to Thomas Burns, July 9, 1945, both in AFL-CIO Region 8, 1933–1969, SLAGSU, Box 1876-13. On ideological tensions, see R. W. Starnes to Allan Haywood, Aug. 6, 1945, ibid., Box 1876-4 (New Orleans); Alex Lichtenstein, "'Scientific Unionism' and the 'Negro Question': Communists and the Transport Workers Union in Miami, 1944–1949," in Zieger, *Southern Labor in Transition*, 68–77 (Miami); and Honey, *Southern Labor and Black Civil Rights*, 214–44. Powell assesses the state of PAC in the South at the time of his assumption of the regional directorship in Daniel A. Powell, "PAC to COPE:

Thirty-Two Years of Southern Labor in Politics," in *Essays in Southern Labor History: Selected Papers*, Southern Labor History Conference, 1976, ed. Gary M Fink and Merl E. Reed (Westport, Conn.: Greenwood Press, 1977), 244–45.

6. After winning the November election, Eugene Talmadge died on December 21, 1946, creating a complex and protracted succession dispute during which Arnall's lieutenant governor, Melvin E. Thompson, assumed the governorship with Arnall's backing amid fierce legislative and judicial disputation. In the special 1948 gubernatorial election to complete the term to which Eugene Talmadge had been elected, his son Herman defeated Thompson. See Gary L. Roberts, "Tradition and Consensus: An Introduction to Gubernatorial Leadership in Georgia, 1943–1983," in *Georgia Governors in an Age of Change: From Ellis Arnall to George Busbee*, ed. Harold P. Henderson and Gary L. Roberts (Athens: University of Georgia Press, 1988), 5–7; Harold P. Henderson, "M. E. Thompson and the Politics of Succession," ibid., 49–65; and Harold Paulk Henderson, *The Politics of Change in Georgia: A Political Biography of Ellis Arnall* (Athens: University of Georgia Press, 1991), 171–89.

7. Joseph L. Bernd, "White Supremacy and the Disfranchisement of Blacks in Georgia, 1946," *Georgia Historical Quarterly* 66, no. 4 (Winter 1982): 492–513; Steven F. Lawson, *Black Ballots: Voting Rights in the South, 1944–1969* (New York: Columbia University Press, 1976), 90–94; Hamilton, *Lister Hill*, 146–49. See also Henderson, *Politics of Change in Georgia*, 137–89. James Boylan, *The New Deal Coalition and the Election of 1946* (New York: Garland, 1981), 85–88, surveys a broad spectrum of setbacks for liberal and labor candidates during the 1946 southern primaries.

8. On the origins and early activities of PAC, see Robert H. Zieger, *The CIO, 1935–1955* (Chapel Hill: University of North Carolina Press, 1995), 177–88, and Foster, *Union Politic*, 3–15. The quotes are in Zieger, *CIO*, 231.

9. Daniel Powell biographical sketch, ca. 1975, Daniel A. Powell Papers, Southern Historical Collection, University of North Carolina, Chapel Hill, Series 3, Union and Personal; application for federal employment, Feb. 7, 1945, ibid.; Paul Christopher to Jack Kroll, Oct. 18, 1945, AFL-CIO Region 8 Papers, Box 1876, Folder 3; Christopher to Tilford E. Dudley, Oct. 22, 1945, ibid., Folder 2. The best recent discussion of the kind of cold war liberalism that men such as Powell and Christopher embraced appears in David Plotke, *Building a Democratic Political Order: Reshaping American Liberalism in the 1930s and 1940s* (Cambridge, U.K.: Cambridge University Press, 1996), 298–335.

10. Biographical Sketch, ca. 1975; Powell, "PAC to COPE," 244–45. Neither Powell's sparse published writings nor his otherwise useful and informative papers contain any broad statements of political philosophy. His views, as summarized in this paragraph, are inferred from his characteristic quotidian utterances, his associates, and the work he performed. On his relations with Popular Front activists, see Powell to Tilford E. Dudley, Feb. 25, 1947, Powell Papers, Series 2, National PAC Correspondence, 1945–1955 (on collaboration with the Food and Tobacco Workers in

Winston-Salem, North Carolina), and Polly Hayden to Daniel Powell, Mar. 2, 1948, Powell Papers, Series 2, Correspondence—PAC, 1945–51. On James Carey, see Zieger, *CIO*, 257, 285; on Copeland, see Honey, *Southern Labor and Black Civil Rights*, 210–11. Powell's views and behavior on the issue of communism closely paralleled those of CIO regional director Paul Christopher, who preceded Powell as Southern PAC director and who recommended him for the position. See Joseph Garrison, "Paul Revere Christopher: Southern Labor Leader, 1910–1974" (diss., Georgia State University, 1976).

11. If Powell submitted regular reports to his Washington PAC superiors, they have not survived in his papers or in other CIO collections. His correspondence with CIO national functionaries, however, does provide a sense of his travels and activities and, often, his day-to-day financial affairs. See, for example, Powell to Tilford E. Dudley, Feb. 25, 1947, Powell Papers, Series 2, National PAC Correspondence, 1945–1955; and Powell to George Rettinger, Aug. 25, 1951, ibid. Rachel Powell's letter, ca. 1953, one of the few personal items in the Powell Papers, is in ibid., Union and Personal, as is the advertising reprint from the *Memphis Press Scimitar-Commercial Appeal*, Feb. 18 and 21, 1952. For a sample of Powell's characteristic schedule, see Frances L. Todd to Powell, Mar. 8, 1949, with attached schedule, Mar. 7–22, 1949, Powell Papers, Series 1, Virginia Correspondence. The difficulties of dealing with medical and financial emergencies are hinted at in Powell to Tilford E. Dudley, Feb. 25, 1947, Powell Papers, National PAC Correspondence, 1945–1955.

12. See, for example, Tilford E. Dudley to CIO Regional Director William J. Smith, Mar. 14, 1947, Powell Papers, Series 1—Florida, 1945–1955; Fred C. Pieper to John Brophy and Jack Kroll, Mar. 18, 1948, Powell Papers, Series 1—Louisiana, 1946–53; Dudley to William Crawford, Georgia CIO PAC, Sept. 21, 1950, Powell Papers, Series 1—Georgia Correspondence. Some of the complexities of PAC funding are revealed in Daniel Powell to Jack Kroll, June 18, 1951, Powell Papers, Series 1—Georgia. Despite the suspicions of southern members, in fact national PAC put a good deal more money into the South than it extracted from members in the region.

13. On Alabama, see, for example, W. T. Adcock to Charles F. Hearn, June 24, 1948, Powell Papers, Series 1—Alabama, 1946–1948.

14. See, for example, Powell report to Jack Kroll on Virginia, Kentucky, North Carolina, South Carolina, Tennessee, Alabama, Georgia, and Florida, Apr. 28, 1955: "It is my estimate that not more than 40% of CIO members in Kentucky are registered to vote."

15. Norrell, "Labor Trouble," 250–72; Draper, *Conflict of Interests*, 3–40; Michelle Brattain, "Making Friends and Enemies: Textile Workers and Political Action in Post–World War II Georgia," *Journal of Southern History* 63, no. 1 (Feb. 1997): 91–138.

16. See, for example, Alabama State Industrial Union Council newsletter (mimeographed), May 9, 1955, Powell Papers, Series 1—Alabama. Mississippi's poll tax

and the state's requirements for residency and voter registration were typical in their complexity and discouragement of political participation. See Robert B. Highsaw and Charles N. Fortenberry, *The Government and Administration of Mississippi* (New York: Thomas Y. Crowell, 1954), 32–35, and Olive H. Shadgett, *Voter Registration in Georgia: A Study in Its Administration*, Public Administration Studies No. 7 (Athens: University of Georgia Bureau of Public Administration, 1955), 9–14; Hamilton, *Lister Hill*, 146–49. The best overall account of southern states' voter requirements and registration procedures is Lawson, *Black Ballots*, 86–95, 132–37, and passim.

17. On this theme, see Bartley, *New South*, 38–73.

18. See, for example, Jack Kroll to Fred C. Pieper, Louisiana State Industrial Union Council Director, Sept. 19, 1947, and Pieper to Hoyt S. Haddock, Jan. 28, 1948, Powell Papers, Series 1—Louisiana, 1946–53; Jack Kroll to Powell, Mar. 24, 1955, Powell Papers, National PAC Correspondence. On the expansion of the black electorate, see Lawson, *Black Ballots*, 134; Michael J. Klarman, "How *Brown* Changed Race Relations: The Backlash Thesis," *Journal of American History* 81, no. 1 (June 1994): 89, n. 14; and Henry Lee Moon, *Balance of Power: The Negro Vote* (Garden City, N.Y.: Doubleday, 1948), 132–45, 174–97.

19. There is virtually no historical literature on non-CIO southern labor political activity in the postwar period. One exception is Charles L. Fontenay, *Estes Kefauver: A Biography* (Knoxville: University of Tennessee Press, 1980), 71–73, 78–80, 119–22. For some of the problems and frustrations involved in attempting to work with the AFL and the brotherhoods in the South, see, for example, John M. Goldsmith to Charles C. Webber (director, Virginia CIO PAC), Apr. 29, 1950; Webber to Goldsmith, May 4, 1950, and Tilford E. Dudley to Powell, May 11, 1950, Powell Papers, Series 1, Virginia—Correspondence. Eric Arnesen, "The Failure of Protest: Black Labor, the FEPC, and the Railroad Industry," a paper presented at the Southern Labor Studies Conference, Williamsburg, Virginia, Sept. 29, 1997, outlines the brotherhoods' postwar legal battles to preserve job discrimination. Powell, "PAC to COPE," comments briefly on AFL southern political activity (p. 245).

20. Walter Truman to Paul Christopher, Jan. 15, 1946; Jack Kroll to Powell, May 24, 1955, both in Powell Papers, Series 2, National PAC Correspondence, 1945–1955; Burgess to Powell, Oct. 25, 1951, Powell Papers, Series 1—Georgia. Burgess may have meant that he understood that white Georgia unionists were biased, not that he sympathized with their prejudices. See also Alan Draper, "Do the Right Thing: The Desegregation of Union Conventions in the South," *Labor History* 33, no. 3 (Summer 1992): 343–56.

21. Carey remarks, minutes of the First Constitutional Convention of the North Carolina State Industrial Union Council, Raleigh, Oct. 31, 1953, Proceedings Files, SLAGSU; Reuther speech, Sept. 25, 1953, Georgia State Industrial Union Council, *1953 Convention Proceedings, Fourteenth Annual Convention of the Georgia State Industrial*

Union Council, Savannah, Sept. 25–27, 1953 (n.p., n.d.), 18–31. When, early in 1955, the national *CIO News* printed a picture of TWUA president Emil Rieve presenting a check to the Urban League's southern fund, southern CIO operatives quickly mobilized for damage control. "I think we can expect to see the picture of Brother Rieve reproduced [widely]," warned TWUA southern director Boyd Payton, "and possibly a story [will be circulated] which will attempt to show that we are trying to upgrade Negroes to supervisory jobs over white people." Payton to All Southern Staff, Feb. 16, 1955, Records of the [TWUA] Northwest Georgia Joint Board, SLAGSU, Folder 1609–8.

22. Affidavit by Tilford E. Dudley, Apr. 27, 1950, Powell Papers, Series 1, General Politics, 1950; Dudley to Deering Danielson, July 29, 1949, Powell Papers, Series 1—Virginia; Powell, "PAC to COPE," 247.

23. G. E. Hathaway remarks, Georgia State Industrial Union Council, *1949 Convention Proceedings: Tenth Annual Convention of the Georgia State Industrial Union Council,* Oct. 8–9, Atlanta (n.p., n.d.), 26; remarks of W. H. Crawford, *1953 Convention Proceedings . . . Georgia State Industrial Union Council,* 15.

24. Syllabus-handbook, PAC Political Action School, 1951, Powell Papers, Series 1, Political Action School, 1951; records and materials relating to Knoxville Political Action Institute, Jan. 26–29, 1954, AFL-CIO Region 8, 1933–1969, Papers, SLAGSU, Box 1916–17; folder on Greensboro Political Action School, June 8–11, 1955, ibid, Box 1916–5.

25. Brattain, "Making Friends and Enemies," 91–138.

26. On Alabama, see Flynt, "From the 1920s to the 1990s," 536–37; on North Carolina, see Julian M. Pleasants and Augustus M. Burns III, *Frank Porter Graham and the 1950 Senate Race in North Carolina* (Chapel Hill: University of North Carolina Press, 1990), 6, and William Smith to Allan S. Haywood, June 28, 1948, copy in Powell Papers, Series 1—North Carolina, 1947–1955; on Tennessee, see Norman L. Parks, "Tennessee Politics since Kefauver and Reece: A 'Generalist' View," *Journal of Politics* 28 (Feb. 1966): 148, 151–52, and Fontenay, *Estes Kefauver,* 137–63; on Florida, see Claude Denson Pepper (with Hays Gorey), *Pepper: Eyewitness to a Century* (San Diego, New York: Harcourt, Brace, Jovanovich, 1987), 106–68, and Jack Kroll to John V. Riffe, Mar. 12, 1953, Powell Papers, National PAC Correspondence.

27. Powell to Louise McGregor, Mar. 15, 1950, Powell Papers, National PAC Correspondence. PAC's efforts to rally African American support are indicated in Phillip Weightman to Jack Kroll, Feb. 16, 1950, and Weightman to George Rettinger, Feb. 27, 1950, Powell Papers, Series 1—Florida, Correspondence, 1946–1955. Smathers is quoted in Price, *Negro and Southern Politics,* 62; see also 59–65 for a discussion of the CIO role and extensive excerpts and reproductions relating to the PAC effort in Florida.

28. Pleasants and Burns, *Frank Porter Graham,* 186; Tilford E. Dudley to Powell, June 2, 1950, Powell Papers, Series 1—North Carolina, 1947–1955.

29. Pleasants and Burns, quoting Willis P. Holmes Jr., *Frank Porter Graham*, 227; Jonathan Daniels to Dave Burgess, July 20, 1950, with Fleet Williams to Daniels, July 19, 1950, enclosed; Samuel Lubell to Judge Johnson, July 3, 1950 (copy), both in Powell Papers, Series 1—North Carolina, 1947–1955. The campaign is covered in Pleasants and Burns, *Frank Porter Graham*, 203–46.

30. Resolution of Florida CIO Political Action, Jan. 27, 1952, Powell Papers, Series 1—Florida, 1947–1955; John Edelman addressing the Sixth Annual Convention of the North Carolina State CIO-PAC, Oct. 30, 1953, minutes in Proceedings Files, SLAGSU. Powell's personal retrospective comments on these two elections appear in Powell, "PAC to COPE," 250.

31. Powell, "PAC to COPE," 249–50; Klarman, "How *Brown* Changed Race Relations," 96–97.

32. The most recent expressions of this perspective are found in Michael Goldfield, *The Color of Politics: Race and the Mainsprings of American Politics* (New York: New Press, 1997), 240–49, 280–86, and passim, and, more implicitly, in Michael K. Honey, "Martin Luther King, Jr., the Crisis of the Black Working Class, and the Memphis Sanitation Strike," in Zieger, *Southern Labor in Transition*, 146–75.

33. Powell, "PAC to COPE," 249–50.

34. Sidney Hillman to Daniel A. Powell, Feb. 27, 1946, Daniel A. Powell Papers, Southern Historical Collection, University of North Carolina, Chapel Hill, Series 2, National PAC-COPE Correspondence.

Affirmative Action and the Conservative Agenda: President Richard M. Nixon's Philadelphia Plan of 1969

Judith Stein

Richard M. Nixon came to the presidency without a personal or political commitment to African Americans. Although no bigot, Nixon was deaf to black voices. Interested in foreign more than domestic affairs, he navigated civil rights waters with a political compass. The president tried to oblige both the new anti–civil rights Republicans from the South and the liberal Republicans from the North.[1] Under these circumstances, his actions were inevitably inconsistent. Still, Nixon entered the White House believing that the nation required no new initiative on civil rights. He publicly assailed the use of busing to achieve racial balance, and he buried open housing enforcement and Model Cities; he warred with the Equal Employment Opportunity Commission (EEOC), nominated Supreme Court justices with questionable civil rights records, and attempted to create a black "silent majority" to rival the traditional civil rights leadership.[2]

Thus, scholars have asked why Nixon launched the Philadelphia plan of 1969, which embodied the "hard" affirmative action he rhetorically excoriated. Under the plan, the government mandated that federal construction contractors hire percentages of black workers in six skilled crafts. Unlike earlier government efforts, which had used incentives and moral suasion, the Philadelphia plan set numbers, even if they were not the fixed quotas forbidden by the law. Hugh D. Graham suggests that the president wanted to split the alliance between blacks and the labor movement.[3] Thus, he concludes that the plan was an "unintended and ironical consequence" of the civil rights era.[4] The concept of irony was picked up by James Patterson in his survey of the United States after World War II and by John David

Skrentny in his *Ironies of Affirmative Action*.[5] Graham and Skrentny also used the word *irony* to characterize the opposition or indifference of leading black figures. Such prominent black leaders as National Association for the Advancement of Colored People (NAACP) lobbyist Clarence Mitchell and U.S. Representative Augustus F. Hawkins, to say nothing of civil rights advocate Bayard Rustin, may have been wrong, but historians have an obligation to explain the way these black spokesmen saw the Philadelphia plan.

Examining this context, one can conclude that the "ironic" view reflects the assumptions of the 1990s, not the 1970s. The plan, which was one of several responses to the urban riots of the late 1960s, was devised before Nixon's election, by Democrats in the Office of Contract Compliance (OFCC) and the Departments of Housing and Urban Development (HUD) and Health, Education, and Welfare (HEW). The question becomes, why did Nixon continue this Democratic policy? It appears that Nixon supported the plan because it harmonized with his attempt to control inflation in construction, a goal he continued to pursue after he disengaged from implementing the plan. Less than two months after the government announced the Philadelphia plan, Nixon discovered that racially integrating a small group of elite trades would not serve his anti-inflation purpose, so he switched to more potent means to address what he believed were high construction wages. The results confirm the purpose. The government kept the lid on wages and trained more construction laborers, but failed to increase minority participation in the elite skilled crafts, the purported target of the Philadelphia plan.[6] In short, historians must look beyond civil rights policy for explanations of the Philadelphia plan.

Three broad conclusions can be drawn from this brief history. First, racial employment policies must be examined within the context of the government's entire economic agenda. Second, affirmative action can be woven into conservative as well as liberal agendas. Third, the history of affirmative action is virgin territory. Much of the work at hand consists of polemical debates over constitutionality and civic culture. The Graham and Skrentny studies are excellent, but they stop at the edge of policy formation. No one dirties her hands to determine whether, and why, policies work or fail.

The Origins of the Philadelphia Plan

The building trades were among the most parochial unions in the AFL-CIO. Long accustomed to using localized market power to achieve their objectives, union leaders lacked both the incentive and the ideology to make a broad appeal to the larger working class and to the general public. Public and commercial construction had been the target of civil rights protests since early in the 1960s, despite the fact that in 1964, blacks composed 13.5 percent of the contract construction industry and that of these black workers, a higher proportion of them were craftsmen than were craftsmen in most other industries.[7] But construction workers labored in full sight of observers, unlike others hidden behind factory gates or office walls. This visibility, and the vigor with which the building trades defended their practices, gave the industry a symbolic significance, despite the fact that their record was slightly better than in blue-collar skilled work in general and much better than in white-collar occupations.

Democratic policy aimed to promote black entrance into the unions. Under an executive order signed by President John Kennedy in June 1963, the government created apprenticeship standards that required merit acceptance and some action to "remove the effects of previous practices under which discriminatory patterns of employment may have resulted."[8] It demanded affirmative action, although no numbers or precise standards were determined. Shortly, the AFL-CIO's civil rights department entered into negotiations with building trades in various cities, urging them to recruit minority apprentices. Then, the labor department opened up apprenticeship information centers in thirty-six major industrial areas to inform young people of the opportunities. Finally, the government embraced preapprenticeship training, funding private groups like the Workers Defense League in New York, the National Urban League, and the unions themselves to tutor and counsel youngsters to pass examinations required for entrance.

Recognizing that agreed-upon policy at the national level did not always translate into local action, Secretary of Labor R. Willard Wirtz, in February 1968, won a pledge from eighteen AFL-CIO building trades union presidents to work with local officials to implement the agreement. Wirtz waved the stick of strengthened sanctions at a time when the government had committed itself to rehabilitate ghettos.[9] The results were uneven, depending upon available slots, local race relations, and the economics of specific trades. Between 1967 and 1968, the number of minority apprentices increased from 4,000 to 10,500, rising from 3.6 to 7 percent of the totals.[10] However one evaluated the changes, numerous protests at building sites could not be ignored in the two years after the Detroit riot. Clashes over construction jobs were a permanent feature of the urban landscape in 1969, and the government was feeling the heat. Reverend Robert F. Drinan of Boston warned Arthur Fletcher, the assistant secretary of labor for wages and standards, that "if serious disorders break out in the near future, the Department of Labor can be cited as the proximate cause of such disorders."[11]

The situation in Philadelphia began badly and ended that way. In March 1963, the Philadelphia AFL-CIO Central Labor Council's civil rights committee issued a report documenting discrimination in the building trades. But neither the council nor the individual unions had any plans to do anything about it.[12] Some movement came as a result of NAACP picketing and AFL-CIO urging. Yet agreement was stymied because the unions refused to accept NAACP participation in the formulation and monitoring of plans. At a meeting of the Building and Construction Trades Council, President James O'Neil announced that his own plumbers' union immediately would put on a black journeyman and enroll two black apprentices and asked the officers of the other unions to take similar affirmative action. Receiving no response, O'Neil resigned, saying that he had tried to lead, but no one wanted to follow.[13] It was a bad sign.

The combination of persistent protests by blacks and resistance from certain unions kept the pressure on. In June 1967, the regional director of OFCC, the labor department body that enforced the executive order governing employment for federal contractors, created a multiagency preaward program requiring affirmative action. Construction contractors were required to submit an affirmative action plan to increase minority group representation in all trades.[14] OFCC received help from compliance officers in the regional HUD and HEW offices. Officials in these new urbanoriented departments were often more attuned to black opinion than their equivalents in older departments, like those managing defense contracts. In the fall of 1967, after the Detroit riots, the labor department developed the Philadelphia plan, which embodied these affirmative action requirements. Warren P. Phelon of HUD surveyed the building crafts and singled out seven unions, comprising 4 percent (between eighty-five hundred and nine thousand) of the area's construction workers. Unions representing electrical and sheetmetal workers, steamfitters, roofers, plumbers, structural ironworkers, and elevator constructors, he believed, underutilized minority workers. Blacks composed 35 percent of the workforce in the city's trades, but only 2 percent of the membership of the seven unions in question. Phelon ruled that no contracts would be accepted until bidders submitted manning tables that analyzed the minority participation in the work-force and set forth plans for improvement. After selecting the lowest bid-der, he would evaluate its affirmative action plan. Phelon set no firm num-bers, which would have suggested illegal quotas. The marriage of a desire to hire more blacks and the prohibition of quotas thus produced a highly unusual procedure. A contract accepted on traditional low-bid criteria would be subject to further negotiation.

Elmer Staats, comptroller-general of the Government Accounting Office (GAO), the fiscal watchdog of the Congress, was alerted to this situation by Congressman William C. Cramer, a Republican from Florida who spoke for the industry. At its convention in Dallas earlier in 1968, the Associated General Contractors of America, representing the large companies, had strongly objected to OFCC's new bidding procedures, which, it claimed, re-quired quotas.[15] On November 18, 1968, after the presidential election, Staats concluded that the procedure was illegal. Principles of competitive bidding would be violated if a contract were withheld from the low bidder on the basis of an unacceptable affirmative action program unless pro-spective bidders had been advised beforehand of the requirements of a sat-isfactory program. (Later, Nixon's OFCC believed it met these objections by requiring an affirmative action plan with goals in the initial bidding.)

Thus, Nixon inherited the Philadelphia plan. The new administration's first instinct was to disassociate itself from such problems by transferring OFCC to EEOC, an independent agency. Indeed, a Johnson administration task force report and a Brookings Institution study already had recom-mended transfer, as did personnel from the Bureau of the Budget and the new secretary of labor, George P. Shultz.[16] However, Shultz wanted to avoid getting into a position that could be interpreted as retreating from the battle against job discrimination, because he was currently under attack over his accommodation with the textile industry. Shultz had relied upon the good faith of the leaders of the industry to devise and implement affir-mative action plans in an industry that had a much worse racial record than construction.[17] Having other goals related to the larger economy, he acted differently in Philadelphia.

Affirmative Action to Combat "Wage Inflation"

Construction unions had been targets of liberals during the Ken-nedy and Johnson years, but in the late 1960s they also became villains for businesses and government because of their alleged role in increasing in-flation. When Nixon took office, he considered his number one domestic issue to be inflation, which had climbed to 5 percent (annualized) in the final quarter of 1968. Before his inauguration, he had declared the funda-mental cause of inflation to be budget deficits at a time of full employment and excessive increases in the money supply.[18] Subsequently, the business community persuaded him that increasing wages were a principal factor in the high cost of construction and thus a significant cause of inflation.[19]

In 1968, U.S. Chamber of Commerce president Winton Blount, a major Alabama contractor, had sponsored a conference on construction prob-lems, which fingered high union wage rates. Blount became convinced that the power of leading industrial corporations that spent heavily on con-struction was needed to bring wages in line. After nearly a year of unpubli-cized meetings, the Construction Users' Anti-Inflation Roundtable, com-posed of the CEOs of sixty of the nation's largest companies, was established in September 1969. Roger Blough, recently retired from U.S. Steel, headed the group, dubbed "Roger's Roundtable." The Construction Users shared the ideology of the Labor Law Study Committee, another business group dedicated to the proposition that the labor laws and machinery of enforce-ment, allegedly biased in favor of labor, had to be reformed. The two joined to form the Business Roundtable in 1972.[20] These new lobbies became the shock troops of the business community's battle to alter the industrial cli-mate in the United States.

Blough told Council of Economic Advisers (CEA) head Arthur Burns in 1969 that the annual rise in construction wages averaged 15 percent. "If this trend spreads to factory labor, we are in real trouble."[21] Blough's figures were wrong. The Bureau of Labor Statistics reported wage increases of 7.6 percent in that year. With a 5 percent inflation rate, the rise was not exces-sive. Moreover, no evidence existed that the leaders of industrial unions in manufacturing paid the slightest attention to construction wage settle-ments.[22] Between 1960 and 1968, the unemployment rate for construction workers averaged 12.1 percent, compared with 5.2 percent for private non–farm workers. Low interest rates, increasing public construction through Model Cities and other Johnson administration programs, and the eco-nomic expansion of the late 1960s permitted wage increases *and* produced historically low unemployment rates.[23]

Reflecting business opinion, Nixon, one month after taking office, asked Shultz to propose measures to increase the number of skilled construction workers and eliminate the "restrictive practices of construction unions."[24] The request harmonized with many of Shultz's own thoughts on inflation and employment. Shultz, a labor economist, had headed the Graduate School of Business at the University of Chicago. Although labor market reform was not intrinsically conservative or liberal, it had become a key element of the new assault by the Right on Keynesianism. Led by Milton Friedman, the Chicago school argued that the Kennedy-Johnson prescription of lowering unemployment through fiscal policy inevitably produced inflation. Friedman believed that labor market policy could reduce unemployment by ending government policies that inhibited the free market. He believed that labor unions, minimum wages, and the Davis-Bacon Act, which guaranteed prevailing (usually union) wages on government construction, enhanced unemployment by interfering with the labor market. The new economists also assumed that much of existing unemployment was voluntary. Thus, taxing unemployment insurance would encourage men and women to take jobs. These ideas offered policy alternatives to the programs of the War on Poverty and current thinking about public service jobs. Shultz was not an orthodox Friedmanite, but he believed that union practices, particularly those in construction, were significant causes of inflation.

The link between the wage and race questions in construction was made by Henrik S. Houthakker, a member of the CEA who specialized in international economics. In May, Houthakker told Nixon that construction wages were currently increasing at twice the rate of industry wages as a whole, "yet the reservoir of labor in the very areas that need construction activity most—the central cities and the ghettos—remain[s] underutilized in the construction industry." The administration should rally "public opinion behind the twin objectives of increasing minority employment in construction and of restraining construction costs." On June 13, Pepsi-Cola's Donald Kendall, head of the National Alliance of Businessmen and a friend of the president, also linked anti-unionism and minority hiring. Kendall urged Nixon to "take on the trade unions." He cited the recommendations of Roy Wilkins and Whitney Young "that the best thing that can happen to hit the unions is the MA-5 contract," a program in the labor department that trained workers.[25] Thus, a strong consensus existed that unions caused rising construction costs and that increased minority training and hiring provided a means of tackling the problem.

Two weeks later, on June 27, the administration announced a revised Philadelphia plan for seven crafts in the city.[26] Then, on August 20, even before the specifics of the plan were worked out, the administration peremptorily cut federal construction 75 percent. If the White House embrace of the Philadelphia plan was motivated by the notion of racial equity, the construction freeze made no sense. The halt was supposed to release labor for residential and small-scale commercial building outside the orbit of government civil rights enforcement. Yet government was asking the unionized public sector, subject to the federal cutback, to hire more minorities.[27] Because Nixon's other policies undercut the racial objectives of the Philadelphia plan but were consistent with a desire to bring down wages, the plan, despite the enthusiasm of its promoters in the OFCC, can best be seen as motivated by the industry's wage bill, not its racial composition.[28] One and a half years later, the Office of Management and Budget (OMB) acknowledged that the cutback in federal construction had curtailed "the influx of minority groups into the higher skilled construction trades."[29] As a result of the freeze, many of the voluntary affirmative action plans were stalled.

In Indianapolis, brickmasons, including many blacks, now suffered 50 percent unemployment and viewed the city's affirmative action plan as one that promised only to add more people to the ranks of the unemployed.[30] Joseph T. Jackson, of the Negro American Labor Committee, bitterly observed, "We fought to get into the trades and now he's [Nixon's] cut back model cities funds which were geared toward helping the black worker."[31] In December 1969, CEA chairman Paul McCracken acknowledged that the 19 percent unemployment rate in construction exceeded the national average. These workers also averaged less time employed per year than those in other sectors of the economy.[32]

Initially, most Republicans had opposed the Philadelphia plan, but not because of quotas. Conservatives wanted action against unions, not contractors. Congressman Cramer told the president and Shultz that the plan was unfair because it put the onus on the contractors to hire black labor. Representative John Rhodes of Arizona complained that contractors were being placed in an "impossible situation."[33] Nixon replied that the unions caused "high construction costs and we have to make every possible effort to reduce those costs by increasing the supply of labor, and this [the Philadelphia plan] is one way" to do it. Just before the final vote, Shultz reassured congressional Republicans that "the Plan expands the potential labor supply. This is among the reasons why many contractors are supporting the Plan and unions are fighting it—vigorously and openly."[34] In the fall, the president told reporters that "America needs more construction workers."[35]

The administration won when the Senate voted against Robert Byrd's rider to an appropriations bill banning "the expenditure of funds for contracts which the Comptroller-General held in contravention of any Federal statue," an opaque reference to the Staats ruling that the bidding procedures of the Philadelphia plan were illegal. The Republican minority stayed with the president. He was helped by the death of Senate minority leader Everett Dirkson in September. Dirkson had earlier told Shultz that the Philadelphia plan violated Section 703(j) of the Civil Rights Act of 1964, which he had inserted in the legislation to ban quotas. The new minority leader, Hugh Scott of Pennsylvania, dependent upon black votes and up for reelection in the fall, supported the plan. The baton of opposition passed to the less credible Democratic senator from North Carolina, Sam Ervin. The Republicans held firm, and enough liberals voted for the Philadelphia plan to defeat the rider. The plan obtained only meager support from the civil rights organizations. Most people believed that other, labor-supported measures, such as the creation of public jobs, were worth more to black workers than the Philadelphia plan. Nixon opposed public employment in 1969 and vetoed legislation toward this end passed in 1970.[36] But underlying this ranking was the plan itself.

Philadelphia Plan: Theory

The construction industry comprised a highly specialized yet diverse collection of trades, crafts, unions, contractors, and associations, differing from city to city and from region to region. Wages and labor relations also varied among the three major branches: large-scale public and industrial construction, commercial construction, and home building. Workers were not employed by one firm, like factory operatives or clerks, but were engaged by contractors for a particular project. Nevertheless, the largest companies tried to retain their "best" workers, those who could work autonomously, which reduced a firm's supervisory costs. The construction trades had strong work cultures, cemented by personal associations. Companies often obtained workers from unions, but not from the mythic hiring hall. In most instances, the hiring process was more informal. Workers were selected from past employment or direct application by the workers themselves.[37] Only for the leading trades and large projects did a company use union rosters. To ensure a trained workforce, contractors and unions jointly operated apprenticeship programs.[38]

The growing nonunion sector of the economy was organized more on an industrial model: fewer fully trained men, greater breaking down of tasks so that unskilled men could perform the work, and more variety in wages. While paying lower hourly wages, open-shop contractors, of necessity, required more supervisors and foremen. Thus, their total outlay for wages was not appreciably lower. Generally, open-shop contractors flourished in areas with weak unions, like the South and Southwest, and in those sectors of the industry where unskilled labor could be substituted easily for skilled labor.[39] But increasingly, open-shop employers were moving out of the residential and small commercial markets and were beginning to perform large-scale industrial and public work. Companies such as the Texas-based Brown and Root were undertaking projects throughout the nation, not simply in the Sunbelt.[40] Even in the union sector, most craftsmen and construction worers did not go through formal apprenticeships. Many journeymen "picked up" requisite skills, although proficiency had to be demonstrated by passing a test or working regularly in the craft. But those completing the apprenticeship programs had access to jobs across the country, to secure employment in hard times, to relatively high wages, and, until the elimination of occupational deferments in 1968, to exemption from military service. For new workers without personal associations, apprenticeship programs were crucial. This was especially true in the Ivy League mechanical and electrical trades, which required skills in mathematics and science. These elite trades were the targets of the Philadelphia plan and most other government efforts.

Although some of the union opposition was based upon race, it would be wrong to see trade action simply as organized bigotry. Declining trades and those trades experiencing unemployment usually resisted affirmative action. Because many of the training programs created by private groups or the government maintained minimal standards, craftsmen feared skill dilution.[41] Poorly educated or motivated youngsters and graduates of inadequate training programs created after the urban riots only confirmed the prejudices of construction workers. Contractors generally opposed government-mandated schemes. The costs of employing the marginally trained were high. When pressed, contractors cynically followed the form, not the spirit, of government requirements and hired enough unskilled persons to obtain the correct numbers. Across the political spectrum, union control was assumed to be the barrier to black employment, partly because black protest focused upon unionized government projects in the North. But the performance of the union sector was superior to the open shop. A Department of Labor study begun in 1976 found that minorities composed 21 percent of the apprentices in union programs and only 10 percent in the nonunion sector. Worse, dropout rates in the open-shop apprentice programs were six times higher than in the union segment of the industry.

In both sectors, blacks predominated in those trades in which they had historic roots, such as the trowel trades.[42] While unions often exaggerated the qualifications necessary to enroll in apprenticeships, in 1966 the NAACP's Herbert Hill, no friend of the building trades, admitted to John A. Morsell, Roy Wilkins's assistant at the NAACP, that "as a result of rapid technological innovation in the economy, the admission standards for such programs are rising and very frequently are a direct barrier to Negroes even where overt anti-Negro practices have been altered."[43] Black high school graduates, the likely candidates for apprenticeships, shared the prevailing bias against manual occupations. Most of the 37 percent of the black population that completed four years of high school had white-collar aspirations. These goals were reinforced by school and employment counselors who, on the basis of past experience, did not advise their best black students to consider apprenticeships, particularly in the 1960s, when racial barriers to white-collar work were falling. People paid a "price," in deferred earnings, for an apprenticeship. With past discrimination in mind and new options available, the risk for blacks often seemed too great.[44]

For those willing to take the risk, three approaches to apprenticeships existed and all were employed. The first, promoted by the Urban League and the Workers Defense League, sought to train blacks to pass tests; the second, sponsored by some civil rights groups and government officials, changed the tests or rules of entrance; the third involved radical Taylorism. Russell Nixon, an activist professor at New York University, argued that "occupations in the construction industry must be analyzed, redesigned, and restructured to permit easier entry of untrained workers and occupational advancement up the skill ladder through on-the-job training. It is absolutely essential and long overdue to apply the well tested and proven procedures of functional job analysis to the construction industry." Nixon recognized that outreach efforts were producing results, but the process was too slow to prevent racial conflict and too feeble to "change significantly the overwhelming white make-up of construction labor."[45] His advocacy of Taylorism reflected fear of urban rebellion and the middle-class assumption that manual work did not, or should not, require skill.[46]

Opening up apprenticeships where they were restrictive was certainly desirable, as were fairer means of certifying journeymen. But often these steps were misrepresented as solutions to ghetto problems, with the false promise of obtaining jobs for those with little education and training. The main effort during the Democratic years had been to expand minority representation in the unionized skilled trades. This goal matched the politics of the party, keeping unions and African Americans together. Yet personnel in the newer, less union-oriented parts of the Democratic bureaucracy formulated the original Philadelphia plan in the wake of the 1967 riots.

President Nixon, who lacked the Democrats' political objective, was attracted to the construction trades because he believed that their unions had too much power and restricted the supply of labor. Thus, the Nixon policy would increase the supply of labor, but not of unionists. The implementation of the Philadelphia plan reveals this changed objective. The revised Philadelphia plan, announced on June 27, 1969, required ranges of percentages for each of seven trades, subsequently reduced to six. But the hastily put together statement advanced intentions, not a plan. August hearings held in Philadelphia sought to formulate the specific goals.

The diversity of construction workers was matched by the variety of the protest groups that sprang up in many cities across the nation in the wake of accelerated urban renewal and the Model Cities Act of 1966. Often, protesters at building sites wanted jobs, some of them being unemployed or underemployed. Many were not those most likely to qualify for apprenticeships, which included both classroom and on-the-job instruction. The work rules and the culture of the crafts were complicated, and few outside of the industry understood them. Often, community groups viewed the rules as explicit barriers designed to exclude. Different black groups demanded different things. Some workers, trained by Reverend Leon Sullivan's Opportunities Industrialization Center (OIC), wanted employment and union membership. The trades refused to accept workers with OIC training. Others wanted to reform apprenticeship testing and entrance requirements.[47] By contrast, the vice president of the heavily black Laborers' Union testified that he opposed the preapprenticeship approach. He wanted opportunities for skilled work to go to his union members who had worked as helpers in the skilled crafts. In the language of labor market theory, he would provide access from the secondary to the primary labor market.

Black contractors had other interests that differed from those of the protesting workers. Two minority contractors had been awarded work in excess of two million dollars, part of an eighty-million-dollar development project awarded to the Tishman Realty and Construction Company, which had invited black contractors to bid on parts of it.[48] These black contractors retreated from the battle to integrate the crafts. Robert Easley, head of the NAACP's Afro-American Builders Corporation, encouraged by Herbert Hill, said, "I am not interested in our people [the black contractors] getting into the union integration fight. . . . It is possible for them to get stuck with all the culls from these groups who will demand that black contractors hire all blacks at going wages, qualified or not. We already have had to fight this situation in Boston and Buffalo."[49] Hiring untrained blacks often was impossible for small contractors of whatever ethnicity or race. The larger black contractors in the North and East generally drew upon the same labor pool as their white counterparts.[50] Thus, several distinct black groups had interests in construction: contractors, adults of various experiences, teenagers with no experience, and construction laborers working on projects. The Philadelphia protests tried to embrace every one of these groups, though not all of their interests could be satisfied.

Given the divisions within the black community and the stonewalling by the unions, OFCC formulated numerical goals on the basis of current black participation in each trade, the availability of blacks for employment in the trade, the black population in the area, the prospects for employment, and the possibility of training.[51] The OFCC guidelines were vague, and the numbers rested upon facts and assumptions that were not axiomatic. Crucially, the plan failed to address the question of training for the elite crafts, the ostensible target. Contractors were required to employ blacks on jobs, but a job offered no career in construction.

Philadelphia Plan: Practice

The underlying assumption of the Philadelphia plan did not match reality. The plan's architects assumed that a pool of skilled minority workers already existed in the elite trades who, but for discrimination, would be employed. Indeed, if that assumption had been accurate, coercion could have worked. One could force a contractor to hire a journeyman. However, the problem was training, and coercion did not work so well in such a situation. Informing that assumption was the omnipresent middle-class view of blue-collar labor. A lawyer who had worked on the Philadelphia plan in the labor department asked, "Since all of the construction industry involves rather rough and heavy work, you would think that segment of society for whom 'bull labor' has generally been reserved would be disproportionately represented in such industry."[52] He had grossly mischaracterized the jobs in question. Because the Philadelphia plan stressed jobs, not training, contractors played musical chairs to reach their goals. They moved skilled blacks from the nonfederal jobs to the federal ones, or they accepted black workers of whatever competence from community organizations, and without providing any training, simply paid them as if they were skilled workers. These tactics guaranteed that they would be found to be in compliance. Thus, meeting employment quotas on federal projects became a surrogate for increasing the number of blacks in the trade. In the first year of the Philadelphia plan, forty-one blacks worked in the targeted trades on twenty-five federal projects. Before the plan went into effect, ninety-seven minority journeymen were members of the relevant local unions. None of the forty-one black workers came from sources other than existing union members or apprentices recruited by existing union outreach plans.[53] Compliance was measured by man-hours of work. Too few compliance officers, and advance warnings about inspections, made even these man-hours figures suspect. Also, the reporting system for Philadelphia and other city plans remained inadequate: Minority group data did not reflect the composition of the contractors' operations on non-federal sites.[54]

But basically, the error lay in formulation, not monitoring. The key to attracting a permanent black labor force involved offering a career ladder that training and a union card represented, but a job did not. Projects come and go, which is why most training programs, including apprenticeships, were not administered by individual employers. Peter Gross, an assistant general counsel for the U.S. Commission on Civil Rights, made this point in 1972. He credited OFCC with progress in facilitating the employment of blacks on public projects but also said: "What is needed now is some mechanism for job continuity for people entering the construction industry under OFCC's goals and timetables."[55] In that same year, the OMB concluded that "bad faith by unions, incompetence by [OFCC] staff and poor construction labor market conditions in 1970 resulted in the failure of the plan."[56] All of this was true, but this analysis missed the mark. The plan had not included a training component.[57]

It is often said that bad cases make bad law. Such was true of the Philadelphia plan. Even its advocates acknowledged that if the six trades were appreciably integrated, such a change "would not substantially improve the total participation of blacks in the economic benefits of the nation."[58] Because black leaders had not given up on the urban unemployed at this time, other items, namely public jobs, were deemed more significant. The AFL-CIO agreed. But the construction demonstrations were not far from the public employment debate. Senator Jacob Javits of New York, who voted for the Philadelphia plan and also backed a public jobs program, asked the AFL-CIO's research director, Nathaniel Goldfinger, in April 1970: "If all you have to do is dump the dustbin into public employment and the Government becomes the employer of last resort, why should the Building Trades Unions break their backs to put blacks on the job or anybody else for that matter?" Goldfinger distinguished among sectors of the black population saying, "I think the public service employment program we are talking about meets one need and that is the need for jobs by the long-term unemployed and seriously underemployed, but there are many other needs in our society and there obviously is the need to open up employment opportunities on an equal basis regardless of race, creed, color, with nondiscriminatory practices."[59] Such distinctions rarely informed discussions of urban unemployment.

Reducing Construction Wages without Affirmative Action

After its congressional victory, the administration retreated when confronted with building trades opposition and the difficulty of the task that it had reluctantly embraced. It eventually discovered that more construction laborers were needed, not skilled tradesmen. First, Shultz reformulated the policy to promote hometown plans. Local communities, not the OFCC, would devise plans, although they still would have to be approved in Washington. Then, in 1970, OMB found an "excessive concentration of OFCC resources on construction." Twenty-five percent of the OFCC staff had worked on that sector, which represented less than 2 percent of the labor force.[60] If the administration considered the Philadelphia plan significant, OFCC reduction of personnel working on construction made no sense.

Meanwhile, Nixon distanced himself from the whole endeavor. The attempt to increase the supply of labor through civil rights enforcement was a one-shot affair, but the administration's attempt to reduce wages in the industry remained a constant. On March 17, 1970, the president reiterated the need to combat construction inflation. Vietnam politics interrupted Nixon's efforts until after the midterm elections. When protests escalated in the wake of the April 30 invasion of Cambodia, Peter Brennan, head of the New York building trades, organized a huge demonstration in support of the president's Vietnam policies. Construction unions in other cities followed suit. Perhaps in gratitude, Nixon ended the freeze on federal construction on June 30. By doing so without condition, a staff person in OMB concluded, the president passed up "an opportunity to establish an incentive to undertake new starts conditioned on meeting certain requirements for minority hiring and job training."[61] After the 1970s elections, the wheel turned again. Nixon inveighed against high construction wages in a speech before the National Association of Manufacturers in December.[62] Two months later, Secretary George Romney at HUD labeled high construction wages "the most dangerous source of inflation in our economy." Romney advocated repeal of the Davis-Bacon Act, changes in the National Labor Relations Board, government training of construction workers, and the promotion of industrialized housing.[63]

The new secretary of labor, James D. Hodgson, prodded by the president, announced a "massive" effort to expand the supply of construction labor. Hodgson had replaced Shultz, who became head of OMB in June 1970. He and Shultz were close ideologically, so the change did not alter policy, and Shultz continued to keep a hand on labor matters. Arnold Weber, Shultz's assistant in OMB, reminded John Ehrlichman that actual training programs were more modest, although Weber shared Hodgson's objective. Weber thought the current slowdown in construction limited many of the union-sponsored training programs. The president should wait until demand picked up and then make a statement to create public approval for "a large non-union labor pool, which is what we will need to meet the immediate demand." In the end Shultz simply used government manpower programs to train more workers, particularly Vietnam veterans, for the industry. Labor department expenditures on training programs in construction increased from $45 million in 1970 to $165.6 million in 1971.[64]

Paul McCracken, who headed a special Cabinet Committee on Construction created in 1969 to review the government's activities, also wanted to repeal the Davis-Bacon Act, but he understood the political difficulties involved. Instead, McCracken suggested changing some of the administrative regulations to permit a range of prevailing wage rates. Once again, civil rights was invoked as a means to the end. He maintained that "a major political advantage [of this approach] is that it opens up opportunities for lower skilled minority workers to work on federal construction projects. As with the Philadelphia Plan, the government can emphasize the benefit to minority workers thereby partially offsetting the expected strong adverse reaction by craft unions. In order to emphasize further this aspect of the proposal, existing regulations can be changed to permit contractors to employ trainees and apprentices on construction projects if their training programs have been approved by the OFCC."[65]

Nixon willingly took on the construction unions, even though it hurt politically in the short run.[66] He suspended the Davis-Bacon Act on February 23, 1971, knowing it would generate opposition from the very unions he had been wooing.[67] Union contractors opposed his move too. While many remained as disenchanted with the unions as their nonunion competitors, they were stuck with them. They saw the suspension as a government preference for the nonunion sector. Despite the criticism, Shultz believed Nixon could get away with the suspension because "the construction industry now is experiencing unemployment, the contractors are hungry, there's lots of non-union help and earnings per hour are off." Nixon reinstated the Davis-Bacon Act on March 29, after the industry and unions agreed to work together to keep wages down. Inflation declined slightly, falling from 6.1 percent in 1969 to 5.5 percent in 1970, then dropping to 5 percent in the first six months of 1971. Both the industry and the administration congratulated themselves that wage increases in 1971 were more reasonable than in 1970.[68]

Having solved the construction inflation problem, Nixon's promotion of affirmative action in the industry all but disappeared. White House aide Leonard Garment, a racial liberal, recommended a public meeting with those contractors, unionists, and minority representatives who were active in the most successful of the "hometown" plans, like the one in Indianapolis. Nixon said no.[69] When Garment urged the president to award more contracts to minorities, he refused.[70] Then, in July 1971, Nixon rejected a plan proposed by Secretary of Commerce Maurice Stans to initiate an affirmative action plan for minority construction firms.[71]

Another sign of Nixon's flagging interest in affirmative action was the decision to remove Arthur Fletcher from the labor department. As assistant secretary for wage and standards, Fletcher was a dynamic, charismatic black Republican who had lost a race for lieutenant governor of Washington in 1968. A former businessman and professional football player, he was bitterly anti-union, whether by conviction or by calculation that anti-unionism was the best vehicle to promote black employment in a Republican administration.[72] Fletcher attacked the apprenticeship approach, preferring instead the manpower programs that tended to be controlled by black institutions. He regularly denounced unions at NAACP conventions and before the Associated Builders and Contractors, the organization of open-shop builders. In 1971, Fletcher declared that "the era of arrogance and discrimination by some trade unions has ended. Corrupted by their sense of power, they have overreached. And the institutional systems which they built up, turned out to rest on sand, not rock. We are within a year of a great influx of minority workers into the construction trades, as the citadel of labor supply control plus overt discrimination is being destroyed." Yet Fletcher knew his audience. He warned them not to repeat the reputed errors of the past when black workers were discarded after "serving the purpose of breaking the union."[73]

Fletcher's gleeful anti-unionism made him anathema to the AFL-CIO. A major supporter, Secretary of Labor Hodgson believed that Fletcher got into trouble with the unions because of a limited understanding of labor relations.[74] Mere grumblings avalanched to calls for Fletcher's removal after he addressed the Associated Builders on March 12, 1971. He told the gathering that the real purpose behind the suspension of the Davis-Bacon Act was not to control inflation but to weaken and even destroy the unions.[75] The building trades started publicly demanding his resignation. By July 2, the administration decided that Fletcher would go. Although Charles Colson, the White House aide who dealt with labor, believed that Fletcher was an able, loyal, and effective Republican, Colson began to view him as an obstacle to wooing back the "hardhats," who had been disaffected by the suspension of Davis-Bacon.[76] Shultz and Hodgson accepted the inevitable and did not resist the move. Fletcher himself remarked, "I've carried this job as far as inspirational rhetoric and limited technical know-how could carry it."[77] He eventually went to work for the Republican National Committee.[78]

Presidential inattention, the complexities of implementation, conflicting goals, and inadequate personnel doomed the hopes of the Philadelphia plan's more enthusiastic champions. Circulating regulations became a surrogate for enforcement. The labor department had issued Order No. 4

on February 3, 1970, requiring all contractors, not simply those doing construction, to file affirmative action plans and incorporate the notion of "underutilization." Such vague standards, married to the enormous scope of coverage, inevitably undercut their impact, and Nixon showed no interest in improving the agency's capabilities.[79] In 1972, only 71 of OFCC's 112 positions were filled. Its competence did not improve under a Democratic president. A GAO report of 1979 concluded that the office only kept up with the paperwork and did not enforce the regulations it issued.[80]

OFCC denied the indictment, arguing that the poor economy explained its meager figures. But whatever the explanation, its record demonstrates why the Philadelphia plan never assumed the significance that commentators in the 1990s have given it. Unlike historians, contemporaries did not perceive the Philadelphia plan as a departure from past policy. Courts, mayors, and governors were ordering similar measures before and afterward. The plan enjoyed broad but shallow support because it had been sold as a solution to urban disorder. Nixon embraced it because he thought it would increase the supply of construction labor, a key element in his anti-inflation program. However, affirmative action in a few elite trades did not affect the larger situation. The president discovered that other measures— training more workers, holding tripartite discussions among the government, the contractors, and the unions, suspending the Davis-Bacon Act, and slowing federal construction projects—better reduced wages and increased the supply of workers. Although these measures did not affect the inflation rate, they did moderate construction wages.[81]

In the 1970s, when Keynesian economics was still alive, macroeconomic measures, public service jobs, education and training, and full employment seemed more potent to many blacks, especially when measured by their actual and disappointing experience with the Philadelphia plan. Only after the policy changes of the Reagan years, when many of these tools were removed from the government's kit, did the Philadelphia plan assume its symbolic role as the fountain of black progress.[82] Even so, it is acknowledged that such plans do not help the "truly disadvantaged." The argument today is that plans awarding contracts to black businessmen and admitting black students at elite universities have created a new middle class. Whether that judgment is true or not, neither effort was supported by President Richard Nixon.

Nixon's interest in affirmative action was hostage to his economic policy and ended when it became clear that there were superior means to control construction wages. Independent of motives, the contract compliance mechanism, involving a project-by-project approach, was not an effective tool to increase the number of black skilled workers. OFCC had improvised the plan out of fear of urban riots, relying upon middle-class assumptions about blue-collar work. Then Nixon added his own hopes to control inflation. The Democrats' civil rights perspective and the president's conservative economic agenda were both inadequate bases for helping black workers because they ignored the character of the construction industry and chose coercion in a situation that required cooperation for success. Whether the experience in construction is typical is unclear because the history of affirmative action in other industries, whether voluntary or coercive, is unwritten. Still, the story of Nixon and the Philadelphia plan suggests that the genesis of affirmative action policies may lie outside concerns regarding civil rights and that announcing a plan is not the same as effecting one. Perhaps because of the implementation question, the Carter administration shifted enforcement from workers to minority business in the wake of the Public Works Act of 1977, which required 10 percent of the government contracts to be given to minorities. That is yet another story that needs to be told.

Notes

1. Nixon also faced a Democratic Congress. The Democrats enjoyed a 58–42 majority in the Senate and a 243–192 majority in the House. Stephen E. Ambrose, *Nixon: The Triumph of a Politician, 1962–1972* (New York: Simon and Schuster, 1989), 220.

2. A. James Reichley, *Conservatives in an Age of Change: The Nixon and Ford Administrations* (Washington, D.C.: Brookings Institution, 1981), 179–86; Haldeman notes, Apr. 28, 1969, box 40; Feb. 21, 1970, box 41; Aug. 4, Nov. 7, 1970, box 42; John C. Whitaker, Memorandum for Members of the Cabinet, June 24, 1969, White House Central Files (WHCF), CF HU2, box 2, Richard M. Nixon presidential papers, National Archives (NA), College Park, Md. (hereinafter Nixon); John Ehrlichman, *Witness to Power: The Nixon Years* (New York: Simon and Schuster, 1989), 220.

3. Graham bases his conclusion on Clarence Mitchell's characterization of the plan as a "calculated attempt . . . to break up the coalition between Negroes and labor unions." *Congressional Quarterly Weekly Report* (Nov. 27, 1970), 28:2859–61.

4. Hugh Graham, *The Civil Rights Era: Origins and Development of National Policy, 1960–1972* (New York: Oxford University Press, 1990), 475.

5. James T. Patterson, *Grand Expectations: The United States, 1945–1974* (New York:

Oxford University Press, 1996); John David Skrentny, *The Ironies of Affirmative Action: Politics, Culture, and Justice in America* (Chicago: University of Chicago Press, 1996).

6. General Accounting Office, *Federal Efforts to Increase Minority Opportunities in Skilled Construction Craft Unions Have Had Little Success* (Washington, D.C.: GPO, 1979).

7. Daniel Quinn Mills, *Industrial Relations and Manpower in Construction* (Cambridge, Mass.: MIT Press, 1972), 141, 148. About 11 percent of the labor force was black. There are many ways to count construction workers, and each way will provide a slightly different estimate of the numbers of black workers in the industry.

8. Press Release, Department of Labor, Oct. 20, 1963, "President's Committee," box 67, RG 174, Records of Secretary of Labor W. Willard Wirtz, NA.

9. C. J. Haggerty to W. Willard Wirtz, Feb. 1, 1968; Wirtz to Haggarty, Feb. 2, 1968, box 54, Records of Secretary of Labor W. Willard Wirtz. The trades also agreed on procedures to implement the Model Cities Act of 1966 and Housing Act of 1968, which required that residents of areas affected be involved in construction work carried out under the programs.

10. See speech by Undersecretary of Labor James J. Reynolds, Nov. 21, 1968, ibid.

11. Robert F. Drinan to Arthur Fletcher, Oct. 14, 1969; Dr. Russell Nixon to George Shultz, July 7, 1969, EEO-2, box 68, RG 174, Records of Secretary of Labor George P. Shultz, NA (hereinafter Shultz).

12. "Minutes of Meeting," Mar. 19, 1963, Chron. file, Civil Rights Committee, AFL-CIO, George Meany Memorial Archives, Silver Spring, Md.

13. Boris Shishkin to William Schnitzler, June 17, 1963, ibid.

14. Edward Sylvester to Secretary Wirtz, June 14, 1967, EEOC-3, box 62, Records of Secretary of Labor W. Willard Wirtz.

15. "Statement of the Associated General Contractors of America," Hearings on S. 2515, Subcommittee on Labor of the Senate Committee on Labor and Public Welfare, 92nd Congress, 1st sess., 138: 339.

16. Jim Gaither to Joseph Califano, Dec. 24, 1968; Gaither to James Frey, Jan. 2, 1969, WHCF, FG 600, file Gaither: CR, box 3, Lyndon B. Johnson Library.

17. Ward McCreedy to Patrick H. Gannon, Jan. 30, 1969; McCreedy to Shultz, Jan. 30, 1969; Shultz to David Packard, Feb. 12, 1969; Packard to Shultz, Feb. 13, 1969; William Rehnquist to Schultz, Feb. 24, 1969, OFCC, box 68, Shultz.

18. *New York Times*, Dec. 19, 1972.

19. Paul McCracken, "Memorandum for Cabinet Committee on Economic Policy," Mar. 5, 1969, POF, box 77; Cabinet Meeting on Economic Policy, Sept. 19, 1969, POF, box 79, Nixon; Herbert Stein, *Presidential Economics: The Making of Economic Policy from Roosevelt to Reagan and Beyond*, 2nd rev. ed. (Washington, D.C.: American Enterprise Institute, 1988), 152.

20. *Wall Street Journal*, Aug. 15, 1969; Clinton C. Bourdon and Raymond E. Levitt,

Union and Open-Shop Construction: Compensation, Work Practices, and Labor Markets (Lexington, Mass.: Lexington Books, 1980), 108–9.

21. Cabinet Meeting on Economic Policy, Sept. 19, 1969, POF, box 79, Nixon.

22. Bourdon and Levitt, *Union and Open-Shop Construction*, 99–100.

23. Ibid., 7.

24. George Shultz to the President, July 30, 1969, WHCF, FG22, box 1, Nixon.

25. Presidential Meetings, June 13, 1969, POF, Nixon.

26. Announced by OFCC, the plan was put together by Solicitor of Labor Laurence H. Silberman and lawyers in the Justice Department to meet the objections of Elmer Staats. Arthur A. Fletcher to Secretary and Undersecretary, July 15, 1969, EEO-1, box 67, Shultz.

27. McCracken, "Memorandum for the President," Aug. 20, 1969, Cabinet Committee on Economic Policy, box 29, Shultz.

28. For Nixon's rejection of aid to minority construction contractors, see Leonard Garment, "Memorandum for the President," July 20, 1971, WHCF, HU2, box 3, Nixon, with the president's "NO" appended to it.

29. William A. Boleyn to Arthur Weber, Dec. 17, 1970, T1-1, ser. 69.1, RG 51, Records of the Office of Management and Budget, NA.

30. Richard L. Rowan and Lester Rubin, *Opening the Skilled Construction Trades to Blacks: A Study of the Washington and Indianapolis Plans for Minority Employment* (Philadelphia: University of Pennsylvania Press, 1972), 134–35.

31. Negro American Labor Committee, executive board minutes, Mar. 14, 1970, 10, 1/2. Richard Parris papers, Schomburg Center for Research in Black Culture, New York, N.Y.

32. Paul McCracken to George Shultz, Dec. 18, 1969, Council of Economic Advisers, box 55, Shultz; *Wall Street Journal*, Jan. 6, 1970, 1.

33. "Memo to President," PJB meeting, July 9, 1969, 2, POF, box 78, Nixon.

34. George Shultz, "Why Vote to Recommit?," EEO-1, box 67, Shultz.

35. Cited in Skrentny, *Ironies of Affirmative Action*, 197.

36. Ward McCreedy, "Memorandum for Secretary Shultz and Assistant Secretary Fletcher," Dec. 23, 1969, WF-2, box 71, Shultz; Lamar Alexander to Bryce Harlow, June 17, 1970, WHCF, HU2 FG1, box 2, Nixon. Nixon signed a Democratic public employment bill, which the president viewed as temporary, only as the 1972 elections approached. Margaret Weir, *Politics and Jobs: The Boundaries of Employment Policy in the United States* (Princeton: Princeton University Press, 1992), 116–18, 122.

37. Walter Licht, *Getting Work: Philadelphia, 1840–1950* (Cambridge, Mass.: Harvard University Press, 1992), 116–17.

38. Bourdon and Levitt, *Union and Open-Shop Construction*, Chap. 4.

39. Ibid., 51.

40. Ibid., 19.

41. Peter B. Doeringer and Michael J. Piore, *Internal Labor Markets and Manpower Analysis* (Lexington, Mass.: Heath, 1971), 150.

42. Bourdon and Levitt, *Union and Open-Shop Construction*, 71–73; Richard L. Rowan and Lester Rubin come to similar conclusions in their *Opening the Skilled Construction Trades to Blacks*, 93.

43. Herbert Hill, "Memorandum," May 3, 1966, IV, box A-73, NAACP papers, Library of Congress.

44. Rowan and Rubin, *Opening the Skilled Construction Trades*, 81; F. Ray Marshall and Vernon M. Briggs Jr., *Equal Apprenticeship Opportunities: The Nature of the Issue and the New York Experience* (Washington, D.C.: National Manpower Policy Task Force, 1968), 19.

45. Russell A. Nixon, "Summary Statement before Opening Meeting on Contract Compliance in the Construction Industry," June 26, 1969, EEO-2, box 68, Shultz.

46. Ray Marshall et al., *Employment Discrimination: Impact of Legal and Administrative Remedies* (New York: Praeger, 1978), 3–9.

47. Arthur Fletcher, "Memorandum for the Secretary," Aug. 29, June 24, 1969, EEO-1, box 67, Shultz.

48. Herbert Hill to Dr. Morsell, Jan. 3, 1969, IV, A-36, NAACP.

49. Robert Easly to Herbert Hill, Nov. 13, 1969, IV, Hill Memos 1966–70, box A-73, NAACP.

50. Mills, *Industrial Relations and Manpower in Construction*, 172–75.

51. "Procedure for Determining Ranges and Targets under the Philadelphia Plan," n.d., EEO-1, box 67, Shultz.

52. James E. Jones Jr., "The Bugaboo of Employment Quotas," *Wisconsin Law Review* 34 (1970): 373.

53. Bob McGlotten to Andrew Biemiller, Nov. 21, 1972, "Placements since Philadelphia Plan," 38/42, Legislation Department, AFL-CIO, Meany.

54. William Boylan to Frank C. Carlucci, June 29, 1972, box 4, Labor Manpower Branch, RG 51.

55. Cited in *Labor Relations Yearbook, 1972*, 273.

56. Evaluation Division, OMB, "Report," May, 1972, 11, 21, ser. 69.1, T1-11, RG 51. Nationally, the proportions rose from 1960, when 2.5 percent of all apprentices were minorities; the figure reached 4.4 in 1966, 8.6 in 1969, and over 14 percent in 1973. But the role of the new OFCC requirements is questionable because it did not promote apprenticeships. *Labor Relations Yearbook, 1972*, 205.

57. Charles R. Perry et al., *Impact of Government Manpower Programs in General and on Minorities and Women* (Philadelphia: Wharton School, 1975).

58. Jones, "Bugaboo of Employment Quotas," 402.

59. Goldfinger, Hearings, Subcommittee on Employment, Manpower, and Poverty, Apr. 1, 1970, 91st Cong., 1st sess., 106:1411.

60. Domestic Council, "Study of Federal Efforts to Reduce Employment Discrimination," n.d., T2-10, ser. 69.1, RG 51.

61. Mark W. Alger to Arnold Weber, Mar. 22, 1971, T1-11, ser. 69.1, RG 51.

62. Cited in Reichley, *Conservatives in an Age of Change*, 216–17.

63. Harry S. Havens to Richard Nathan, Dec. 28, 1970, box 37, Labor-Manpower Branch, 1969–76, RG 51.

64. John D. Ehrlichman, "Memorandum for Secretary Hodgson," Feb. 11, 1971, WHCF, FG22, box 2, Nixon; Arnold Weber, draft for John Ehrlichman, "Expansion of Labor Supply for the Construction Industry," Feb. 10, 1971; Weber to Ehrlichman, Feb. 10, 1971, Weber to Ehrlichman, n.d. [Feb., 1971], T1-11, box 37, ser. 69.1, RG 51.

65. McCracken, "Memorandum for the Cabinet Committee on Construction," Nov. 13, 1970, T2-2, ser. 69.1, RG 51.

66. "Memorandum for the President's File," Nov. 19, 1970, box 83, Charles W. Colson papers, Nixon.

67. Charles W. Colson, Memorandum for the President, Mar. 4, 1971, WHCF, PQ2, box 2; Secretary of Labor, Memorandum for the President, Dec. 28, 1970; George Shultz, Memorandum for John R. Brown III, Dec. 30, 1970, Labor, box 129, Haldeman papers; Ehrlichman, Notes of President Meetings, Jan. 15, 1971, box 4, Nixon.

68. Shultz, Memorandum for the President's File, Jan. 28, 1972, box 87, Colson papers, Nixon. Shultz was wrong; wages increased by 11.8 percent in 1972, more than the 11.6 the year before. Bourdon and Levitt, *Union and Open-Shop Construction*, 7.

69. Leonard Garment, "Memorandum for the President," Nov. 23, 1970, 4–5, POF, box 8, Nixon.

70. Garment, "Memorandum for the President," July 29, 1971, WHCF, HU2, box 3, Nixon.

71. Garment, "Memorandum for the President," July 20, 1971. The plan was supported by most of the relevant agencies, including OMB, and Charles Colson, who also supported the attempt to woo the construction unions. See Colson, "Memorandum for Staff Secretary," July 26, 1971, ibid. The year before, Stans became director of the Minority-group Contractors Assistance Project, funded by the Ford Foundation and Commerce Department, to provide seed money and assistance to minority group contractors. *Wall Street Journal*, July 21, 1970, 23.

72. *Daily Labor Review* 224 (1970): A-1.

73. *Labor Relations Yearbook, 1971*, 106–7.

74. Fred Malek to John Ehrlichman, Sept. 24, 1971, WHCF, CF FG22, box 20, Nixon.

75. *Daily Labor Report*, Mar. 2, 1971, A-15, 16.

76. Colson to Haldeman, Apr. 7, 1971, Malek, box 10, Colson papers, Nixon.

77. *Wall Street Journal*, Sept. 21, 1971, 1.

78. Department of Labor, News Release, Aug. 6, 1969, EEO-1, box 67, Shultz.

79. Allan G. Patterson, to Arnold R. Weber, Jan. 22, 1971, T1-11, ser. 69.1, RG 51.

80. General Accounting Office, *Federal Efforts*, 27.

81. Stein, *Presidential Economics*, 161.

82. Some argue that the source of the contemporary black middle class was the affirmative action initiated first in the Philadelphia plan. Others argue that it was the general antidiscrimination measures begun in the 1964 Civil Rights Act. For thoughtful assessments see James P. Smith and Finis R. Welch, "Black Economic Progress after Myrdal," *Journal of Economic Literature* 27 (June 1989): 519–64, and John. J. Donohue III and James Heckman, "Continuous Versus Episodic Change: The Impact of Civil Rights Policy on the Economic Status of Blacks," *Journal of Economic Literature* 29 (Dec. 1991): 1603–43.

The Serendipitous Historian: Gary M Fink and the Shaping of Southern Labor History

Clifford Kuhn

Since his arrival at Georgia State University in 1970, Gary Fink has played a leading role in developing the field of southern labor history. He is the author and editor of nine books in labor and political history, covering a wide range of topics, from the politics of the Missouri labor movement to the 1914–15 strike at Atlanta's Fulton Bag and Cotton Mills to the presidency of Jimmy Carter. In addition to his scholarship, Fink has been a key supporter of the Southern Labor Archives since its infancy, helping it grow to one of the leading labor repositories in the country. He also was central to the establishment of the biennial Southern Labor Studies Conference, first held at Georgia State in 1976, and the Atlanta Seminar in the Comparative History of Labor, Industry, Technology, and Society (SCHLITS).

Yet despite his last name, it was not at all foreordained that Fink would become a labor historian, much less a southern labor historian. The descendant of German and Estonian immigrants, Fink was born in 1935 on a farm in eastern Montana. After high school, he entered the army, where he experienced something of an intellectual awakening after overhearing a conversation between two of his fellow soldiers about American literature. "I was just sort of stunned," he later recalled. "I thought, I want to be able to talk about those sorts of things."

Upon his discharge, Fink entered the University of Montana as a business major. Under the influence of such teachers as Leslie Fiedler and historians Morton Borden, Melvin Wren, and Paul Carter, he became more interested in history, and ended up with a degree in business education and a minor in history. After graduation, he got a job teaching business and coaching at a high school in Astoria, Oregon, where his wife, Mary, taught second grade. "My first year was all business courses. And then the second and third year I added more history courses. That's really when I figured out what I really wanted to do was teach high school history and not coach."

Toward that end, Fink entered a one-year master's program at the University of Missouri. Not coincidentally, Columbia was also the hometown of Mary Fink, who was pregnant at the time, and the couple looked forward to having her mother close by after their child's birth. "That seemed a very practical sort of thing, which became very embarrassing in later years, when people asked me why I went to Missouri, and I had to come up with stories like, 'Oh, I went there to work with Dick Kirkendall,' who I hadn't even heard of before we went there! Of course, as with a great many people, one year turned into five. I was really taken with graduate school."

In addition to Richard Kirkendall, Fink's professors and associates at Missouri included Noble Cunningham, David Thelen, Allen Davis, Richard Dalfiume, and Alonzo Hamby, among others. Another important influence was Harold Woodman. It was Woodman who first introduced Fink to labor history, supervising a readings course in the absence of any formal course being offered in the subject. Yet Fink's dissertation, which was published as *Labor's Search for Political Order: The Political Behavior of the Missouri Labor Movement, 1890–1941*, was conceived and carried out primarily as a work of political history rather than labor history.[1]

Fink's first academic job was at Mankato State in Minnesota, where he became caught up in bitter history department politics, breaking down largely along generational lines. Dissatisfaction with his position at Mankato led him to apply to Georgia State, although, as with much of his career trajectory, in a serendipitous manner. The following selection, excerpted from three oral history interviews conducted with Fink in late 1997 and early 1998, picks up the story at that point, and traces Fink's involvement with the field of labor history and, more particularly, of southern labor history.

Fink: A good friend and labor historian, Don Sofchalk, and I went to an OAH meeting in Los Angeles, and we were both very unhappy with our situation. But jobs already—this was 1970—were beginning to dry up. We went to the professional register that the OAH was running and looked at the jobs listing. Only two jobs were posted in labor history. One was at Georgia State and the other was at the University of Wisconsin at Parkside, which then was a very new school that had not yet become operational. The professional register cost ten dollars to enroll, and we were trying to figure out whether or not to do that, since there were only two jobs listed anyway. So we flipped a coin and lost, and decided to register. Then the question became which of us would apply for which job. So we flipped again, and I lost. Don registered for an interview for the job at Parkside, and I interviewed for the job at Georgia State. Well, it turned out that the representative from Parkside never showed, so Don never had an interview. Don stayed at Mankato, and retired a couple of years ago.

Kuhn: That's really the story of how you got to Georgia State?

Fink: I got a call from Joe Baylen, the department head, asking me to come down for an interview. I talked it over with Mary. We had just had our third child a few months earlier, in December, and I think the call came in the spring, shortly after the OAH. I said, "We really don't want to go to the South, do we? Mankato is bad, but it can't be as bad as Georgia." But we decided to go at their expense just to see what it was like.

We came in May. Of course, Atlanta was gorgeous. Still snow in shaded places in Minnesota. Mary spent a day just riding urban transit, and whatever direction from downtown she rode, she found beautiful residential areas and really fell in love with the city. In the meantime, I went through all the interviews at Georgia State and was very impressed with the people I met here. So by the time we got on the plane to go back, we saw Georgia State as a very good alternative to Mankato and would have been disappointed if we weren't offered the job. It was, of course, a labor history position, and I had never previously defined myself as a labor historian. I was a political historian who happened to do a labor-related dissertation, but the jobs in political history were scarce relative to the number of applicants, and there were still labor jobs, so I became a labor historian.

Kuhn: So now let's go back over this. You had a turning point in your life while hiding in a boiler room in Fort Lewis. You went to graduate school because you had a pregnant wife and a mother-in-law in the city where you were going to go. You flipped a coin and lost twice and came to Georgia State University. You're saying that the pivotal events of your life are all this kind of . . .

Fink: It really is amazing. And I don't think that I'm alone in this. I think that most of us go through life and at a critical time serendipitous things happen that take us from one course to another. The person we happen to marry or the first job we happen to get or a teacher who happened to influence us at a particular time. I bet it happens to most of us.

Kuhn: So you arrived at Georgia State soon after the establishment of the Southern Labor Archives.

Fink: Merl [Reed] had contacted [Al] Kehrer. Al had a master's degree in economics from Yale, and he headed the AFL-CIO Civil Rights Office here in Atlanta, covering the South. They had met on some social occasion. They started talking about [labor attorney] Joe Jacobs and some way of recognizing Joe's contributions to the labor movement in the South. Merl, I think, mentioned that what we really needed to do was establish an archive in Joe's name, as a fitting tribute to his contribution. That idea took hold and grew. Merl took it to Joe Baylen, and Baylen eventually took it to the administration, although the administration was not enthused about the idea at all. But Al Kehrer had George Busbee's support. Busbee was the House majority leader in the General Assembly. Kehrer worked through Democratic connections. So the pressure came on the administration from that source to move on this. I think that helped pave the way.

Kuhn: What was your relationship with the Labor Archives?

Fink: It was very close. Merl and I would meet on a regular, almost a weekly, basis with David Gracy [first director of the Southern Labor Archives] and talk about various issues and try to figure out where our collecting efforts should be—and, of course, always the problems of how to approach the [GSU] administration for funding, and how to cultivate close ties with the local labor movement, which none of us really had. I mean, we really depended almost exclusively on Al Kehrer to represent us. But the [archive] was an infant, and we cared for it like an infant.

Kuhn: Maybe you could talk about the evolution of the Southern Labor Studies Conference.

Fink: The first four or five were held at the Urban Life Conference Center at Georgia State. One of the things that strikes me clearly is that in the early conferences, there was a great deal of labor involvement— retirees, active labor people—which diminished as we moved along. I'm not sure exactly why. I remember the session with the auto workers.

Kuhn: 1982.

Fink: In many ways, for me that [was] a highlight of the conferences, when we had Eric Hobsbawm and [David] Montgomery on the same platform, so to speak. I recall Eric Hobsbawm saying at the conclusion of that session that it was the best session he had ever attended. So for me, that became a highlight. I recall that Merl and Les [Hough] and I, and a few other people, were sitting around afterward reviewing the quality of the program, and we concluded that we had had two of the top ten historians in the English-speaking world on the program. I am not sure where that rating came from, but I didn't disagree with it.

I think Jacquelyn Hall's address [in 1991], especially because so many of us were working on the Fulton Bag strike, was one of the most memorable. She developed her discussion as the detective/historian so effectively that it just captivated everyone. We got more positive feedback from her talk and Montgomery's address than any others.

Kuhn: The 1986 one was the one with Karin Shapiro and Dan Letwin.

Fink: And Eric Arneson.

Kuhn: And Earl Lewis was here.

Fink: That's right. Earl was still in graduate school at Berkeley. I remember a Saturday afternoon after a conference had adjourned, and Earl and I went off to have a cup of coffee, and we had a very long conversation. He was sort of thinking through his future at that point. He has done very well.

Kuhn: Speak to the experience of seeing these younger scholars—in '82, Dolores Janiewski, Bob Korstad, Jim Leloudis, that cohort. And then in '86, Arneson and Letwin and Shapiro and Lewis. Tera Hunter was another, in '91.

Fink: This has been one of the real services of the conferences. It provided a forum for young scholars, many of them working on dissertations at the time, to expose their work and get their feet into the profession. I think in almost every conference, there [has] been a cohort of these young historians, many of whom have gone great guns since they were here.

Kuhn: How did the publications come about? The three different volumes of essays from the conferences.[2]

Fink: Well, those volumes were in some ways an outgrowth of the reference books I did on labor leaders and labor unions.[3] Again, serendipity fits into all of this [*chuckling*]. I became very intrigued with labor leaders at the state and local level while doing my dissertation. There was a fellow in Missouri who was an active Socialist by the name of Reuben Wood, who was a cigar maker out of Springfield, Missouri, and became, at quite a young age, the president of the Missouri State Federation of Labor. For a long time, he maintained his Socialist ties. The southern part of Missouri had a very strong radical heritage, a sort of prairie radicalism, as opposed to the ethnic radicalism of Saint Louis. Reuben Wood eventually served two or three terms in Congress, as a Democrat, and had ties with Harry Truman and so forth. But he's just an absolutely forgotten figure in American politics.

I thought there were a lot of people like this at the state and local level who were just unknown, so I thought of putting together a collection of short biographies, of people like Reuben Wood. I talked to some people—this was in the early '70s—around the country that I knew who had been working in local and state histories, and had enough of a group together that I thought this would be a project worth pursuing.

So I sent a prospectus around to three or four publishers. One of the publishers I approached was Greenwood Press, which had been doing some work on labor. Milton Cantor and Bruce Laurie were editing a series on labor history. It turns out that at that time the founder of the Greenwood Press was an Atlantan. In fact, he used to deliver newspapers as a boy around Atlanta neighborhoods and went to Emory and eventually got a Ph.D.

But anyway, he was coming to Atlanta shortly after I wrote that letter, to give something like a quarter of a million dollars to Emory. He arranged a meeting with me at the time to talk about this proposal I had made. It turned out he wasn't much interested in my proposal, but they were very interested in developing a series of reference books on leaders in various areas and institutions. So we ended up talking about a directory of labor leaders. I eventually went to Westport, Connecticut, and they had also contracted Milton Cantor as a senior advisor to the project. We all met in Westport for a couple of days, and fleshed out what we were going to do and who we were going to bring into the project and so forth.

Kuhn: Who were you going to bring in?

Fink: Well, we had an impressive series of advisory editors. We brought David Montgomery and Philip Taft into the same project [*chuckling*]. We had almost all of the major labor historians at the time involved in one way or the other: Albert Blum, Mel Dubofsky, Walter Galenson, Sidney Fine, Leon Stein, Maurice Neufeld, Howard Quint, Edward Pessen, and many others. Milton had been the editor of *Labor History*, and he brought most of these people in. Most of them checked lists of potential entries and/or read finished sketches for accuracy. I would submit a list of labor leaders in particular areas, and they would identify the people they felt made the most significant contribution to the labor movement. We eventually got this down to about five hundred people.

For me, it was a tremendous experience. I got to meet so many people. I was still an assistant professor at the time. My first book hadn't come out at that point, so it was just a really good arrangement.

I learned a great deal. I imagine I researched and wrote 60 percent of the sketches and plagued friends and acquaintances [*chuckling*] with other sketches. Most of them were drawn out of primary sources. There just weren't that many secondary sources available on most labor leaders, especially when [we got] beyond the most important unions on the national level, so I think I developed a real feel for the labor movement at different levels and for the character, the nature of labor leaders at different levels, and the conflicts between them. So it was, more than anything else, a learning experience of studying a lot of people at a lot of different levels and how they reacted to various events.

Oh, and also the library experience. I can't imagine how this would go with the World Wide Web and all that today, but then you just plowed through all kinds of primary sources. I spent more time reading obituaries than you can possibly imagine. Every time the biennial AFL-CIO convention report came out, they listed all who had died. I couldn't wait to get my hands on those [*chuckling*]. Sort of a gruesome approach to history. But one gets to know obituary sources very well in that enterprise. The official publications carried sometimes very informative obituaries.

Kuhn: How did the labor leaders book lead to the labor unions book?

Fink: Well, the first series of reference books that Greenwood did included leaders in various fields of endeavor, and then the second was a series on American institutions. So they were shopping around for editors for that series. They asked me about the labor unions, and at this time I was pretty excited about the labor leaders volume, so I agreed to do the unions volume. I agreed to do it also with the stipulation I could write complete sentences and do a more lengthy analysis, rather than the one-page sketches with no sentence subjects.

Kuhn: So that's the progression of Greenwood picking up the southern labor studies essays. Maybe you could speak to those three volumes.

Fink: Okay. Because of the connection with Greenwood on the labor leaders and labor unions volume, when we were considering publishing the proceedings of the 1976 conference, we approached a number of publishers, including Greenwood. The biggest problem we had was the necessity of having the printers' union bug on the book. The problem was that that jacked up the price of printing to the point that no publisher was willing to do it. So again we turned to Al Kehrer. He talked to the folks at the typographers' union here in Atlanta, and they agreed that if we did an offset, then they would permit the union bug on the publication, so that's what we ended up doing. So that's the way we did the first two volumes. And then the last time we worked through Malcolm MacDonald and the University of Alabama Press.

Kuhn: What do you think [is] the impact those volumes [have] made in the field?

Fink: Well, I like to think that, along with the conferences, they were fundamental to the development of southern labor history. For one, they provided a forum for southern labor historians, young historians, to get into print. If you look at the names in those first couple of volumes, most of them are very well established by this time. I think the books established southern labor history as a distinct field of labor history and of southern history, which had pretty much been ignored up to that time. The volumes that Bob Zieger edited are a wonderful complement to those volumes.[4] At least six anthologies on southern labor, and there aren't many bad articles in any of them.

Kuhn: As you look back over a twenty-five-year period, as southern labor history has evolved, in what directions has it evolved?

Fink: Well, it has evolved in many of the same ways that labor history and southern history generally have evolved. Certainly, issues of gender have been late in coming. I mean, they were always there, but I think at the end of every conference, we sat around and rehashed, and we would see the absence of any direct effort to address gender issues as a weakness in the conferences. Finally, we're catching up with that.

Interracial unionism has been a theme that has developed with the conferences. We have moved from an emphasis on institutional history and unions to a greater emphasis on worker culture and an effort to identify a southern working class. So in many ways it seems very parallel to the changes that have occurred in labor history generally, just the distinctive southern application of all of this.

Kuhn: That's an issue, of course, raised implicitly and explicitly—the existence of southern exceptionalism. You've had people weighing in on different sides of that, too.

Fink: I'd like to make a distinction. I don't know if I'm just playing a semantic game here, but—a distinction between *exceptionalism* and *distinctiveness*. I think *exceptionalism* carries all kinds of ideological weight in terms of exclusivity and the value judgments associated with it. *Distinctive-*

ness, to me, suggests it's just different in some ways. It's hard for me to deny distinctiveness. Exceptional, no. I think that the second volume that Bob Zieger edited focused to some extent on southern exceptionalism or distinctiveness, so it's a real issue.

Kuhn: Although I think, especially over the last few years, given the trends in the American economy, that the rest of the nation is becoming more like the South. The "Dixification" of America certainly is a theme.

Fink: A few years ago we had a session at the Southern on the twenty-fifth anniversary of Ray Marshall's *Labor in the South*. I was involved in that, and Bob Zieger and a couple of others. We were generally reassessing *Labor in the South* from the perspective of a quarter century later. Ray Marshall was there, too. One of the conclusions we all came to was that—I think it was in 1967 that Marshall published his book—Marshall had it backwards when he predicted that eventually the South would become more like the rest of the nation. To the contrary, the rest of the nation has become more like the South.

Kuhn: As you look back, what are some of the things that you're proud of, that you accomplished?

Fink: I'm very proud of the development of the Southern Labor Studies Conference and southern labor history. And this just isn't me. This is a whole bunch of people. Wayne Urban and Merl, David Gracy, Les Hough, and Bob Dinwiddie, and the folks in the labor studies area. We have made Atlanta sort of a center for labor history in the South, and I think to some extent SCHLITS [the Atlanta Seminar in the Comparative History of Labor, Industrialization, Technology, and Society] is an outgrowth of that emphasis. So, in a way, I see that as something that I was involved with that I think has flowered very nicely.

I'm quite proud of the years I served as chair. I think I probably served a couple of years too many, but at least the first three years I think were very interesting. I saw the academy from a much different perspective than I had previously. I came out of there with the opinion that there ought to be a rotating chairmanship. I don't think this should be a lifetime job in any way. I think the more time [one spends] in that position, the less sensitive one becomes to basic faculty and student interests. It's just a natural insulation that grows as one stays in the position, maybe even an arrogance that develops. But I just think the department chair ought to be responsible, almost exclusively, to the faculty and not to the administration.

Other legacies? I think the faculty I helped recruit and the students I've dealt with. I go [to] the Meany Archives and I see Lee Sayres, and I think, "Yes, that's pretty good." Bill Holland wrote a fine dissertation and published a very good article in *Prologue*. Sally Brown has done so well.[5] You have to be proud of that; there are so many others in whose professional development I have shared.

Notes

1. Gary M Fink, *Labor's Search for Political Order: The Political Behavior of the Missouri Labor Movement, 1890–1940* (Columbia: University of Missouri Press, 1973).

2. Gary M Fink and Merl E. Reed, eds., *Essays in Southern Labor History* (Westport, Conn.: Greenwood Press, 1977); Merl E. Reed, Leslie S. Hough, and Gary M Fink, eds., *Southern Workers and Their Unions, 1880–1975* (Westport Conn.: Greenwood Press, 1981); Gary M Fink and Merl E. Reed, eds., *Race, Class, and Community in Southern Labor History* (Tuscaloosa: University of Alabama Press, 1994).

3. Gary M Fink, *Biographical Dictionary of American Labor Leaders* (Westport, Conn.: Greenwood Press, 1974); Fink, *Labor Unions* (Westport, Conn.: Greenwood Press, 1977).

4. Robert H. Zieger, ed., *Organized Labor in the Twentieth Century South* (Knoxville: University of Tennessee Press, 1991); Zieger, ed., *Southern Labor in Transition* (Knoxville: University of Tennessee Press, 1997).

5. James William Holland, "The Mugwumps and Modern America: An Analysis of Change, 1870–1918" (Ph.D. diss., Georgia State University, 1995); Sarah Hart Brown, *Standing against Dragons: Three Southern Lawyers in an Era of Fear* (Baton Rouge: Louisiana State University Press, 1998).

Afterword

Gary M Fink

Although Ray Marshall, an institutional economist, is appropriately recognized as the founder of southern labor history, this branch of American working-class history grew and matured during the postinstitutional phase of the larger discipline.[1] With the exception of Marshall's initial foray, an "old" southern labor history remains to be written. Indeed, this is one of its more unique features. As it has evolved over the years, southern labor history lacks the institutional underpinning (much maligned though it may have been) that provided the structural context—organized labor, the capitalist economy, the state—for the "new" labor history. It is ironic, therefore, that one of the more enduring questions about southern labor involves the absence of labor institutions. That same question perplexed Marshall some forty years earlier.[2]

Near the end of his inaugural volume on southern labor, Marshall perused his crystal ball and concluded that the circumstances of organized labor in the South would gradually change until it came more closely to resemble the labor movement elsewhere in the country. As it turned out, Marshall's prediction came true, though not in the way that he had envisioned. In reality, the conditions of southern labor changed very little, but the strength of organized labor nationally diminished significantly as industrial jobs disappeared, unionization rates fell, and real wages failed to keep pace with those in other sectors of the economy. To paraphrase a recent study, it constituted the Dixification of American labor.[3]

Perhaps inevitably, the continuing debate over American and, more specifically, southern exceptionalism has had its working-class counterpart. There can be little doubt that southern labor was different, but was it exceptional? Used in this context, *exceptionalism* is a term so value-laden as to immediately raise red flags (or perhaps red, white, and blue flags). Because of the emotional and ideological baggage it carries, the term ultimately does more to irritate and offend than to illuminate.[4]

From a social or cultural perspective, southern workers closely resembled their northern counterparts. Both espoused republican values and displayed a patriarchal disposition; both sought some measure of control over the circumstances of their labor, often through collective action; both resisted management's growing hegemony over the workplace, and at times both permitted ethnic and racial antagonism to undermine class unity. Such similarities have led some social historians to challenge even the notion of southern distinctiveness.

Still, history and its legacy of structural differences did significantly alter the character of labor and the form and effectiveness of working-class movements in the South. Even more so than New England or the Southwest, for example, the South has been shaped by history. The legacy of plantation slavery endowed the region with a biracial labor force that effectively deterred the waves of immigrants who created the multicultural, multiethnic workforce so common to northern industry. Further, the general absence of ethnic diversity in the South robbed labor of the radical perspective and trade union experiences so common in other sections of the country. History also contrived to produce a unique southern political culture that featured a one-party system with an unusual degree of elite dominance. Even those workers, black and white, who did manage to avoid disfranchisement found their political participation qualified in a variety of other ways, especially through paternalistic arrangements and economic coercion.

As a result of these and other factors, a distinctive, largely underdeveloped southern economy emerged that continued to vex the South until recent years. Textiles and coal remained the dominant industries in the South through much of the twentieth century. Both were labor-intensive enterprises with relatively low levels of capitalization that existed in a highly competitive market economy. Staying in business meant continuous pressures to reduce labor costs through cutting wages and increasing labor productivity. The result was intermittent industrial warfare that did little to promote economic stability and development.

Similarly, southern agriculture featured a cotton crop that became less and less competitive on the international market. Like the industrial labor force, the sharecroppers and tenant farmers who comprised much of the agricultural workforce sometimes revolted but more often simply left the farm for more promising opportunities outside the South or, more typically, moved to mill towns, joining the textile labor force. Such geographical mobility, though common throughout the United States, produced an especially high rate of working-class transience within the South.

Much of the particularity of the South relates to race. The legacy of plantation slavery meant that African Americans—first bound, then supposedly free—would comprise a large segment of the workforce. Ray Marshall once again anticipated the significance of this circumstance with the publication of *The Negro and Organized Labor* (1965) and *The Negro Worker* (1967).[5] But race was not to become a major theme of American labor history without considerable controversy. Herbert Gutman served as the lightning rod in the acrimonious debate over the relative significance of race and class in working-class history.[6] Although model academic demeanor sometimes degenerated in this spirited debate, it nevertheless proved productive, providing considerable enlightenment on such issues as occupational segmentation, the strengths and weaknesses of interracial unionism, and the psychology of "whiteness." Recent studies of interracial unionism among southern miners and the Gulf Coast waterfront reflect just how sophisticated and how productive that debate has been for southern labor history.[7]

Although late arriving, gender also has taken its place as a major theme of southern labor history. *Like a Family*, the award-winning study that evolved from the collective efforts of the Southern Oral History Program at the University of North Carolina, dramatically revealed the value of such an approach to an understanding of the "southern cotton mill world."[8] The three gender-based essays that appear in this volume further evidence the importance of such an analysis and the quality of the scholarship being done.[9]

Because in the South everything seems to work out a bit differently, a "new" southern labor history could well involve an effort to reconstruct the structural organization of southern society that did so much to influence and condition social and cultural arrangements.[10] Thus does the new become the old and vice versa. It hardly seems coincidental that three of the essays in this volume deal specifically with the relationship between labor and the state.

Provocative analyses of the relationship between labor and politics in South Carolina clearly have demonstrated the value of examining working-class political behavior.[11] Before we can generalize about labor and politics in the region as a whole, however, we need similar studies of other states as well as of major southern cities. Did southern workers establish a distinctive political culture? From the South Carolina studies, we know that race dominated labor politics in the Palmetto State at particular times. But was this typical of the region, or did class and other issues occasionally come to the fore as they did in South Carolina during the 1930s?

We also need to know more about skilled workers in the South. Students of the region's labor history have been transfixed by millhands and miners, particularly in textiles and coal. But what of the critically important building and construction trades and craftsmen in such occupations as the printing trades, iron workers and machinists, teamsters, and urban and interstate transit employees? And what of white-collar and service workers, such as those employed in education, government, and retailing? The evolution of industrial relations in the South and collective bargaining where it existed needs further study.[12] There is still much we do not know about paternalistic arrangements in various industries, labor recruitment and apprenticeship, the introduction of scientific management, and the battle to control the shop or mill floor.

But to itemize how much is left to do is to ignore how much has been done in the few short years since the publication of Ray Marshall's inaugural volume on the subject. The time now seems propitious for the writing of a revised general history—a "House of Southern Labor" that puts the many fragments of the region's labor and working-class history together into a new synthesis.

Clearly, southern labor history has come of age. In addition to the impressive list of methodologically and analytically sophisticated monographs that have appeared in recent years,[13] seven substantial anthologies have been published and two historical quarterlies have devoted special editions to the subject.[14] Southern labor history has its own archival repository and its own dedicated conference. Moreover, sessions devoted to southern labor topics regularly appear on the convention programs of national and international historical organizations and in the published articles of their journals. The essays that appear in this volume further testify to the general excellence of work in the field. To reword an old adage, perhaps southern labor history's best days are yet to come.

Notes

1. F. Ray Marshall, *Labor in the South* (Cambridge, Mass.: Harvard University Press, 1967).

2. Bryant Simon, "Rethinking Why There Are So Few Unions in the South," *Georgia Historical Quarterly* 81, no. 2 (Summer 1997): 465.

3. Stephen D. Cummings, *The Dixification of America: The American Odyssey into the Conservative Economic Trap* (Westport, Conn.: Praeger Press, 1998).

4. Robert H. Zieger reviews the "exceptionalist" literature and examines the issue in the context of southern labor in *Southern Labor in Transition, 1940–1995* (Knoxville: University of Tennessee Press, 1997), 1–8.

5. F. Ray Marshall, *The Negro and Organized Labor* (New York: Wiley, 1965) and *The Negro Worker* (New York: Random House, 1967).

6. Herbert Hill, "Myth Making as Labor History: Herbert Gutman and the United Mine Workers of America," *International Journal of Politics, Culture, and Society* 2, no. 2 (Winter 1988).

7. On southern waterfront workers, see Bruce Nelson, "Organized Labor and the Struggle for Black Equality in Mobile during World War II," *Journal of American History* 80, no. 3 (Dec. 1993): 952–88, and Eric Arnesen, *Waterfront Workers of New Orleans: Race, Class, and Politics, 1863–1923* (New York: Oxford University Press, 1991). On southern miners, see, for example, Joe W. Trotter, *Coal, Class, and Color: Blacks in Southern West Virginia, 1915–1932* (Urbana: University of Illinois Press, 1990), and Daniel Letwin, *The Challenge of Interracial Unionism: Alabama Coal Miners, 1878–1921* (Chapel Hill: University of North Carolina Press, 1998). On "whiteness," see David Roediger, *The Wages of Whiteness: Race and the Making of the American Working Class* (London: Verso Books,1991), and Bruce Nelson, "Class, Race, and Democracy in the CIO: The New Labor History Meets the Wages of Whiteness," *International Review of Social History* 41 (1996): 351–88.

8. Jacquelyn Dowd Hall et al., *Like a Family: The Making of a Southern Cotton Mill World* (Chapel Hill: University of North Carolina Press, 1987).

9. See also Mary E. Frederickson, "Heroines and Girl Strikers: Gender Issues and Organized Labor in the Twentieth-Century American South," in Robert H. Zieger, ed., *Organized Labor in the Twentieth-Century South* (Knoxville: University of Tennessee Press, 1991), 84–112, and Bess Beatty, "Gender Relations in Southern Textiles: A Historiographical Overview," in Gary M Fink and Merl E. Reed, eds., *Race, Class, and Community in Southern Labor History* (Tuscaloosa: University of Alabama Press, 1994), 9–16.

10. The value of such an approach is demonstrated in Douglas Flamming, *Creating the New South: Millhands and Managers in Dalton, Georgia* (Chapel Hill: University of North Carolina Press, 1992). Flamming combined a structural analysis with social history and a century-long time perspective to produce this sweeping study.

11. David L. Carlton, *Mill and Town in South Carolina, 1880–1920* (Baton Rouge: Louisiana State University Press, 1982), and Bryant Simon, *A Fabric of Defeat: The Politics of South Carolina Millhands, 1910–1948* (Chapel Hill: University of North Carolina Press, 1998).

12. Particularly provocative in this respect are Daniel J. Clark, *Like Night and Day: Unionization in a Southern Mill Town* (Chapel Hill: University of North Carolina Press,

1997), and Timothy J. Minchin, *What Do We Need a Union For?: The TWUA in the South, 1945–1955* (Chapel Hill: University of North Carolina Press, 1997).

13. See Michelle Brattain's essay in this volume.

14. Jeffrey Leiter, Michael D. Schulman, and Rhonda Zingraff, eds., *Hanging by a Thread: Social Change in Southern Textiles* (Ithaca: ILR Press, 1991); Edwin L. Brown and Colin J. Davis, eds., *It Is Union and Liberty: Alabama Coal Miners, 1898–1998* (Tuscaloosa: University of Alabama Press, 1999); Gary M Fink and Merl E. Reed, eds., *Essays in Southern Labor History: Selected Papers, Southern Labor History Conference, 1976* (Westport, Conn.: Greenwood Press, 1977); Merl E. Reed, Leslie S. Hough, and Gary M Fink, eds., *Southern Workers and Their Unions, 1880–1975: Selected Papers, the Second Southern Labor History Conference, 1978* (Westport, Conn.: Greenwood Press, 1981); Fink and Reed, *Race, Class, and Community in Southern Labor History*; Zieger, *Organized Labor in the Twentieth-Century South* and *Southern Labor in Transition*; *Atlanta History: A Journal of Georgia and the South* 36 (Winter 1993): *Georgia Historical Quarterly* 81 (Summer 1997).

About the Authors

Michelle Brattain. A native of Charlotte, Michelle Brattain earned a bachelor's degree from the University of North Carolina at Chapel Hill in 1990. She continued her training at Rutgers University, where in January 1997 she completed her doctorate. A book based on her dissertation, "The Politics of Whiteness: Race, Workers, and Culture in the Modern South," is forthcoming from Princeton University Press. Brattain taught at the California Institute of Technology and the University of Auckland, New Zealand, before coming to GSU in the fall of 1998.

Gary M Fink. A native of Montana, where he studied at the state university, Gary M Fink undertook graduate training at the University of Missouri, whose press in 1974 published a book based on his dissertation as *The Search for Political Order: The Political Behavior of the Missouri Labor Movement, 1890–1940*. Other studies in labor history by Fink include the *Biographical Dictionary of American Labor*, published by Greenwood Press in 1974 and reprinted in 1984; *Labor Unions*, published by Greenwood Press in 1977; *Organizing Dixie: Alabama Workers in the Industrial Era*, coauthored with Philip A. Taft and published by Greenwood Press in 1980; and several edited volumes of AFL and CIO *Proceedings*. The use of espionage by Fulton Bag's management during the 1914–15 strike provided Gary Fink with the subject of his latest monograph, *The Fulton Bag and Cotton Mills Strike of 1914–1915: An Episode in New South Industrial Relations*, published by ILR Press of Cornell University in 1993. The intersection of politics and labor has interested Fink for years, as demonstrated by his seminal study, *Prelude to the Presidency: The Political Character and Legislative Leadership Style of Governor Jimmy Carter*, published by Greenwood Press in 1980, and the coedited volume of essays *The Carter Presidency: Policy Choices in the Post–New Deal Era*, published by the University Press of Kansas in 1998 and based on a conference held at the Carter Center in 1997. Indeed, setting up conferences and then editing the proceedings has long been a staple of Fink's professional career. He chaired the program committees of the Southern Labor Studies Conference from 1976 to 1995 and coedited with Merl E. Reed and others three volumes of essays derived from those meetings: *Essays in Southern Labor History*, published by Greenwood Press in 1977; *Southern Workers and Their Unions*, published by Greenwood Press in 1981; and *Race, Class, and Community in Southern Labor History*, published by the University of Alabama Press in 1994. While Fink's scholarly contributions and interests make him much more than simply a student of southern labor history, his numerous contributions to a field he helped develop and nurture warrant his reflections in the afterword included in this volume. Indeed, because of his unfaltering support on behalf of southern labor history, and because of the high esteem held for him by his peers, this volume of essays is dedicated to honor Professor Gary M Fink.

Douglas Flamming. Douglas Flamming moved to Atlanta in 1997 after leaving the California Institute of Technology for a position at the Georgia Institute of Technology. He now heads Tech's Center for the Study of Southern Industrialization. A native Texan, Flamming grew up in Abilene and graduated from the University of Texas at Arlington in 1981. He finished a doctorate in history at Vanderbilt University in 1987. His research interests include African Americans in Los Angeles and the southern working class in the Vietnam era. His first book, *Creating the Modern South: Millhands and Managers in Dalton, Georgia, 1884–1984*, published by the University of North Carolina Press in 1992, won the Philip A. Taft Labor History Prize.

Tera W. Hunter. The working lives of black women in the urban South and their efforts at unionization has provided Tera Hunter with a fruitful subject for her research. The essay in this volume continues a discussion begun in her book, *To 'Joy My Freedom: Southern Black Women's Lives and Labors after the Civil War*, which Harvard University Press published in 1997 and which won the H. L. Mitchell Award of the Southern Historical Association. Born and raised in Miami, Florida, Hunter graduated from Duke University with a bachelor's degree in 1982 and Yale University with a doctoral degree in 1990. After six years on the faculty at the University of North Carolina, Chapel Hill, Hunter moved to Pittsburgh, where she now teaches at Carnegie Mellon University.

Clifford Kuhn. In many ways mentored by Gary M Fink, Cliff Kuhn has worked closely with his colleague since first exploring the Southern Labor Archives in 1984. Now Kuhn heads GSU's Georgia Government Documentation Project and teaches history. After earning his bachelor's degree from Yale University in 1974, Kuhn honed his oral history skills by producing documentaries for radio. One such project resulted in *Living Atlanta: An Oral History of the City, 1914–1948*. Kuhn received a doctoral degree from the University of North Carolina, Chapel Hill, in 1993. A book based on his dissertation, which concerns a strike at Atlanta's Fulton Bag and Cotton Mills, will be published by the University of North Carolina Press.

Alex Lichtenstein. An associate professor of history at Florida International University in Miami, Alex Lichtenstein earned a bachelor's degree from Yale University in 1984 and a doctoral degree from the University of Pennsylvania in 1990. Verso published his dissertation in 1996 as *Twice the Work of Free Labor: The Political Economy of Convict Labor in the New South*. Lichtenstein has published numerous introductions, book chapters, and articles. The contribution in this volume reflects his new research on the Communist Party and the Congress of Industrial Organizations.

Merl E. Reed. In the essay in this book, Merl Reed expands the institutional analysis he offered in *Seedtime for the Modern Civil Rights Movement: The President's Committee on Fair Employment Practice, 1941–1946,* published in 1991 by the Louisiana State University Press. LSU Press published Reed's first book in 1966, *New Orleans and the Railroads: The Struggle for Commercial Empire, 1830–1860,* which was a revision of his 1957 LSU dissertation. Since then, Reed has written numerous articles and coedited with Gary M Fink several significant collections of essays on southern labor history. Now an emeritus professor, Reed is writing an institutional history of GSU.

Bryant Simon. Although he was born in Pittsburgh, Bryant Simon grew up in south Jersey. He attended the University of North Carolina, Chapel Hill, twice, first to earn the bachelor's degree in 1983 and then to complete a doctorate in 1992. He also earned two master's degrees, one from Yale University in 1985 and the other from the University of Warwick in 1987. For two years, Simon held an Ahmanson postdoctoral fellowship at the California Institute of Technology, and he taught for a year at Drake University before coming to the University of Georgia in 1995. In 1998 the University of North Carolina Press published his first book, *A Fabric of Defeat: The Politics of South Carolina Textile Workers, 1910–1945.* A lengthy entry in the *Eleanor Roosevelt Encyclopedia* provided the subject for the essay in this volume.

Judith Stein. A 1960 graduate of Vassar College, Judith Stein completed her doctorate at Yale University in 1968. She published *The World of Marcus Garvey: Race and Class in Modern Society* with Louisiana State University Press in 1986. The essay in this volume explores issues raised in her most recent book, *Running Steel, Running America: Race, Economic Policy, and the Decline of Liberalism,* published by the University of North Carolina Press in 1998. Stein is a professor in the graduate school and university center of the City University of New York.

Robert H. Zieger. After graduating from Montclair State College in New Jersey in 1960, Robert H. Zieger went on to earn a master's degree from the University of Wyoming in 1961 and a doctoral degree from the University of Maryland in 1965. He taught at the University of Wisconsin–Stevens Point, Kansas State University, and Wayne State University before accepting a position at the University of Florida. Zieger has written numerous books and edited two significant collections of essays on southern labor history. His study, *The CIO, 1935–1955,* which the University of North Carolina Press published in 1995, won the Philip A. Taft Labor History Prize.

Index

affirmative action, in the Philadelphia plan: and apprenticeships, 190–97; to combat "wage inflation," 182–83, 186–90, 193, 197–201; failure of, 197–201; origins of, 182 86

AFL: discriminatory practices of, 105–8, 127, 138–43, 150, 167; relations with CIO, 12–13, 120, 137–43, 166–67; strikes discouraged by, 66–67

AFL-CIO, 183–86, 196, 198

American Cigar Company, 65–71

Andrews, George H. (black applicant at Bell), 121

anticommunism, 11, 28, 42 (n. 36), 158–60, 163, 168, 174

antidiscrimination efforts, 76–78, 103–16, 119, 126–29, 133 (n. 82), 135–39, 142–51; of the Philadelphia plan, 182–86, 189–96, 199–201. *See also* CIO PAC; FEPC (Fair Employment Practices Commission); segregation: CIO's efforts to combat

anti-unionism, 4–5, 27–28, 55–56, 198–99

apprenticeships, in building trades, 190–97

Atlanta: antidiscrimination efforts in, 103–16, 119, 126–29, 133 (n. 82); domestic workers in, 62, 72–78; FEPC investigations in, 103, 106, 109–13, 115, 117–28; labor resources in, 102–4, 116–21

Atlanta Daily World (black newspaper), 105, 111–12

Atlanta Urban League (AUL). *See* Atlanta: antidiscrimination efforts in

Bartley, Numan V., 36 (n. 4), 44 (n. 55), 159

Baylen, Joe, 210

Beecher, John, 103, 109–12, 143

Bell, Lawrence D. (Larry), 102–3, 109

Bell, William Y., 104–7, 111, 115–16, 119, 126, 133 (n. 82)

Bell Aircraft Corporation, 102–3, 109–12, 118–29

Benson, Lester, 109–10

Blease, Cole, 23, 33, 57

Blough, Roger, 187

Blount, Winton, 187

Boilermakers: black auxiliaries of, 138, 141; race discrimination of, 138–43

Boydston, Jeanne, 15

Brin, Leonard, 142, 145

Brown, Joseph M., 72–73

Brown, Sally, 216

Brown v. Board of Education, 2, 32–33, 35 (n. 4)

building trades. *See* affirmative action, in the Philadelphia plan

Bunker, Archie (quoted), 95

Busbee, George, 210

Business Roundtable, 187

Carey, James B., 168

Carlton, David, 5, 57

Carmichael, James V., 161

Cash, Wilbur J., 5, 36–37 (nn. 8, 9)

CDT (Council on Defense Training for Negroes), 107–16

Cigar Makers International Union, 71

CIO: antidiscrimination efforts of, 11–14, 126–29, 135–39, 142–51 (*see also* segregation: CIO's efforts to combat); relations with AFL, 12–13, 120, 137–43, 166–67. *See also* CIO PAC

CIO PAC: and anticommunism, 11, 158–60, 163, 168, 174; founding of, 160–62;